The History Student Writer's Manual

Mark Hellstern
Tulsa Community College

Gregory M. Scott
University of Central Oklahoma

Stephen M. Garrison
University of Central Oklahoma

Prentice Hall
Upper Saddle River, New Jersey 07458

Library of Congress Cataloging-in-Publication Data

HELLSTERN, MARK
   The history student writer's manual/Mark Hellstern, Gregory M. Scott, Stephen M. Garrison
   P. CM.
   Includes bibliographical references and index.
   ISBN 0-13-874728-8 (alk. paper)
   1. Historiography—Handbooks, manuals, etc.   2. Academic writing—Handbooks, manuals, etc.   3. History—
Research—Handbooks, manuals, etc.   I. Scott, Gregory M.   II. Garrison, Stephen M.   III. Title.
D13'H4147 1998
808' .066907—dc21   97-30907

Editorial director: *Charlyce Jones Owen*
Production editor: *Edie Riker*
Cover design: *Bruce Kenselaar*
Buyer: *Lynn Pearlman*

This book was set in 10/12 Baskerville by East End Publishing Services
and was printed and bound by Victor Printers. The cover was
printed by Phoenix Color Corp.

Printed in the United States of America

10   9   8   7   6   5

ISBN   0-13-874728-8

Prentice-Hall International (UK) Limited, *London*
Prentice-Hall of Australia Pty. Limited, *Sydney*
Prentice-Hall Canada, Inc., *Toronto*
Prentice-Hall Hispanoamericana, S.A., *Mexico*
Prentice-Hall of India Private Limited, *New Delhi*
Prentice-Hall of Japan, Inc., *Tokyo*
Pearson Education Asia Pte. Ltd., *Singapore*
Editora Prentice-Hall do Brasil,Ltda., *Rio de Janeiro*

To:

Gene and Dorothy Hellstern
Carolyn and Hannah, Bethany, Jason, and Christopher Hellstern

Geraldine Tidd Scott and Mahlon E. Scott

Martha and Gene Garrison
Melissa Garrison

Contents

To the Student

It should come as no surprise to you to learn that success in academia, in politics, or in the business world is linked to the ability to express yourself well in writing. Whether it is a class grade, a persuasive political argument, or advertising that reaches a select group of consumers, effective communication is a vital tool to possess in this world. As historians, we utilize the past to gain clearer insight into the way human beings behaved (and therefore *behave)* under certain circumstances. We read, ponder, and interpret the historical record left by previous generations in this or other places. Then we present our ideas, often in written form so that others may share the insight we have gained. *We write to record what we observe, to explain what we record, and to defend what we explain.*

The History Student Writer's Manual is designed to help you do two things: 1) improve your writing and 2) learn about history. These two central objectives are addressed in the three major sections of this book. The **Introduction** offers you thought-provoking commentary on the nature of history itself, a brief history of history, and some thoughts on the current state of the discipline. **Part One** of the *Manual* addresses fundamental concerns of all writers, exploring the reasons *why* we write, describing the *writing* process itself, and examining those elements of grammar, style, and punctuation that cause the most confusion among writers in general. A vital concern throughout this part, and the rest of the book as well, is the three-way interrelationship among writer, topic, and audience. Effective writing is not some magical, mystical dispensation granted only to a few privileged geniuses. Writing is a series of interconnected skills that are common and which may be honed through instruction and practice. While William Shakespeare, Thomas Jefferson, Willa Cather, or Langston Hughes need not fear that we will endanger their niche in the hallowed annals of writing greatness, there are things we all can learn to enable us to turn words into powerful communication.

Part Two of the *Manual* focuses on research. The book will guide you step by step from organizing the research process through probing the mysteries of that foreboding but essential place called the library. It will tell you what you need to know to present your writing project in its proper format and demonstrate how to cite your sources correctly and ethically. **Part Three** offers advice concerning specific kinds of papers, such as book reviews, biographies, military papers, and archaeology papers. We have even included a chapter on how to produce historical scripts. Your professor may give you a specific paper assignment from one of these types. If not, Chapter 12 presents several creative writing exercises, not only to give you a chance to practice your writing skills but also to provide opportunity to become part of history by seeing it in new and different ways.

This manual is a reference book. It has been written to help you become a better writer than you are now. We wish you all success as you accept a primary challenge of academic and professional life: to write, and write well.

Mark Hellstern, Greg Scott, and Steve Garrison

To the Teacher

How many times have you assigned papers in your history classes and found your-self teaching the class *how to write the paper*—not only content, but form and grammar as well? This text may accompany the primary text you assign in any undergraduate or grad-uate level history course, or it may stand on its own. It allows you to assign one of the many types of standard or unique papers explained in Part Three with the knowledge that virtually everything the student needs to know—from grammar to sources of infor-mation to citing sources—is here within one book.

You can direct your students, for example, to write a book review according to the directions in Chapter 8, and follow the instructions in Parts One and Two for conduct-ing research, organizing the material, formatting, grammar, and source citations. Almost every question a student might ask about the paper is answered in this book, but you will be able to supplement your assignment with special instructions.

If you intend for your students to write any of the traditional types of history papers, such as book reviews or standard research papers, these specialized forms are discussed in Part Three. If you are interested in unique and more adventuresome experiments with historical writing, perhaps you could direct your students to the creative writing exercises in Chapter 12.These enable the student not only to gain valuable writing expe-rience but also permit an immersion into the basic nature of history itself—a look into the actual processes which transmit ideas from one generation to another across time. Whether you are teaching an undergraduate American History survey, a graduate semi-nar in the military history of the ancient Mediterranean, or a continuing education class in general archaeological methods, you will find this manual to be an invaluable tool in helping you to achieve your course objectives.

As you know, writing skill is essential to professional success in history as in other professions. This book is written to assist you in leading students toward that success.

Mark Hellstern, Greg Scott, and Steve Garrison

1 *The Discipline of History*

That was my *least* favorite subject in school.

All history teachers have heard that line. We expect it when we reveal our occupation in casual conversation. From cashiers at the local discount store to cab drivers in New York to barbers in Oslo, the message is the same: High school history was a less-than-rewarding experience. How many of you remember taking a high school history class in which, at the beginning of a typical class session, your teacher told you something like this: "Read the next two sections in the chapter. Then answer the study questions at the end of each section. Here is a list of terms. Make sure you have them defined by Wednesday. Now, read quietly at your desks."

How many of you enjoyed that class? How many of you learned something in it?

1.1 What History Is *Not*

For one thing, the study of history is *not* the meaningless memorization of countless names, dates, and places—names of dead, forgotten people, dates of meaningless battles or treaties, and places where students will never visit. Nor should the academic study of history consist, simply, of long hours spent reading the dense prose of a textbook—at least, not without the stimulation of class discussions or lectures. This sort of unleavened textbook reading induces more comas than it does any genuine understanding of the past. When history is taught as it should be taught, and when students participate at the height of their creative abilities, the questions that occur too often in high school history classes—"Why do we have to study this stuff?" "How will learning this help us in real life?"—are never asked.

1.2 What History *Is*

In the first place, it is a topic that a large percentage of the American population—as well as the rest of the world—finds fascinating. Think about the distinguished historical documentaries that keep turning up on television. There are even cable television channels devoted entirely to history. And then there are the movies with historical themes, dramas like *Dances with Wolves* and *Braveheart* and *Gettysburg*, that garner prizes as well as huge audiences. Why?

How many of you know a history buff—someone who can spew battle accounts and generals at you all day; someone who knows every type of aircraft that flew during the Second World War, their rates of climb, their armaments, and the dates when they were placed in service? History buffs can provide specifics for every major battle of the Civil War. They collect war memorabilia. They get together and play war games in clubs. Whether you find what the history buffs do to be annoying or admirable, meaningless playtime or meaningful ritual, the phenomenon of the buff is a further indication of our culture's preoccupation with history.

The truth is that history is not the mindless retention of thousands of irrelevant facts. Nor is it being able to impress your friends with how much trivia you can recall on cue. The reason for our fascination with history is that it is a way of coming at the oldest question the human race has ever asked: *Who are we?* While exploring who we were yesterday, a hundred years ago, or two thousand years before the Christian era, we are also gathering clues about who we are today. It is the most fundamental of all unanswered questions. And no other discipline moves us closer to an answer than the study of history.

In this book, we hope not only to help you prepare quality research papers, but also to assist you in seeing what our profession is all about. As you begin to glimpse history through the eyes of historians, perhaps you will be among those students who exclaim, "Wow! I never knew this stuff could be so much fun!" or "The more I learn about this, the more fascinating it becomes."

1.3 History Is a Social Science

In its primary goal, history is related to other academic disciplines, such as economics, geography, philosophy, political science, psychology, and sociology. Sociologists, for example, study the way groups of people act. So do historians, only in the past tense. Psychologists explore the mysteries of the mind and of individual patterns of behavior. So do historians, in the past tense. Perhaps the subject matter or the approach to it changes from discipline to discipline, but each of them represents a different approach to the common goal of gaining a clearer, fuller understanding of the way human beings are. The objective is not facts, grade point averages, or publications (although we often forget this). The objective is to discover why we do the things we do—what makes us tick.

This human factor is what is most often missing from boring history classes, whether at the high school or college level. It is the missing ingredient in lists of aircraft, tanks, and warships. When students begin to see that history is the study of real people, it takes on a wondrous new perspective. When we view history as the real hopes, dreams, ambitions, and anxieties of living, breathing folks like ourselves, it naturally piques our curiosity.

AN EXAMPLE

Take a quarter from your purse or pocket (assuming that you, a poor college student, actually have one). You have used these round metal objects since you were a young child, but have you ever looked at one closely? Suppose you are an archaeologist two thousand years from now. You are digging through the rubble of an ancient civilization, and all you manage to find is the object you are holding. What silent clues does it hold about the culture that manufactured it? What can you learn about these people by examining the surface attributes of this artifact? Let us suggest a few.

- Even before you begin to take a close look at the object's attributes, you notice that it is metal. So the civilization that created it had advanced to the point of having metallurgy.
- The object is probably a coin. As an experienced archaeologist, you have seen other items like this one before. This tells you . . .
- The civilization had a currency. Its people were advanced enough to employ a medium of exchange, as opposed to a barter system.
- As you begin to examine the side of the coin with a human likeness on it, no doubt the first question you will ask is, "Who was this?" He must have been important to have had his face on a coin. You might guess that he was a religious or political ruler, a king, perhaps. You already know that the Romans imprinted their coins with the image of whoever was emperor at that moment. Perhaps this civilization did the same thing.
- Is it possible to tell anything about the type of relationship that existed between the genders in this society? Is it significant that the likeness on the coin is that of a male?
- There is some sort of language here. You do not know what it is yet or how to decipher it, but you can discern that the writing on both sides of the coin is an alphabetic language, as opposed to pictograph. There is little chance that one small coin could provide enough linguistic help to reconstruct an entire language. (There are inherent problems also, which our future historian may suspect are present but will not know about with certainty. Some of the characters on the coin represent numeric values, not sounds. These will present another huge dilemma. In addition our coins reveal two languages—English and Latin. Were these people multilingual?)
- Let us say that you have managed to decipher this alphabet. You then notice that the biggest word on the coin is "Liberty," stamped in an arch

above the head of the male likeness, who may, therefore, have been the god of liberty. In any event, you can guess that the concept of liberty was very powerful and important for these people. Also, near the face just below the chin you find the words "In God we Trust." It seems likely to conclude, then, that this was a polytheistic, male-dominated society.

- What else may the "head" side of the coin tell us? Clothing styles? There is no observable collar; perhaps the figure is naked. What about the hair style? Is that a wig tied with a ribbon? Is it possible that the people of that long ago time wore elaborate wigs and nothing else?
- What about those numbers under the neck? If it is a date, are we to assume that it refers to a year in which the person on the coin ruled? Or does it instead refer to the value of the coin?
- The "tails" side presents new problems. If the guy on the front is a god, then the bird on the back could be his eternal symbol. The Egyptians portrayed gods as beasts. Perhaps these people did as well. And what is that thing that the bird is clutching in its talons? Could it be a weapon of some kind?

Perhaps you are surprised at the amount of information that can be gleaned from a single little coin—and the confusion that it can cause. What we have tried to give you here is a small historical record. Archaeologists employ such silent, hand-held artifacts to reconstruct parts of the distant past that existed before or apart from written, documentary evidence. Historians work with documents, but written records are imbedded with clues just as surely as the artifact we have examined.

We should also remind you that much of the information suggested above was entirely a matter of speculation. We do not know with certainty that the face on the front was a god or that the building on the back was his temple. They are absolutely reasonable guesses, but they are guesses nevertheless. Many of our speculations can be, in fact, completely erroneous. If the person was a ruler, he did not rule on the date listed near his face. Washington died in 1799, a date significantly prior to the one on the coin you examined. We guessed that this civilization was multilingual, one of the languages being Latin. It is an unfortunate fact that most Americans are not fluent in their own language, much less another one or two, and unless you are a priest or a fan of classical studies, you probably do not speak or write Latin.

Written history also contains the same potential for conjecture—for making reasonable guesses that, in the light of later revelation and/or study, may turn out to be completely wrong. We all know, for example, that Andrew Jackson served as seventh President of the United States from 1829 to 1837. That is a fact. No one seriously doubts it. But what kind of president was Andrew Jackson? What were Americans experiencing and doing during the years Jackson was president? Was this period of time really the "Age of the Common Man" as we have been told, or is there another version of the story?

Some historians are fans of "Old Hickory," while others are not so fond of him. Times change. New generations of historians look at the old stories through new lenses. New evidence appears to challenge conventional wisdom.

In our profession, there is an old adage: If you gathered one hundred historians in a room and asked the simple question "Why did Rome fall?" you would receive one hundred different answers, including some saying that Rome never actually fell at all. In other words, just as the clues on the coin could mean many different things, so can we examine the same documentary evidence but arrive at different conclusions about what it means. This is historical interpretation, and it is part of what makes history come alive.

Our understanding of the events and ideas of the past is undergoing constant revision. Let us take the era of Reconstruction, for example. Most historians agree that the way the government handled problems in the post-Civil War South was a disaster. Historians used to learn (and then teach) that the debacle was entirely the fault of vengeful Northerners whose meddling drove Southern whites to unorthodox measures simply for self-defense and survival. Some historians still believe this version of the story.

Most of us in the profession, however, have revised our previous understanding. We now teach more or less the opposite of the conventional wisdom, asserting instead that while the South may have been beaten on the battlefield, their basic beliefs and values were not affected by Lee's surrender to Grant in April of 1865. In fact, Southern whites worked quickly to restore as much of their old order as possible, defying and evading postwar constitutional amendments. The nagging problems of race relations are still with us, not because the North pushed the South into a corner, but because the postwar North, absorbed with growing industrialism and thinking that problems were solved just because the war was over, turned their backs, leaving southern blacks in a worse predicament than before. *Traditionalists,* therefore, maintain that the North went too far, while *revisionists* argue that the North did not go far enough.

The introduction of varying interpretations is one of the reasons history is a dynamic, creative process and not a dusty, lifeless collection of memorized facts.

1.4 A Brief History of History

You may know something of Herodotus and Thucydides, who in the fifth century before the Christian era (B.C.E.) wrote accounts of the Persian and Peloponnesian wars, respectively. In several important ways, these two Greeks established patterns for writing about historical events that are still employed today. For example, their concentration on war, constitutional matters, and the actions of notable leaders (in other words, on political and diplomatic history) has served as the emphasis of historical writing for almost twenty-five centuries. Most historians still view political activity and the behavior of nation-states as the supreme expression of the human mind, will, and emotions.

Polybius, a Greek of the second century B.C.E., investigated the rise of the rival Romans and their political institutions. A century later, Plutarch wrote his famous *Parallel Lives,* in which he employed quotations and anecdotes to illustrate the qualities of character. The Romans themselves contributed to historical literature through the writings of Cato the Elder, Tacitus, and Seutonius.

During the Christian era, in the later years of the third century or the early years of the fourth, Eusebius wrote a history of the early church from its Judean beginnings through the infamous persecutions to acceptability during the reign of Constantine. Breaking from the traditional historical method, Eusebius emphasized the lives of common folk and was the first writer since the Old and New Testament times to mingle a chronological narrative with a discussion of ideas. This attempt to see history as the interplay of events and ideas was carried forward into the fifth century by Augustine, whose *Civitas Dei* (*City of God*) described a complex relationship between secular, Roman history and that of Christianity.

The Middle Ages brought a temporary disruption of standard, classical historical writing, though for generations, monastic scribes transmitted not only copies of religious manuscripts but also year-by-year records of the events they witnessed. In time, these chronologies were organized by, among others, Gregory of Tours and the Venerable Bede. The integration of secular and church history diminished with the Renaissance, as Europeans began to rediscover ancient and classical writers and their works. Niccolò Machiavelli recast human events in human rather than divine terms, placing renewed emphasis on secular rulers and the secular state as the defining characteristic of human life and history.

With the exception of the work of Eusebius, most classical, medieval, and Renaissance historical literature emphasized the literary aspect of historical writing rather than research. In other words, they were more interested in telling a good story than in getting the facts right. In the sixteenth century, however, this began to change. A generation of antiquarians began to delve into archival preservation and establish basic parameters for future historical work. By the eighteenth century, however, Enlightenment thinkers began to shun the rigors of research and to focus their energies on producing a philosophical interpretation of the past. Writers such as Montesquieu, Voltaire, and David Hume sacrificed documentary evidence for a more vigorous, enjoyable style.

Those who desire to read about the past could choose, therefore, from work that was either accurate but cold and dreary or less than precise but enjoyable to read. From 1776 through 1788, Edward Gibbon successfully synthesized research and quality writing in his masterful classic *The History of the Decline and Fall of the Roman Empire*. Widely consulted today, Gibbon's work established a standard for historical presentation which we still employ.

Nineteenth-century historian Leopold von Ranke introduced to the writing of history the idea of an impartial, unbiased examination of the past. He insisted that the proper approach to the past should be made through an era's documentary evidence, with the further admonition that researchers should take into account the contemporary situation of the source and therefore form their opinions judiciously. This advance lifted historical studies out of the dark, dusty realm of the antiquarians as well as away from the flashing pens of Enlightenment philosophers. Von Ranke, in other words, transformed history from merely another literary genre into a modern science and a recognized academic discipline. German methods became the standard by which the past was recaptured and presented.

George Bancroft was the first American to study the history of the United States, though his views were influenced by the nationalist fervor of the times in which he wrote. By the turn of the twentieth century, history was an established professional field, firmly fixed in universities on both sides of the Atlantic. Writers were making consistent, methodical use of primary sources to discover, interpret, and present the past to scholars and lay persons alike.

Two Stories

Years ago a young man in an American history survey course became incensed during class. The lecture that day was devoted to an overview of Puritan theology as it applied to the colonization of seventeenth-century New England. As the discussion drifted toward the complex philosophical reasons for their insistence on conformity of thought, the student became more and more tumultuous. He decried the bigotry of the Puritans. He despised their hate. He blasted any view that said, "Our way of seeing things is the only way of seeing things." As his tirade continued, it became more and more apparent to professor and students alike that there was indeed a bigot in the room, one who believed that his way of seeing things was the only way.

On another occasion, the Arts and Humanities Council of Tulsa, Oklahoma sponsored its annual Chautauqua program, where scholars are invited to assume the identities of famous or not-so-famous characters and present these historical individuals to an audience under a huge tent. Among the very fine portrayals that year were one of William Jennings Bryan and one of Clarence Darrow. As a fitting climax to the evening's performance, the two scholars reenacted the final moments of the famous Scopes trial, the "monkey" trial, held in Dayton, Tennessee, in 1925, in which an insular, fundamentalist community challenged a teacher's right to teach the theory of evolution. When the two finished and began to ask for questions from the audience, a young man rose at the back of the tent and for several minutes blasted the scholar who had portrayed Bryan, claiming that his interpretation was too sympathetic and not harsh enough. The crowd listened with a mingled air of embarrassment and disgust as the man continued. He decried the bigotry of religious fundamentalists. He despised their closed mindedness. He blasted any view that said, "Our view of the origin of things is the only view of the origin of things." As the diatribe went on, it became clear that there was indeed a fundamentalist in the tent, one whose mind was tightly closed, who believed that his way of seeing things was the only way.

1.5 The Discipline of History Today

The two true stories above illustrate a phenomenon characteristic of modern historical studies. Since the turn of the century, the study of history has experienced a tremendous fragmentation. There are now many approaches to analyzing the past, and most of them are needed and welcomed. Other approaches, however, have been less useful, falling victim to passing academic fads and in some cases replacing instruction with indoctrination. It has become fashionable for the holders of various politically driven historical viewpoints to attack those who disagree with them. In the process of their attack, however, these agenda-driven thinkers become smug and self-righteous as well, often exacerbating the problem by failing to recognize in themselves the arrogance they perceive in others.

Both ends of the political spectrum, liberal and conservative, fall prey to this sort of monolithic thinking, as well as those who occupy the turf in the middle. This is the point of the two stories above.

Our desire is that you view history and write about it as objectively as possible. What we are urging is balance. It is fine, even laudable, to be passionate about certain things, but often passion short-circuits reason. With this in mind, let us present for your consideration a list of the areas in which current historiography has ventured boldly and sometimes, perhaps, too far.

Revisionism

Basically, revisionism means to look into long-held opinions to see if they still hold up as objective truth, and then, if they do not, to revise them for greater accuracy. On the surface, what could be wrong with this? What could be worse than burying one's head in a fable just because it is traditional while neglecting the truth because the truth might be uncomfortable? The answer, of course, is that there is nothing wrong with seeking truth. Replacing the traditional belief that a vengeful North pushed Southern whites to extremes during Reconstruction with the current view that an unrepentant white South craftily replaced many prewar institutions is a work of revisionism. While the new view may not please everyone, for the moment it does seem to a majority of historians to be closer to the truth of what happened in the postwar South.

The problem lies not in replacing fiction with fact but rather with practicing revisionism for its own sake or for the sake of advancing a new ideology. Many scholars are driven by a desire not to find the correct story but merely to vindicate an alternative story. This tendency is sometimes aggravated by political bias and personal agendas. In other words, it is possible for a revisionist version of history to be just as slanted in one direction as the older view that it attempts to displace is in another.

Social History

As you shall see later in this book, we are fans of social history. Knowing about prime ministers and presidents is fine, but what about common people, those who served as models for characters in Austen, Dickens, or Michener novels? How did they live? How were nineteenth-century Plains farmers able to enjoy ice cream in the summer? Looking into the lives of insignificant people is often more fun and more enlightening than studying popes and potentates. But sometimes this focus on the common person becomes too intrusive, supplanting a necessary grounding in the larger tide of events. We need to know about the ordinary people, but we need to know about the popes and queens and generals, too. Otherwise, our understanding of the details of everyday life in small communities remains fragmented and shallow, because the larger cultural context that gave meaning to those details remains unexplored.

The result of an overemphasis on social history is an imbalance in our understanding of the past. This imbalance, often actuated by politics and agendas, can be seen in one very popular American history textbook, which discusses the savage beating of Rodney C. King in Los Angeles. No page reports the name Neil Armstrong, the first man to walk on the moon. In another text, a full page is devoted to the Salem witch hunt phenomenon but only a single sentence is given to the Lewis and Clark expedition.

Pluralism

Who is not delighted to see, after decades of nonmention, a more complete discussion of the roles of women and minorities in shaping history? A multicultural approach to the past is long overdue. Those of us who have specialized in the study of particular racial or ethnic groups are encouraged to see newer textbooks with more space given to the stories of deserving American groups. With this vital improvement, however, comes the potential once again for imbalance. Consider this conundrum.

What happens when a multiculturalist encounters a member of an ethnocentric society? It is important for you to know that multiculturalism is a predominantly Western notion; many cultures in the world are not multicultural. If the multiculturalist in our story tries to persuade the enthnocentrist to change, then has not the multiculturalist presumed moral superiority over the ethnocentrist and become ethnocentric in the process? On the other hand, if the multiculturalist accepts the other's ethnocentrism, is he or she not tacitly admitting that there is an acceptable place for ethnocentrism? True multiculturalism would, in fact, accept all the facets of another culture, including that culture's refusal to be multicultural. While the value of multiculturalism is not in question, there is still the old problem of balance. How far should a historian work to advance the banner of ethnic equality? Far enough to destabilize the culture of another country? It is a difficult question to answer.

Political Correctness

Political correctness can be seen as an attempt to enforce a doctrine of equality upon a culture that has trouble giving up outmoded notions of acceptable behavior. It is a doctrine that requires its adherents to acknowledge that certain cultural values are absolute, regardless of time or place. In a sense, political correctness is a refutation of the relativism that permeated the 1960s and 1970s. The old catch phrase "different strokes for different folks" is not acceptable to the politically correct. Now all folks must be treated with the same strokes—and the strokes must be approved by . . . whom? By the politically correct, who presume their way to be the correct way, the only acceptable way.

While its end—equality of treatment for everybody—may sound noble, the problem with political correctness is that it can too easily become a kind of neo-Puritanism, "correcting" the behavior of everyone according to a model approved by only a few who believe that what is proper for them must be proper for everyone. The politically correct believe in freedom of thought, but only as long as your thought conforms with theirs. The politically correct preach toleration, but only of the same things they themselves find acceptable. Ironically, in the name of open-mindedness, the minds of the politically correct can become closed. A real searcher for the truth would listen carefully and evaluate a position that contradicts theirs instead of automatically condemning it because it is outside the realm of acceptability.

Our Goal

We would like you to become an excellent researcher, a fine writer of historical papers, and a successful student in each of your college classes, not just those taught in the history department. Beyond that, however, we would like you to be as impartial and unbiased as possible when you examine historical topics. We hope you develop a passion for history, as we have, but we also hope that you do not let passion about a subject keep you from a dispassionate assessment. We urge you to be a seeker of truth rather than a follower of fads. We want you to think for yourself, not think to please instructors. That should be the goal of academia itself—not to propagate arrogant viewpoints and not to replace one dogma with another equally rigid. Read, research, consider, and write. And enjoy this book, too!

2 *Writing as Communication*

2.1 Writing to Learn

Writing is a way of ordering ideas or recording them for future reference. The earliest use of written language probably arose from the need to enumerate the details of commercial transactions. We do many kinds of writing every day. We make grocery lists, "things-to-do" lists, lists of people to invite to a party. We enter payments in a checkbook registry. We receive monthly bank and credit card statements. Written memos from employers appear on our desks. Certainly our technology has taken us far from the days of quill pens, yet our modern lives are characterized by more writing, not less. We use fax machines, photocopiers, and E-mail. We go through life leaving behind us a "paper trail." Writing is indeed a fact of life, and those who write well distinguish themselves from those who do not. They rise above the crowd. They stand out. They may be selected for employment ahead of those who have never honed such basic skills.

When we write, we are ordering our experiences. We are putting pieces of our world together in new ways and making ourselves freshly conscious of these pieces. This is one reason why writing is so hard. From the flood of data our minds continually collect, process, and lock into our memories, we are selecting only certain items significant to the immediate task, connecting these with other items and rephrasing them in new relationships. We are constantly remapping part of our universe, gaining a little more control over the processes by which we interact with the world around us.

For all these reasons, the act of writing is never insignificant. Writing is communication, if not with another human being, then with ourselves. It is a way of making a fresh connection with our world.

Writing therefore is also one of the best ways to learn. This statement at first may seem odd. If you are an unpracticed writer, you may share a common notion that the only purpose of writing is to express what you already know or think. According to this view, any learning that you as a writer may have experienced has already occurred by the time your pen meets the paper or your fingers touch the keyboard. Your task is to inform, entertain, or even surprise the reader. But if you are a practiced writer, you know that at any moment as you write, you are capable of surprising *yourself*. And it is surprise that you desire: the shock of seeing what happens in your own mind when you drop an old, established opinion into a batch of new facts or bump into a cherished belief from a different angle. Writing synthesizes new understanding not only for the prospective reader but also—and perhaps more importantly—for the writer. We make meaning as we write, jolting ourselves by little, surprising discoveries into a larger, more interesting universe.

2.1.1 The Irony of Writing

As we have said, history is more than the mere memorization of names, dates, and places. Each of the social sciences, including history, has as its main focus the search for a better understanding of who we are as human beings. All of us, not just the social scientist or the historian, benefit by this deeper understanding. An artist's masterpiece is created with thousands of brush strokes on a canvas. Individually, these strokes mean very little, but seen together and from a wider vantage point, they blend to produce a clear image. Historians look for facts, to be sure, but the true historian looks for the larger picture revealed by the individual facts. Internalizing the facts, therefore, is only the first step in the learning process. Starting with a knowledge of the essentials, we begin to synthesize the facts until new shapes begin to emerge.

Archaeology, a discipline in which laboratory science and history converge, specializes in turning a mountain of seemingly unrelated, individual facts into a cohesive and interesting story. If, for example, the same types of broken pottery, or "sherds," are unearthed from various sites scattered across the northern Mediterranean rim, and if it can be determined that these artifacts are related by time, place of origin, and method of manufacture, the picture that could emerge is one of a society whose economy involved an extensive trade network, with advanced navigation abilities, a useful language for recording day-to-day commercial necessities, or even possible engagement in ancient wars for "turf." The many ceramic fragments are important. Even more important, however, is the understanding they help us gain of a culture and a time period in human history.

It is to test this broader understanding of larger concepts that many professors prefer to use an essay form of examination. Short answer questions—multiple choice, matching, and the like—tend to test the recall of facts. Essays require deeper comprehension: "What can you tell me about A, B, and C?" is not as significant or sophisticated as "What do A, B, and C tell us about D?" Writing not only helps the professor determine what has been learned but also aids the student in focusing, ordering, and assessing the facts in new ways. It is a forced look at the big picture and an internalizing of concepts. An essay exam, therefore, can be both a testing tool and a teaching tool. It is but one of many examples of the vital act of "writing to learn."

| EXERCISE | *Learning by Writing* |

One way of testing the notion that writing is a powerful learning tool is by rewriting your notes from a recent class lecture. The type of class does not matter; it can be history, English literature, or anthropology. In class, you probably did not have clock time to capture more than the bare essentials, mostly nouns and perhaps a few verbs. As you rewrite, add transitional elements such as prepositions and conjunctions as well as adjectives and adverbs, if you wish, to "flesh out" your notes. Furnish your own anecdotes or illustrations to add more meaning.

Another way to accomplish similar results is to read a portion of your textbook—a section, subsection, or even a paragraph—and then rewrite that segment in your own words. Again, supply you own illustrations to help you understand the points the text was trying to make. By becoming an author yourself for a few minutes, you will begin to experience the assessing and decision making—the ordering of ideas—that lie at the heart of the writing process. And you will learn by writing.

Challenge Yourself

There is no way around it: Writing, for most people, is a struggle. Of course, there have been a few Mozarts for whom creating seemed as effortless as breathing. Remember that there have been Beethovens as well, who at times had to work and rework certain passages again and again until they satisfied him. Some never did! Bringing order to the world is never easy. The 1978 Nobel Prize winner in literature, Isaac Bashevis Singer, once wrote, "I believe in miracles in every area of life except writing. . . . The only thing that produces good writing is hard work" (qtd. in Lunceford and Conners 1992, 2).

Thomas Jefferson's original draft of the Declaration of Independence is not the same version you will find reprinted in the appendices of history textbooks. Not only did he revise his own work, but the Second Continental Congress also took their turn dismantling and rewording major provisions in the document. The cogent, frugal wording of Abraham Lincoln's Gettysburg Address emerged only through intense care, finesse, and frustration. When he gave the speech, he was given sparing applause by a crowd who deemed it either a bore or an insult to a dignified occasion. Then he was roundly criticized by the national newspapers, who relegated the address to "back page" status. Yet Edward Everett, who had spoken just before Lincoln that day, said of the president's work, "I wish I could flatter myself that I had come as near to the central idea of the occasion in two hours as you did in two minutes" (Microsoft. *Encarta.* 1994, Microsoft Corporation. Copyright © 1994 Funk and Wagnall's Corporation).

Enjoy the eloquence of Jefferson:

We hold these Truths to be self-evident, That all men are created equal, That they are endowed by their Creator with certain unalienable rights, That among these are Life, Liberty, and the Pursuit of Happiness, That to secure these rights, governments are instituted among men, deriving their just powers from the Consent of the Governed, That when any government becomes destructive of these ends, it is the Right of the People to alter or abolish it.

and of Lincoln:

Now we are engaged in a great civil war, testing whether that nation or any nation so conceived and so dedicated can long endure. We are met on a great battlefield of that war. We have come to dedicate a portion of that field as a final resting place for those who here gave their lives that that nation might live. It is altogether fitting and proper that we should do this.

But, in a larger sense, we cannot dedicate—we cannot consecrate—we cannot hallow this ground. The brave men, living and dead, who struggled here, have consecrated it far above our poor power to add or detract. The world will little note, nor long remember, what we say here, but it can never forget what they did here. It is for us the living, rather, to be dedicated here to the unfinished work which they who fought here have thus far so nobly advanced. It is rather for us to be here dedicated to the great task remaining before us—that from these honored dead we take increased devotion to that cause for which they gave the last full measure of devotion—that we here highly resolve that these dead shall not have died in vain—that this nation, under God, shall have a new birth of freedom—and that government of the people, by the people, for the people, shall not perish from the earth.

Hard work was evident in the words of John F. Kennedy's Inaugural Address. Each word was crafted to embed an image in the listener's mind. As you read the following excerpt from Kennedy's speech, what images does it evoke? Some historians consider a president "great" when his words live longer than his deeds in the minds of the people. Do you think this will be—or has been—true of Kennedy?

We observe today not a victory of party but a celebration of freedom—symbolizing an end as well as a beginning—signifying renewal as well as change. For I have sworn before you and Almighty God the same solemn oath our forebears prescribed nearly a century and three quarters ago. The world is very different now. For man holds in is mortal hands that power to abolish all forms of human poverty and all forms of human life. And yet the same revolutionary beliefs for which our fore bears fought are still at issue around the globe—the belief that the rights of man come not from the generosity of the state but from the hand of God.
We dare not forget that we are the heirs of that first revolution. Let the word go forth from this time and place, to friend and foe alike that the torch has

been passed to a new generation of Americans—born in this century, tempered by war, disciplined by a hard and bitter peace, proud of our ancient heritage—and unwilling to witness or permit the slow undoing of those human rights to which this nation has always been committed, and to which we are committed today at home and around the world. . . .

In the long history of the world, only a few generations have been granted the role of defending freedom in its hours of maximum danger. I do not shrink from the responsibility—I welcome it. I do not believe that any of us would exchange places with any other generation. . . . And so, my fellow Americans: ask not what your country can do for you—ask what you can do for your country. My fellow citizens of the world: ask not what America will do for you, but what together we can do for the freedom of man. (qtd. in Boller and Story)

One reason that writing is difficult is that it is not actually a single activity at all but a process consisting of several activities that overlap, with two or more sometimes operating simultaneously as your considerations and labors range from small to large. An artist faces the same series of decisions during the act of visual creating. Which brush? What color? What about perspective, shape, form, and line? A composer has similar worries concerning not only notes but also instrumentation, phrasing, thematic structure, and so forth. You as a writer have many constant decisions to make, from individual word choices to varied sentence structure to paragraph organization to overall format. And while all of these mundane decisions are being made, you cannot forget your main purpose in writing in the first place: To convey some worthwhile message. In other words, you are constantly deciding what to say, how to say it, to whom you will be saying it, when to say it, why to say it, and even whether to say it! The writing process is often a frustrating search for meaning and for the best ways to express that meaning.

Frustrating though that search may be, it need not be futile. Remember this: The writing process uses skills we all have. The ability to write well, in other words, is not some mystical dispensation bestowed on the rare, fortunate individual. While few of us may achieve the lofty proficiency of a Jefferson, Lincoln, or Kennedy, we are all capable of phrasing thoughts clearly and in well-organized fashion. But learning how to do so takes practice. The only sure way to improve your writing is to write.

2.1.2 Maintain Enthusiasm

One of the toughest but most important jobs in writing is to maintain enthusiasm for your writing project. Such commitment may sometimes be hard to achieve, given the difficulties that are inherent in the writing process and that can be made worse when the project is unappealing at first glance. Suppose that your main interest in history concerns gender roles in the United States in the nineteenth century. Then suppose that your Western Civilization teacher has assigned a fifteen-page research paper on eleventh century Scandinavia! How can you manufacture sufficient excitement and desire to plunge into a topic that does not fit your interests exactly?

One of the worst mistakes that unpracticed student writers make is to fail to assume responsibility for keeping themselves interested in their writing. No matter how hard it may seem at first to drum up interest in your topic, you have to do it—that is, if you want a paper you can be proud of, one that contributes useful material and a fresh point of view to the topic. One thing is guaranteed: If you are bored with your writing, your reader will be, too. So what can you do to keep your interest and energy level high?

Challenge yourself! Think of the paper not as an assignment but as a piece of writing that has a point to make. To get this point across persuasively is the real reason why you are writing, not the simple fact that a teacher has assigned you a project. If someone were to ask you why you are writing your paper, and your immediate, unthinking response is, "because I've been given this assignment," or "Because I want a good grade," or some other nonanswer along these lines, your paper may be in trouble. If, however, your first impulse is to explain the challenge of your main point—"I want to show the important place women occupied in Norse society," or "I want to demonstrate that the Vikings were more interested in trade than in pillage and plunder"—then you are thinking usefully about your topic.

2.1.3 Maintain Self-Confidence

Having confidence in your ability to write well about your topic is essential for good writing. Every writer experiences uncertainty in each phase of the writing process. You are not alone in your struggle to weigh evidence, to test hypotheses, to reject hypotheses if necessary, and to experiment with organizational strategies and wording. Be ready for temporary confusion and for seeming dead-ends, and remember that every writer faces these obstacles. It is from your struggle to combine facts and buttress opinion with evidence that order arises.

Do not be intimidated by the amount and quality of work that others have already done in your field of inquiry. Remember that no important topic is ever completely exhausted. There always will be gaps in the historical record. For example, just when we think everything that possibly could be written about some aspect of the American Civil War has been written, someone will discover some new facts or take a fresh and interesting look at the existing facts. Look for the gaps, questions that have not been satisfactorily explored in either published research or the prevailing popular opinion. It is in these gaps that you establish your own authority, your own sense of control.

Remember also that the various stages of the writing process reinforce each other. Establishing solid motivation strengthens your sense of confidence about the project, which in turn influences how successfully you organize and write. If you start well, use good work habits, and give yourself ample time for the various activities to coalesce, you should produce a paper that your audience will find both readable and useful.

2.2 Learning to Write: The Writing Process

2.2.1 The Nature of the Process

As we have said, the writing process involves doing many things at once. This multidirectional awareness begins even before your pen first touches the paper or your fingers begin pounding the keyboard. The earliest stages of the planning process require defining and refining your topic, maintaining your thesis focus, making decisions about your audience which will in turn determine your writing style, and handling the raw results of the research process. Different aspects of the writing process overlap, and much of the difficulty of writing occurs because so many things are happening at once. You will feel like the circus performer who spins all those plates on vertical rods. Just when you think everything is finally under control—when all your plates are spinning just fine—you will notice one or two things you had missed before—a crash about to happen. Perhaps you will develop a wonderful outline only to realize that it does not really lend enough support to your thesis. Maybe your command of basic grammar is so good that you expend your efforts in flawless sentence construction, only to face the grim reality that you have wandered from the central issue and are taking your readers down some very interesting but irrelevant tangent. Through practice—that is, through writing—it is possible to learn how to control those parts of the process that in fact can be controlled and to encourage those mysterious, less controllable activities.

No two people engage in writing in exactly the same way. It is important to recognize the routines—modes of thought as well as individual exercises—that help you negotiate the process successfully. It is also important to give yourself as much time as possible to complete the process. Procrastination is one of the writer's greatest enemies. It saps confidence, undermines energy, destroys concentration, and increases stress. It is much easier to pick up your TV's remote control than a pen and yellow pad. It is more fun to click to a computer game than to a word processing program. Writing regularly and following a well-planned schedule as closely as possible can often make the difference between a confident piece of work and an obvious, last minute "rush job"—between a successful paper and an embarrassment.

Although the various parts of the writing process are interwoven, there is naturally a general order or flow to the work of writing. You have to start somewhere! What follows is a description of the various stages you will encounter as you write: planning, drafting, revising, editing, and proofreading. We also will share some suggestions and tips on how to approach each of these stages successfully. Remember that these tips are suggestions, not rigid rules. You do not need more things to worry about. You will not be arrested if you change the order of the stages or even leave one out completely. Do what ultimately works for you!

2.2.2 Planning

A little planning at the beginning of the writing process will give shape and direction to your work. It will help you stay focused on the purpose you are trying to accomplish. If you are planning to eat tonight at a new restaurant whose location you are not sure about, you could drive up and down each and every street of your town until you happen to come across the right place. A better way, however, might be to plan ahead so you do not wander long and aimlessly. As silly as the first example might seem, there are students who begin writing this same way. This risky start usually produces one of two results: Either they find that they run out of things to say in a few, very general pages, or their narrative rambles without end. Their paper becomes either a shallow and superficial gloss-over of their topic, or it is a bore that drones on and on. A basic game plan established before you begin will help you to avoid both of these needless disasters.

During the important planning stage, at least three early choices must be made. These concern topic, purpose, and audience—elements that constitute the writing context, or the terms under which we all write. Every time you write anything, whether it is a grocery list or an application for a job, each of these elements is present. You are not conscious of these in mundane, everyday matters, but you must think carefully about them when you are writing a history paper. Some or all of these defining elements may be dictated by the exact nature of the assignment, yet you will always retain a certain degree of control over them.

2.2.3 Selecting a Topic

No matter how restrictive an assignment may seem, there is no reason to feel trapped by it. Within any assigned subject you can find a range of topics to explore. What you are seeking is a topic that engages your own interest. Let your curiosity take you where it will. Perhaps you have been assigned the subject of Medieval Scandinavia. At first you may think this topic has nothing whatsoever to do with your interest in Native American history. Any good topic comes with a set of questions. You may well find that your interest increases if you simply begin asking questions. For example, did or does Scandinavia have its own indigenous people? If so, who were or are they? Where did they come from? When did they arrive? What was the experience of these people during the Middle Ages? Are there any links between their experience and that of America's native people? One strong recommendation: Ask these questions on paper! The process of exploring your way through a topic is transformed when you write down your thoughts as they come instead of letting them fly around through your mind unrecorded.

While it is vital to be interested in your topic, you do not have to be an expert on it at the outset of your investigation. You may in fact know nothing at all about it. Wanting to know more may be what triggers your interest in the first place. In some cases, knowing too much about a subject may cause you to experience some "burnout." In other cases, an intimate knowledge of a subject may have supplied you with preconceptions that could cause you to approach the topic with too much excess emotional baggage, thus blurring your judgment and jeopardizing your ability to remain objective.

2.2.4 Narrowing a Topic

Although it often seems to be a burden to many students, the task of narrowing your topic will afford you a great opportunity to reestablish a degree of control over your project. You may take the instructor's broad assignment and hone it to suit both your own interests and the specific requirements of the assignment. If you do a good job here, you could almost guarantee yourself sufficient motivation and confidence for the tasks ahead. If you do not do this well, somewhere along the way you may find yourself overwhelmed, directionless, and out of energy, asking yourself, "Why did I enroll in this class?"

Almost always, the first topics that come to your mind will be much too large for you to handle in your research paper. Many students make mistakes by failing to narrow their topic enough. They find so much available material that they feel overwhelmed and burdened. Their complaint is often that they "don't know where to begin." They may either lose interest entirely or submit a very general rehashing of well-known facts.

Sometimes (but not often) students may narrow too much. The problem here could be a scarcity of readily available or easily accessible research materials. Papers with too narrow a focus often wind up restating the same few facts over and over, only in different words. The idea is to find a topic that is both interesting and manageable. Despite the volumes that have been written on the Second World War, it is still not an exhausted subject. The battle for Iwo Jima, for example, has already been the subject of books and even a John Wayne movie. A ten- or twelve-page paper on the basics will add little that is new. Perhaps, however, you have a relative or acquaintance who was there. If he is willing to share his memories, he will know particulars and have personal anecdotes and perspectives that no book can supply. Maybe you could investigate the story of a particular regiment in a particular battle. Maybe an aspect of the war on a homefront (not just the American homefront) may interest you, such as the problems of rationing food or collecting metal for the war effort. Again, start with your own questions. What would you like to know more completely? Think through the possibilities that occur to you and, as always, jot down your thoughts.

EXERCISE   *Selecting a Topic*

Here is a variation of the famous "ink blot" test. Write each very general topic listed below, then jot down as many related topics as you can think of. Allow yourself only a couple of minutes for each general topic.

Greek Democracy	The Papacy	Theodore Roosevelt
The Crusades	The Aztecs	The Labor Movement
Tudor England	Transcendentalism	Watergate

EXERCISE	*Narrowing Topics*

Without doing research, see how you can narrow the following general topics. (Hint: Try narrowing by time and/or place.)

EXAMPLE   General topic: The Roman Empire

               Narrowed topics: Roman Architecture

                                       The Emperor Tiberius

                                       The Roman Navy

                                       Religion in pre-Christian Rome

GENERAL TOPICS

Ancient Mesopotamia   British Government

Classical Greece   The American Revolution

Medieval Feudalism   The French Revolution

The Protestant Reformation   Manifest Destiny

The Renaissance   The Gilded Age

Sub-Saharan Africa   The New Deal

Pre-Columbian North America   The Cold War

Japan   The Civil Rights Movement

2.2.5 Finding a Thesis

As you conduct your research and as you begin to plan your writing, look for and begin to formulate a central idea that can serve as your thesis. A thesis is not a fact, which can immediately be verified by data, but an assertion worth discussing—an argument with more than one possible conclusion. Your thesis sentence will reveal to your reader not only the argument you have chosen but also your orientation toward it and the conclusion that your paper will attempt to prove. Be flexible about your initial conclusions. As your research continues, you may often encounter bits of factual information which could shed new light on your subject. If you stumble across such facts, you will have a decision to make: You may "sit on" the new information, as if you had never seen it and hope that no other researcher ever will find it. Or you will have to rethink your thesis. Choose the latter.

In looking for a thesis, you are doing many jobs at once:

• You are limiting the amount and kind of material that you must cover, thus making it manageable.

- You are increasing your own interest in the narrowing field of study.
- You are working to establish your paper's purpose, the reason why you are writing about your topic. (If the only reason you can see for writing is to earn a good grade, you will probably be disappointed!)
- You are establishing your notion of who your audience is and what sort of approach to the subject might best capture their interest.

In short, you are gaining control over your writing context. For this reason, it is a good idea to formulate a thesis early—a working thesis. No doubt by the time your research phase is very far along you will have begun to form opinions about the topic on which you are working. As we have said, these opinions may evolve as you uncover new evidence and your thinking deepens. An early thesis idea will allow you to establish a measure of order in the planning stage.

The introduction of your paper will contain a sentence that expresses the task you intend to accomplish. This *thesis sentence* communicates your main idea—the one you are going to prove, defend, or illustrate. It creates an expectation in the reader's mind, and it is your paper's job then to satisfy that expectation. But in the planning stage, a thesis sentence is more than just a statement that informs your reader of your goal. It is a valuable tool to help you to narrow your focus and confirm in your own mind your paper's purpose.

At some point during your preliminary thinking about a topic selection, you should visit a library to get an idea about how much published work on your area of interest exists. This search has at least two benefits:

- It acquaints you with a body of writing that will become very important in the research phase of your paper.
- It gives you a sense of how your topic is generally addressed by the community of scholars you are joining. Is the topic as important as you think it is? Has there been so much research on the subject as to make your inquiry in its present, raw form irrelevant?

As you determine your topic, remember that one of the goals of history writing in college is to enhance your own understanding of the science of history itself. You want to learn how history works—what the role of the historian is: To examine past human behavior in order to give present humans a clearer understanding of themselves. Let this goal help you aim your research into those areas that you know are important to your understanding of the discipline.

2.2.6 Defining a Purpose

There are many ways to classify the purposes of writing, but in general most writing is undertaken either to inform or to persuade an audience. The goal of informative or expository writing is simply to impart information about a particular subject. Here the historian remains more aloof, an objective, third-person observer. The aim of persuasive writing is to convince your reader of your point of view on a issue. This purpose may be both easier and harder for the historian, who will have no trouble expressing opinions but will have a harder time retaining enough detachment to be taken seriously. After all, everyone has opinions. Many (if not most) people do not hesitate to express them. Why should readers take the time to consider yours? They will, if your opinion is sufficiently buttressed by careful and meaningful research, which gives credibility to your opinions. Often the distinction between expository and persuasive writing is blurred, and most historical writing has elements of both. Historians who care enough about an issue to spend, in some cases, years in research and writing about it obviously have invested too much caring in that topic to remain absolutely dispassionate. (For that matter, is it possible to be *completely* objective about anything?)

EXERCISE   *To Explain or to Persuade?*

Here is an easy one. Can you tell from the titles of each of these two papers, both on the same topic, which is an expository paper and which is a persuasive paper?

    1. Everyday Life in Eleventh-Century Norway

    2. The Vikings: Raiders or Traders, A Reassessment

      Learn what you want to say. Do you want to bring your reader to a clearer, deeper understanding or a completely different understanding of an issue? By the time you write your final draft, you must have a very sound notion of the point you wish to make and the purpose for which you want to make it. If, as you write that final draft, someone were to ask you to state your thesis, you should be able to give a satisfactory answer with a minimum of delay and no prompting. If, on the other hand, you fumble for an answer because you cannot express your thesis easily, you may not be ready yet to write a final draft. You may have to engage in some prewriting activities or even write a complete preliminary draft to allow yourself to arrive at a secure understanding of your task.

EXERCISE   *Knowing What You Want to Say*

Three student writers have been asked to state the thesis of their papers. Which two better understand the writing task?

"My paper is about the Civil War."

"My paper examines and explains the Confederate government's treaty negotiations with the so-called 'Five Civilized' Tribes of Indian Territory."

"My paper argues that the Richmond government manipulated the tribes of Indian Territory in order to obtain needed food supplies for Southern armies, so that the planters could continue to raise profitable cotton instead of wheat and corn."

Even though you may be writing a persuasive paper, watch out for bias! No historian is a machine. No matter how hard we try to produce a pristine, objective paper, the fact is that every choice we make as we write is influenced to some extent by a multitude of factors. All of us, like it or not, write about the past through the lens of our own experience, and what we write is colored by personal beliefs and opinions. If you are black, you likely will view slavery in the ante-bellum American South in a vastly different light than a student of another ethnic heritage will. If you are Catholic, your views on the Protestant Reformation will differ from those of a student from another religious background. What we tell our readers as truth, in other words, is shaded, sometimes without our knowing, by factors such as our environment, our upbringing, our religion, and our education; by our attitude toward our audience; by our political party affiliation; by our race and gender; by our career goals; even by our reasons for writing. Perhaps, for example, you are the only Native American student in a graduate writing seminar. This situation will shape the development of your paper. The influence of such factors can be very subtle, and it is something you must work to identify in your own writing as well as in the writing of others in order not to mislead or be misled. Remember that one of the reasons for writing is self-discovery. The writing that you do in your history classes, as well as the writing you will do for the rest of your life, will give you a chance to discover and confront honestly your own views on your subjects. Responsible writers keep an eye on their own biases and are honest about them with their readers.

2.2.7 Defining Your Audience

Many aspects of the writing process depend upon the audience to whom you direct your writing. A "Things to Do" list written to yourself obviously requires a different approach than a formal, twenty-page research paper written for a college professor's seminar. Regardless of the audience, whether it is yourself, a professor, the other members of a class, or the readers of an esoteric historical journal, the object of your work is not to jump through a set of technical hoops. The fundamental point of a list, a scholarly monograph, or any writing project in between is communication. In historical writing this involves the transmission of your knowledge and your conclusions to your reader or readers in a way that suits you. Your task will also include the passing of the spark of your enthusiasm for your topic. Readers who may have been indifferent to your topic before reading your paper should look at it in a new way after finishing it. This is one of the greatest challenges of writing: To enter into your reader's mind and leave behind new answers and new questions!

The discrepancy between the understanding of the writer and that of the audience is one of the greatest impediments to communication, but it is also the basis and beginning of effective communication. To overcome this barrier, you must consider the needs of your audience. By the time you begin drafting, most if not all of your ideas will have begun to attain coherent shape in your mind, so that virtually any words with which you try to express those ideas will reflect your thoughts accurately—*to you.* Your readers, however, have not spent the time in the library that you have. They have not observed, mulled, considered, ruminated, and pondered as you have. You have them, as the saying goes, at a disadvantage. In the number of pages allotted by the restraints of time or the assignment, you must bring your readers carefully along the same path you recently have traveled yourself—that is, if you want them to share your knowledge, your conclusions, and your enthusiasm. If you succeed, even in part, you will have communicated.

You must ask the same questions and make the same decisions a professor makes when he or she designs course content or plans a lecture. What do my students know now? What do they need to know when they are finished? How do I transport them from where they are to where they need to be in terms of knowledge, understanding, and enthusiasm? The same considerations apply in the planning stage of a writing project. What do your readers know already about your subject? What would you like them to know when they finish your paper that they do not know now? What would you like them to see in a different way? What would be the best ways to lead your readers from their current level of understanding to the point where they will at least consider your ideas? The answers to these critical questions will depend, of course, upon the audience. A group of eight or ten fellow students in an undergraduate seminar will produce different answers than a group of scholars at a professional meeting. Probably.

2.2.8 Organizing Your Writing

Few good joke tellers begin with the punch line. The listener must be "set up" with the right premise before the key phrase is added, usually at the end. If certain details or elements are left out, the punch line will fail to trigger laughter. In the same way, a random, disjointed presentation of the facts you have uncovered during your research will fail to have the effects you wanted for your readers. A paper may contain many fascinating factual tidbits, but if these gems are presented in a rambling, ineffective order, the unhappy result will be confusion, boredom, or both! You will neither inform nor persuade, and it is almost certain that you will not pass along the enthusiasm you have for your topic. There are various methods of grouping your ideas, but none is potentially more effective than outlining. The very word, however, conjures unfortunate memories of high school grammar exercises or an ineffective teacher's misguided idea of having students read and comprehend textbook chapters. Good outlining need not be dull or pointless! But it is always a challenge.

2.2.9 Outlining

Outlining for Yourself

Outlining can do a least two vital jobs. First, it can force you, the writer, to gain a better and clearer understanding of your own ideas by arranging them according to their interrelationships. There is one primary rule of outlining: Ideas of equal weight are placed on the same level within the outline. This rule requires you to determine the relative importance of your ideas. You have to decide which ideas are of the same type or order and into which subtopic each idea best fits. If, in the planning stage, you carefully arrange your ideas in a coherent outline, you will greatly enhance your own grasp of the topic. You will have given a logical linkage to your ideas and a basic structure to the body of the paper. Ideas will flow naturally from one to another, and you will take your readers more effectively to the place you want them to be when they finish reading the paper.

The second job an outline can do for you is to decrease inertia when you begin to draft your paper. Many writers experience great anxiety when facing a stark, blank piece of paper, the first glimmer of white as it emerges from a typewriter carriage, or that frightening blank screen on the computer monitor. Having an outline from which to begin writing your first draft has the added effect of providing not only a direction but also any number of starting places. If you cannot muster the inspiration yet to begin with the very first, intimidating word of the introduction, find another place to start for the time being. No immutable writer's law requires you to begin a draft at the beginning. You can always return to the task of writing the first sentence after you have established a rhythm and the creative "juices" are flowing. An outline provides you with little "bites" to chew one at a time, which is an easier task than wading straight into twenty ominous uninterrupted pages of prose!

EXERCISE   *Organizing Thoughts*

Take some time to consider the following ideas or facts. Then number them in logical order.

_____   The exact cause of the death of Alexander the Great remains a mystery.

_____   The young Alexander studied with Aristotle.

_____   Alexander was wounded in battle.

_____   Alexander showed uncommon skill in logistics management.

_____   Following Alexander's death, his generals had difficulty trying to govern his far-flung empire.

_____   Alexander was the son of Philip II of Macedon.

_____   Alexander campaigned successfully from Asia Minor through Palestine, Egypt, and Mesopotamia.

Outlining for Your Reader

In order for your paper to communicate—to escort your readers from their current level of understanding to the point where you want them to be—your ideas must follow a logical pattern. Perhaps you have asked directions about how to find a certain business, a town, or a friend's house. Some people will simply provide an address, which is fine if you happen to have some degree of familiarity with the town already. If you do not, however, you may wander in the hope of finding where you want to go by chance, or you will have to stop and ask directions again. In either case your arrival at your destination will be delayed and frustrated. When presenting your good ideas in a paper, you do not want your readers' arrival at the intended destination to be delayed or frustrated either. You do not want them to have to consult another source to figure out what in the world you were trying to say.

A better way to give instructions to lost motorists is to provide a step-by-step, logical unfolding of their journey, so they will be able to form a mental picture of the proper directions, turns, traffic signals, street numbers, landmarks, and so forth to get them to the place they need to be. A map, whether commercially prepared or quickly sketched, would be better still, because the traveler would have a permanent image to which to refer to keep him or her on the right track.

In the same way, a logical, step-by-step presentation of facts and ideas on paper will see your readers to your desired stopping point. Omitting a key direction, turn, or landmark could make the difference between successful communication and confused, annoyed readers. How do you keep from leaving out something important? You guessed it: Start with an outline!

The Formal Outline Pattern

Following this pattern accurately during the planning stage of your paper helps to guarantee that your ideas are placed logically.

Thesis sentence
I.   First Main Idea
    A.   First subordinate idea
        1.   Reason, example, or illustration
           a.   Supporting detail
           b.   Supporting detail
        2.   Reason, example, or illustration

            a. Supporting detail
            b. Supporting detail
    B.   Second subordinate idea
 II. Second Main Idea

Notice that the thesis sentence *precedes* the outline. This may at first seem puzzling. Why wouldn't the thesis be the first main idea in the outline? Remember that each of the main ideas, I, II, II, and so on, are in some qualitative way equal to each other in importance, and that each of them refers, with equal weight, to your thesis. The thesis, in other words, is the most important sentence in the entire paper; placing it on an equal footing with the main ideas—all of which are actually subordinate to the thesis—throws the outline off balance. The best spot for your thesis sentence is at the top of the outline page, just above the first main idea, so you can refer to it as you organize your thoughts.

Notice also that each level of the outline must have more than one entry; for every A there must be at least a B (and, if required, a C, D, etc.), and for every 1 there must be at least a 2, and so forth. This arrangement forces you to compare ideas, looking carefully at each one to determine its place among the others. The insistence on assigning relative values to your ideas is what makes an outline an effective organizing tool.

You need to make one final decision about your outline: Is it going to be in topic form or sentence form? A topic outline is one in which no numbered entry is a complete sentence:

Thesis: Patrick Henry's homosexuality changed the shape of the Declaration
    of Independence.
 I.   Homosexuality in Colonial times
    A. Religious scruples
    B. English law
 II. Jefferson's reaction to Henry's editing
    A. Confusion at the Convention
    B. Wording amended to delete reference to "sailors"

As you might expect, topic outlines are faster and easier to compile than sentence outlines; there are few complications concerning grammar and syntax in a topic outline. Why, then, would anyone want to use the sentence form of outline, which requires that each numbered entry be a complete sentence? See if you can answer this question by comparing the following sentence outline with the topic outline above:

Thesis: Patrick Henry's homosexuality changed the shape of the Declaration
    of Independence.
 I.   In Colonial times homosexuality was given harsh treatment.
    A. Theologians taught that homosexuality was a mortal sin.
    B. English law condemned practicing homosexuals to lengthy jail terms
       or hanging.

II. Thomas Jefferson's faith in Henry's editorial ability was shaken by Henry's announcement of his homosexuality.
   A. The Convention lost two days of debate in gossip about Henry.
   B. Realizing its true import, Jefferson took out of the Declaration the comment Henry had added about the endurance of the typical British seaman.

As you can see, a sentence outline is more elaborate than a topic outline and requires more thought from the writer. And that is exactly its strength: It forces the writer to think with greater clarity about the points he or she is making and about the order in which they should go.

Here is a trite but effective way to explain the basic presentation of a history paper: Say what you are going to say. Say it. Then say what you have just said. This may seem flippant, but it conveys the essentials: the introduction with thesis, the main points needed to support your thesis, and a conclusion, where you knit together the thesis and its confirming points one last time to seal your message in your readers' minds. Keep this little statement in mind, and you will not stray too far from what you need to accomplish with your paper.

EXERCISE   *Effective Outlining*

Along with the ideas you saw in the previous exercise, you will find here main ideas, subordinate ideas, and so on. Arrange them in a logical outline, in sentence form.

The exact cause of the death of Alexander the Great remains a mystery.

The young Alexander studied with Aristotle.

Alexander was wounded in battle.

The young Alexander was primed for the role he would assume.

Alexander's army advanced into India before turning back.

Alexander showed uncommon skill in logistics management.

Following Alexander's death, his generals had difficulty trying to govern his far-flung empire.

Alexander was the son of Philip II of Macedon.

Alexander's military career was astounding.

Alexander campaigned successfully from Asia Minor through Palestine, Egypt, and Mesopotamia.

Alexander's death was a direct result of his push for empire.

Alexander outmaneuvered the Persians by leaving them in a strategic pass where they had no access to supplies.

Alexander the Great did more than conquer. He spread Greek culture across the Eastern Mediterranean and mingled it with those of the peoples he encountered.

The world after Alexander was shaped by his deeds.

Alexander may have contracted a disease in Asia.

> Alexander's navy sailed along the coast of Palestine with provisions to keep his army fed.

2.2.10 Drafting

You have concluded your research and you have finished your preliminary planning. No longer are you gathering and arranging material from other sources; you are about to become a source yourself! Using your thesis and outline as direction markers, you must now write a first draft, weaving your amalgam of ideas, data, and persuasion strategies into logically ordered sentences and paragraphs. Although some prewriting techniques such as brainstorming or free writing may facilitate the drafting, it still will not be easy. Writers establish their own individual methods of encouraging themselves to forge ahead with the draft, but here are some tips.

1. *Remember that this is only a rough draft, not the final paper.* At this stage, it is not necessary that every word be the best possible choice. You do not need to put that sort of pressure on yourself; you must not allow anything to slow you down now. Writing is not like sculpting in stone, where every chip is permanent. You can always go back to your draft and add, delete, reword, and rearrange. No matter how much effort you have put into planning, you cannot be sure how much of this draft you may eventually keep. It may take several drafts to get one that you find satisfactory.

2. *Give yourself plenty of time!* Avoid delaying the first draft by telling yourself that there is still more research to do. You cannot uncover all the material there is to know on a particular subject, so do not fool yourself into trying. Remember that writing is the process of discovery. You may have to begin writing before you can see exactly what sort of research you still may need to do. Keep in mind that there are other tasks waiting for you after the first draft is finished, so allow for them as you determine your writing schedule.

It is also very important to give yourself time to write because the more time that passes after you have written a draft, the better your ability to view it with greater objectivity. It is very difficult to evaluate your own writing accurately soon after you complete it. We all tend to take criticism of our writing very personally. After spending huge quantities of time in the library and at the typewriter or computer, we think we merit automatic applause. We are proud of our effort, and if the professor does not like our work, it is because "he is such a moron that he cannot really appreciate high quality work." Sound familiar? If you have become so intimately involved in your project that you reject other readers' criticisms, how can you accept your own? You need time to cool down, to recover from the effort of putting all those words together. The "colder" you get on your writing, the better able you are to read it as if it were written by someone else and thus acknowledge the changes you will need to make to strengthen your paper. (Of course, the "I-was-up-typing-until-four-this-morning" papers will lack the strength of those which were given time for careful and honest revisions.)

3. *Stay sharp.* Keep in mind the plan you created as you narrowed your topic, composed your thesis sentence, and outlined your material. But if you begin to feel a strong need to change the plan a bit, do not be afraid to do so. Your goal is to record your best thinking on the subject as accurately as possible.

2.2.11 Language Choices

To be convincing, your writing has to be authoritative. That is, you have to sound as if you have complete confidence in your ability to convey your ideas in words. Sentences that sound stilted or suffer from weak phrasing or the use of clichés are not going to win supporters for the positions that you express in your paper. So a major question becomes: How can I sound confident? Here are some points to consider as you work to convey to your readers that necessary sense of authority.

Level of Formality

Europeans eat with the fork upside down in the left hand and the knife held constantly in the right hand. Most Americans pick up and put down their utensils over and over again through the course of an average meal. Your eating style at a fine San Francisco restaurant would probably differ from that which you would use to consume a hot dog at a Giants' baseball game at Candlestick Park. Conventions and expectations change according to context. The same goes for the language and style you use when you write.

Tone is one of the primary methods by which you tell your readers who you are and what your attitude is toward them and toward your topic. Your major decision is which level of language formality is most appropriate to your audience. The informal tone you would use in a letter to a friend might well be out of place in a paper on New York City voting patterns during the 1830s. Remember that tone is only part of the overall decision that you make about how to present your information. Formality is, to some extent, a function of individual word choices and phrasing. For example, contractions such as "isn't" or "they'll" will not be found in most historical journal articles. How about rhetorical questions such as this one? Or sentence fragments? We have obviously opted to use the more informal first person and second person to be able to communicate more intimately with you, although we would not choose to do so in a paper to be delivered to a group of colleagues at a professional meeting. Usually, in formal writing, you should avoid beginning a sentence with an adverb such as "usually." Part of the challenge of writing a formal paper is simply how to give your prose sufficient impact while staying within the conventions, and different audiences, purposes, and types of papers will require learning various conventions. One of the best ways to acquaint yourself with those conventions is by paying attention to the style employed by writers when you read journal articles or books.

Jargon

One way to lose readers quickly is to overwhelm them with jargon—phrases that have a special, usually technical, meaning within your discipline but which are unfamiliar to the average reader. The very occasional use of jargon may add an effective touch of atmosphere, but anything more than that will severely dampen a reader's enthusiasm for the paper. Often a writer uses jargon in an effort to impress readers by sounding lofty or knowledgeable. The unfortunate result, however, is usually confusion. Worse still, an audience who already has a high degree of knowledge in the subject will see past the facade and recognize the inflated style of writing as an attempt to compensate for scarcity of facts and/or faulty logic. Jargon fools no one.

Some fields of history are more susceptible to jargon usage than others. Specialized fields such as archaeology or military history, to name but two, carry with them their own special terminologies. Most readers will not have words such as "obsidian hydration," or "Minnie ball," in their everyday, working vocabularies.

Some students may feel that, in order to be accepted as historians, they must load their papers with words they probably would not use anywhere else. If you do not use words such as "Oclosyliabic" or "vituperative" on a regular basis, refrain from sprinkling such verbiage in your writing. We could advise, as the bumper sticker says, to "eschew obfuscation." Or we could simply warn against clouding the issue unnecessarily.

Clichés

In the heat of composition, as you are looking for words to help you form your ideas, it is easy to slip in a cliché that has attained universal recognition by overuse. (Note: Clichés differ from jargon in that clichés are part of the general public's everyday language, while jargon is specific to the language of experts in a field.) Our vocabularies are brimming with clichés:

The idea hit him like a ton of bricks.
The Whig Party was forced to face the music.
He passed the test with flying colors.
Truman rose to the occasion.

The problem with clichés is that they are virtually meaningless. Once colorful means of expression, they have lost their color through overuse, and they tend to detract from the quality of other, surrounding word choices. When revising, replace clichés with fresh wording that more accurately conveys your point.

Descriptive Language

It is no secret that historians disagree when it comes to the interpretation of the past. We have said that if one hundred historians gathered in a room and were asked the question "What caused the Fall of Rome?" they would offer one hundred different answers. Historians also disagree about what constitutes a correct historical writing style. Some prefer a language replete with colorful, descriptive prose, writing that is entertaining and enjoyable to read. Others think that historians should write as simply and forthrightly as possible, leaving all those colorful but unnecessary adjectives and adverbs to writers of novels, newspaper columns, and sophomore creative writing assignments.

All languages evolve (some might say, "devolve") through time, and English has been no exception. It was almost a required ritual for Europeans in the eighteenth and nineteenth centuries to sneer at the way the Americans abused English. It was the same animus that caused and causes some Easterners to decry the direct, pragmatic, earthy speech patterns of Westerners. This difference was perhaps never more apparent than in the juxtaposition of the two Gettysburg speeches we mentioned earlier. The famous Eastern orator Edward Everett filled his two-hour discourse with the obligatory allusions from classical literature and with wording that today would be described conservatively as "flowery."

Abraham Lincoln's concluding speech, by contrast, required two minutes, ten sentences, and only 268 words, most of them only one syllable long. He said everything he needed to say in simple, direct, cogent words, using no proper names and no references to Greece or Rome.

When you write your historical paper, among the decisions you will face is how "literary" to make the tone of your prose. Perhaps you admire writing that is entertaining for the reader. Perhaps you view this style as silly or "sophomoric" and prefer a narrative that gets right to the heart of the issue. To an extent, once again, your choice will be determined by context: the type of paper you are presenting, your purpose in writing, your audience, and so on. For each set of potential readers, you will need to arrive at the most effective balance between wording that is so straightforward as to use only simple sentences (and achieve the result of being dull, dry, and boring) and that which appears to be less history and more of a "how-many-adjectives-can-you-cram-into-each-sentence," exercise. Again, pay attention to the styles of established historians and learn from them.

Other Language Considerations

Words can be a very powerful method of either reinforcing or destroying certain cultural stereotypes. By treating the sexes in subtly different ways in your language, you unknowingly may be committing an act of discrimination. A common example is the use of the pronoun "he" to refer to a person whose gender has not been identified. Some writers, when faced with this dilemma, alternate the use of male and female personal pronouns; others use the plural to avoid the need to use a pronoun of either gender.

Remember that language is more than the mere vehicle of your thought. Your words will shape the perceptions of your readers. If your purpose in writing is to inform, your writing style will need to be more objective and therefore less passionate and less descriptive. If your purpose is to entertain with history, you will have more latitude in using colorful words and phrases. If you intend to persuade, you probably can use more potent words to convey your ideas. You should be careful, however, that you retain a certain degree of objectivity; otherwise, your work may be dismissed by readers who will see through your heated prose all the way to your "agenda."

2.2.12 Revising

As we have said, writing is a highly personal activity. Most student writers tend to think that once they have produced their first complete draft, their immortal words should be chiseled on some Washington, D.C. monument. It is hard to accept the idea—from the professor, their seminar classmates, or themselves—that there is room for improvement. The job is finished. It will do fine. Turn it in as is.

As we have also said, some of the most majestic examples of written English have been subjected to intense revision by the writers themselves or by others.

Revising is one of the most important steps in assuring the success of your paper. Unpracticed writers often think of revision as little more than making sure all the i's are dotted and all the t's are crossed, but it is much more than that. Revising is reseeing your work, looking at it from other perspectives, trying always to read your work through the eyes of your audience. Subjecting your entire, hard-fought draft to cold, objective scrutiny is one of the toughest activities to master, but it is absolutely necessary. You must make certain that you have said everything that needs to be said clearly and logically. All it takes is one confusing passage or muddy sentence for the reader's attention to be diverted. You do not want your readers to have to interrupt their concentration to try to discern what you could have stated better had you been honest with your original draft. Here are some tips to help you with revision.

1. *Give yourself adequate time for revision.* As we said earlier, you need to give yourself time to become cold on your paper in order to analyze it objectively. After you have written your draft, spend some time away from it. Then try to reread it as if it had been written by someone else.

2. *Read the paper carefully.* This is tougher than it sounds. One good strategy is to read it aloud to yourself or to have a friend read it aloud while you listen. (Note, however, that friends are usually not the best critics. They are rarely trained in revision techniques and are often unwilling to risk disappointing you by giving your paper a thorough examination.) If you are married, you have a more-or-less captive audience. You can do what countless other married students have done before you: Have your spouse read through your paper. (Couples who have been married a while tend to be more frank with each other.)

If you must read the paper yourself, it may be a good idea to visualize your professor reading the paper. How will she or he view each word? Each sentence? Your thesis? If you will be reading your paper to a group such as seminar participants or a session at a professional meeting, visualize that. How will these strangers receive what you have written?

3. *Have a list of specific items to check.* It is important to revise in an orderly fashion, in stages, looking first at large concerns, such as the overall organization. Does the flow of the draft match what you had intended with the outline? Then read the paper again, this time for possible problems in the small details.

4. *Check for unity, the clear and logical relation of all parts of the thesis.* Make sure that every paragraph is doing its job—that it relates well to the whole of the paper and is in the right place.

5. *Check for coherence.* Make sure there are no gaps between the various parts of the argument. Look to see that you have adequate transition everywhere it is needed. Transitional elements are markers indicating places where the paper's focus or attitude changes. Transitional elements can be one word long—"however," or "although"—or as long as a sentence or an entire paragraph.

Transitional elements rarely introduce new material. Instead, they are direction pointers, either indicating a shift to a new subject matter or signaling how the writer wants certain material to be interpreted by the reader. Because you, the writer, already know where and why your paper changes direction and how you want particular passages to be received, it can be very difficult for you to catch those places where other readers need transition.

6. *Avoid unnecessary repetition.* Two types of repetition can annoy a reader. Repetition of content usually occurs when you return to a subject that you have already discussed. What may seem to you to be a logical and effective use of material a second time may serve only to slow a reader's progress through your paper. Again, constructing a careful and effective outline before you begin can eliminate some of this tendency. Repetition of phrasing occurs when you overuse certain phrases or words. This can make your prose sound choppy or uninspired. Sometimes, repetition can add rhetorical emphasis and drama: I came. I saw. I conquered. Repeated items, however, are usually not intentional, and unless you read your draft effectively, readers will spot the repetitions that you miss. You may have noticed, for example, that this brief paragraph contained three uses of "effective(ly)" and six uses of the word "repetition(s)."

2.2.13 Editing

Editing is sometimes confused with the more involved process of revising. But editing occurs later in the writing process, after you have wrestled through your first draft—and maybe your second and third—and arrived at the final draft. Even though your draft now contains all the information you want to impart and has arranged the information to your satisfaction, there are still many factors to check, such as sentence structure, spelling, and punctuation.

It is at this point that an unpracticed writer might be less than vigilant. After all, most of the work on the paper is finished, since the "big jobs" of research, organizing, and drafting information have been completed. But watch out! Editing is as important as any other part of the writing process. Any errors which slip through in the final draft will count against you in the reader's mind. This may not seem fair, but even a minor error—a misspelled word or the confusing placement of a comma—will make a greater impression on your reader than perhaps it should. Remember that everything about your paper is your responsibility, including performing even the supposedly little jobs correctly. Careless editing undermines the credibility of your paper. It would be a shame if all the hard work you put into research, drafting, and editing were to be damaged because you failed to catch a comma splice.

Most of the tips given above for revising hold for editing as well. It is best to edit in stages, looking for only one or two kinds of errors each time you reread the paper. Focus especially on errors that you remember committing in the past. If, for instance, you know you have a tendency to misplace commas, go through the paper looking at each comma carefully. If your past papers have had red marks on them because you have a weakness for writing sentence fragments, read each sentence aloud to be certain that each one has its subject and verb and that you are not about to present dependent clauses or prepositional phrases as if they were complete sentences. Check verb tenses. The unnecessary or abrupt shifting of tenses is a common problem in history papers that deal naturally in past tenses, and many students have the urge to switch back and forth from past to present tense in a historical narrative.

Watch out for miscues, problems with a sentence that the writer simply does not see. Remember that your search for errors is hampered in two ways. First, as the writer, you hope not to find mistakes in your work. This desire can cause you to miss little things that could amount to big problems. Second, because you know your material so well, it is easy as you read to supply missing material—a word, a piece of punctuation—unconsciously, as if it were actually on the page in front of your eyes.

These days, many student writers rely on their computers' "spell check" features to do the work of editing for them. While they are handy tools, most spell check programs do not detect many types of errors. One tactic for catching mistakes in sentence structure is to read the sentences aloud, starting with the last one in the paper and then moving forward one sentence at a time (reading each sentence in the normal, left-to-right manner, of course) until you reach the first sentence of the introduction. Strange as this procedure may seem, it strips each sentence of its rhetorical context and helps you to focus on its internal structure.

Editing is the stage where you finally answer those minor questions that you had put off when you were wrestling with wording and organization. Any ambiguities regarding the use of abbreviations, italics, numerals, capital letters, titles, hyphens, dashes, apostrophes, and quotation marks have to be cleared up now. You must also check to see that you have used the required formats for footnotes, endnotes, margins, and page numbers.

Guessing is not allowed. Sometimes unpracticed writers who realize that they do not quite understand a particular rule of grammar, punctuation, or format do nothing to fill that knowledge gap. Instead, they rely on guesswork and their own logic—which is not always up to the task of dealing with so contrary a language as English—to get them through problems that they could solve if they referred to a writing manual. Remember that it does not matter to your reader why or how your mistakes slipped onto the page, only that they are there. You must not allow a few careless errors to sabotage all the good work you have done.

Proofreading

This may seem like overkill, but after you have revised and edited and before you hand in the final version of your paper, it is vital that you check it one more time to make sure that there are no errors of any sort. This job is called proofreading or proofing. In essence, you are looking for many of the same things you had checked for during editing, but now you are doing it on the last draft, which is about to be submitted to your audience. Proofreading is as important as editing. As diligent as you may have been before, you may nevertheless have missed something you still have time to find. Like every other stage of the writing process, proofreading is your responsibility.

At this point, you must check for typing mistakes, especially if you have employed a professional typist to prepare your final draft. Though this individual may have a reputation for top-quality work, he or she does not know your subject or your topic as well as you do. Perhaps this person guessed at something you meant. Again, the ultimate responsibility for your paper is yours! It may give you some comfort to be able to mutter to yourself or to your professor that "my typist made this mistake," but shifting blame does not erase the error or the negative impact it may have had on the communication of your good ideas. Remember that communication is the reason you are writing, and you want nothing to interfere with its success.

3 Writing Competently

3.1 Grammar and Style

3.1.1 The Competent Writer

Good writing places your thoughts in your reader's mind in exactly the way you want them to be there. Good writing tells your readers just what you want them to know without telling them anything you do not wish to say. That may sound odd, but the fact is, writers have to be careful not to let unwanted messages slip into their writing. Look, for example, at the passage in the box below, taken from a paper analyzing the impact of a worker-retraining program in the writer's state. Hidden within the prose is a message which jeopardizes the paper's success. Can you detect the message?

> What's wrong here?
>
> Recent articles written on the subject of dislocated workers have had little to say about the particular problems dealt with in this paper. Since few of these articles focus on the problem at the state level.

Chances are, when you reached the end of the second "sentence," you sensed something missing, a gap in logic or coherence, and your eye ran back through both sentences to find the place where things went wrong. The second sentence is actually not a sentence at all. It does have certain features of a sentence—a subject, for example ("few"), and a verb ("focus")—but its first word ("Since") subordinates the entire clause that follows, taking away its ability to stand on its own as a complete idea. The second "sentence," which is properly called a subordinate clause, merely fills in some information about the first sentence, telling us why recent articles about dislocated workers fail to deal with problems discussed in the present paper.

The sort of error represented by the second "sentence" is commonly called a sentence fragment, and it conveys to the reader a message that no writer wants to send: The writer either is careless or—worse—has not mastered the language he is using. Language errors such as fragments, misplaced commas, or shifts in verb tense send up little red flags in the reader's mind. The result is that the reader loses a little of her concentration on the issue being discussed. She becomes distracted and begins to wonder about the language competency of the writer. The writing loses effectiveness.

Remember: Whatever goal you set for your paper, whether you want it to persuade, describe, analyze, or speculate, you must also set another goal: To display language competence. Without it, your paper will not completely achieve its other aims. Language errors spread doubt like a virus; they jeopardize all the hard work you have done on your paper.

You say "potato"; Quayle says "potatoe"

Credibility in politics depends upon language competence. Anyone who doubts this should remember the beating that Dan Quayle took in the press when he was vice president of the United States for misspelling the word "potato" at a Trenton, New Jersey, spelling bee on 15 June 1992. His error caused a storm of humiliating publicity for the hapless Quayle, adding to an impression of his general incompetence.

3.1.2 Correctness Is Relative

Although they may seem minor, the fact is that the sort of language errors we are discussing, which are often called surface errors, can be extremely damaging in certain kinds of writing. Surface errors come in a variety of types, including misspellings, punctuation problems, grammar errors, and the inconsistent use of abbreviations, capitalization, or numerals. These errors are an affront to your reader's notion of correctness—and therein lies one of the biggest problems with surface errors. Different audiences tolerate different levels of correctness. You already know that you can get away with surface errors in, say, a letter to a friend, who will not judge you harshly for them, while those same errors in a job application letter might eliminate you from consideration for the job. Correctness depends to an extent upon context.

Another problem is that the rules governing correctness shift over time. What would have been an error to your grandmother's generation—the splitting of an infinitive, for example, or the ending of a sentence with a preposition—is taken in stride today by most readers.

So how do you write correctly when the rules shift from person to person and over time? Here are some tips.

3.1.3 Consider Your Audience

One of the great risks of writing is that even the simplest choices you make regarding wording or punctuation can sometimes prejudice your audience against you in ways that may seem unfair.

For example, look again at the old grammar "rule" forbidding the splitting of infinitives. After decades of counseling students to never split an infinitive (something this sentence has just done), composition experts now concede that a split infinitive is not a grammar crime. But suppose you have written a position paper trying to convince your city council of the need to hire security personnel for the library, and half of the council members—the people you wish to convince—remember their eighth-grade grammar teacher's outdated warning about splitting infinitives. How will they respond when you tell them, in your introduction, that librarians are ordered "to always accompany" visitors to the rare book room because of the threat of vandalism? How much of their attention have you suddenly lost because of their automatic recollection of a nonrule? It is possible, in other words, to write correctly and still offend your readers' notions of language competence.

Make sure you tailor the surface features of your writing to the level of competency that your readers require. When in doubt, take a conservative approach. The same goes for the level of formality you should assume. Your audience might be just as distracted by contractions as by a split infinitive.

3.1.4 Aim for Consistency

When dealing with a language question for which there are different answers—such as whether or not to place a comma after the second item in a series of three ("The mayor's speech addressed taxes, housing for the poor, and the job situation.")—always use the same strategy. If, for example, you avoid splitting one infinitive, avoid splitting all infinitives in your paper.

3.1.5 Have Confidence

It is easy for unpracticed writers to allow their occasional mistakes to depress them about their writing ability. The fact is, most of what we know about writing is right. We are all capable, for example, of phrasing utterances that are grammatically sound, even if we cannot list the grammar rules by which we achieve coherence. Most writers who worry about their chronic errors have fewer than they think. Becoming distressed about errors makes writing more difficult.

Grammar

As various composition theorists have pointed out, the word "grammar" has several definitions. One meaning is "the formal patterns in which words must be arranged in order to convey meaning." We learn these patterns very early in life and use them spontaneously without thinking about them. Our understanding of grammatical patterns is extremely sophisticated, despite the fact that few of us can actually cite the rules by which the patterns work. Patrick Hartwell tested grammar learning by asking native English speakers of different ages and levels of education, including high school teachers, to arrange these words in natural order:

French   the   young   girls   four

Everyone he asked could produce the natural order for this phrase: "the four young French girls." yet none of Hartwell's respondents said they knew the rule that governs the order of the words (1985, 111).

3.1.6 Eliminate Chronic Errors

All right, then, the question arises: If just thinking about our errors has a negative effect on our writing, then how do we learn to write more correctly? Perhaps the best answer is simply to write as often as possible. Give yourself practice in putting your thoughts into written shape, and get lots of practice in revising and proofing your work. As you write and revise, be honest with yourself, and patient. Chronic errors are like bad habits; getting rid of them takes time.

You probably know of one or two problem areas in your writing that you could have eliminated but have not done so. Instead, you have "fudged" your writing at the critical points, relying upon half-remembered formulas from past English classes or trying to come up with logical solutions to your writing problems. (Warning: The English language does not always work in a way that seems logical.) You may have simply decided that comma rules are unlearnable or that you will never understand the difference between the verbs *lay* and *lie*. And so you guess, and you get the rule wrong a good part of the time. What a shame, when just a little extra work would give you mastery over those few gaps in your understanding and boost your confidence as well.

Instead of continuing with this sort of guesswork, instead of living with the gaps, why not face the problem areas now and learn the rules that have heretofore escaped you? What follows is a discussion of those surface features of a paper where errors most commonly occur. You will probably be familiar with most, if not all, of the rules discussed, but there may be a few you have not yet mastered. Now is the time to do so.

3.2 Punctuation

3.2.1 Apostrophes

An apostrophe is used to show possession; when you wish to say that something belongs to someone or to another thing, you add either an apostrophe and an *s* or an apostrophe alone to the word that represents the owner.

When the owner is singular (a single person or thing), the apostrophe precedes an added *s:*

> According to Mayor Anderson's secretary, the news broadcast has been canceled.
> The union's lawyers challenged the government's policy in court.
> Somebody's briefcase was left in the auditorium.

The same rule applies if the word showing possession is a plural that does not end in *s:*

> The women's club sponsored several debates during the last presidential campaign.
> Governor Smith has proven himself a tireless worker for children's rights.

When the word expressing ownership is a plural ending in *s*, the apostrophe follows the *s:*

> The new legislation was discussed at the secretaries' conference.

There are two ways to form the possessive for two or more nouns:

1. To show joint possession (both nouns owning the same thing or things), the last noun in the series is possessive:

> The president and first lady's invitations were sent out yesterday.

2. To indicate that each noun owns an item or items individually, each noun must show possession:

> Mayor Scott's and Mayor MacKay's speeches took different approaches to the same problem.

> The apostrophe is important, an obvious statement when you consider the difference in meaning between the following two sentences:
>
> Be sure to pick up the senator's things on your way to the airport.
>
> Be sure to pick up the senators' things on your way to the airport.
>
> In the first of these sentences, you have only one senator to worry about, while in the second, you have at least two!

3.2.2 Capitalization

Rules of Capitalization

Here is a brief summary of some hard-to-remember capitalization rules.

Rule 1. You may, if you choose, capitalize the first letter of the first word in a sentence which follows a colon. Whichever method you choose, be consistent with it throughout your paper.

CORRECT: Our instructions are explicit: do not allow anyone into the conference without an identification badge.

ALSO CORRECT: Our instructions are explicit: Do not allow anyone into the conference without an identification badge.

Rule 2. Capitalize proper nouns (nouns naming specific people, places, or things) and proper adjectives (adjectives made from proper nouns). A common noun following the proper adjective is usually not capitalized, nor is a common adjective preceding the proper adjective (such as a, an, or the):

PROPER NOUNS	PROPER ADJECTIVES
Poland	Polish officials
Iraq	the Iraqi ambassador
Shakespeare	a Shakespearean tragedy

Proper nouns include

> Names of famous monuments and buildings: the Washington Monument, the Empire State Building, the Library of Congress
> Historical events, eras, and certain terms concerning calendar dates: the Civil War, the Dark Ages, Monday, December, Columbus Day
> Parts of the country: North, Southwest, Eastern Seaboard, the West Coast, New England.

Note: When words like *north, south, east, west, northwest* are used to designate direction rather than geographical region, they are not capitalized: "We drove east to Boston and then made a tour of the East Coast."

> Words referring to race, religion, or nationality: Islam, Muslim, Caucasian, White (or white), Oriental, Negro, Black (or black), Slavic, Arab, Jewish, Hebrew, Buddhism, Buddhists, Southern Baptists, the Bible, the Koran, American

Names of languages: English, Chinese, Latin, Sanskrit

Titles of corporations, institutions, businesses, universities, organizations: Dow Chemical, General Motors, the National Endowment for the Humanities, University of Tennessee, Colby College, Kiwanis Club, American Association of Retired Persons, the Oklahoma State Senate

Note: Some words once considered proper nouns or adjectives have, over time, become common: french fries, pasteurized milk, arabic numerals, italics, panama hat.

Rule 3. Titles of individuals may be capitalized if they precede a proper name; otherwise, titles are usually not capitalized.

The committee honored Senator Jones.
The committee honored the senator from Kansas.
We phoned Doctor Jessup, who arrived shortly afterward.
We phoned the doctor, who arrived shortly afterward.
A story on Queen Elizabeth's health appeared in yesterday's paper.
A story on the queen's health appeared in yesterday's paper.
Pope John Paul's visit to Colorado was a public relations success.
The pope's visit to Colorado was a public relations success.

When Not to Capitalize

In general, you do not capitalize nouns when your reference is nonspecific. For example, you would not capitalize the phrase *the senator*, but you would capitalize *Senator Smith*. The second reference is as much a title as it is a mere term of identification, while the first reference is a mere identifier. Likewise, there is a difference in degree of specificity between the phrase *the state treasury* and *the Texas State Treasury*.

Note: The meaning of a term may change somewhat depending on capitalization. What, for example, might be the difference between a Democrat and a democrat? (When capitalized, the word refers to a member of a specific political party; when not capitalized, the word refers to someone who believes in the democratic form of government.)

Capitalization depends to some extent on the context of your writing. For example, if you are writing a policy analysis for a specific corporation, you may capitalize words and phrases—*Board of Directors, Chairman of the Board, the Institute*—that would not be capitalized in a paper written for a more general audience. Likewise, in some contexts it is not unusual to see titles of certain powerful officials capitalized even when not accompanying a proper noun: "The President took few members of his staff to Camp David with him."

3.2.3 Colons

There are uses for the colon that we all know. A colon can, for example, separate the parts of a statement of time (4:25 A.M.), separate chapter and verse in a Biblical quotation (John 3:16), and close the salutation of a business letter (Dear Senator Keaton:). But there are other uses for the colon that some writers sometimes don't know that can add an extra degree of flexibility to sentence structure.

The colon can introduce into a sentence certain kinds of material, such as a list, a quotation, or a restatement or description of material mentioned earlier:

> *List:* The committee's research proposal promised to do three things: (1) establish the extent of the problem, (2) examine several possible solutions, and (3) estimate the cost of each solution.
>
> *Quotation:* In his speech, the mayor challenged us with these words: "How will your council's work make a difference in the life of our city?"
>
> *Restatement or Description:* Ahead of us, according to the senator's chief of staff, lay the biggest job of all: convincing our constituents of the plan's benefits.

3.2.4 Commas

The comma is perhaps the most troublesome of all marks of punctuation, no doubt because so many variables govern its use, such as sentence length, rhetorical emphasis, or changing notions of style. Here are the most common problems.

Comma Splices

Joining two complete sentences by only a comma makes a comma splice:

> An impeachment is merely an indictment of a government official, actual removal usually requires a vote by a legislative body.
> An unemployed worker who has been effectively retrained is no longer an economic problem for the community, he has become an asset.
> It might be possible for the city to assess fees on the sale of real estate, however, such a move would be criticized by the community of real estate developers.

In each of these passages, two complete sentences (also called independent clauses) have been "spliced" together by a comma. When a comma splice is taken out of context, it becomes easy to see what is wrong: The break between the two sentences is inadequate.

There is one foolproof way to check your paper for comma splices. Locate the commas in your draft and then read carefully the structures on both sides of each comma to determine if you have spliced two complete sentences together incorrectly. If you find a complete sentence on both sides of a comma, and if the sentence following the comma does not begin with a coordinating connective (*and, but, for, nor, or, so, yet*), then you have found a comma splice.

Simply reading the draft through to try to "hear" the comma splices may not work, since the rhetorical features of your prose, its "movement," may make it hard to detect this kind of sentence completeness error.

There are five commonly used ways to correct comma splices.

1. Place a period between the two independent clauses:

SPLICE: A political candidate receives many benefits from his or her affiliation with a political party, there are liabilities as well.

CORRECTION: A political candidate receives many benefits from his or her affiliation with a political party. There are liabilities as well.

2. Place a comma and a coordinating connective (*and, but, for, or, nor, so, yet*) between the sentences:

SPLICE: The councilman's speech described the major differences of opinion over the economic situation, it also suggested a possible course of action.

CORRECTION: The councilman's speech described the major differences of opinion over the economic situation, and it also suggested a possible course of action.

3. Place a semicolon between the independent clauses:

SPLICE: Some people feel that the federal government should play a large role in establishing a housing policy for the homeless, many others disagree.

CORRECTION: Some people feel that the federal government should play a large role in establishing a housing policy for the homeless; many others disagree.

4. Rewrite the two clauses of the comma splice as one independent clause:

SPLICE: Television ads played a big part in the campaign, however they were not the deciding factor in the challenger's victory over the incumbent.

CORRECTION: Television ads played a large but not a decisive role in the challenger's victory over the incumbent.

5. Change one of the two independent clauses into a dependent clause by beginning it with a subordinating word. A subordinating word introducing a clause prevents the clause from being able to stand on its own as a complete sentence. Words which can be used as subordinators include *although, after, as, because, before, if, though, unless, when, which,* and *where.*

SPLICE: The election was held last Tuesday, there was a poor voter turn out.

CORRECTION: When the election was held last Tuesday, there was a poor voter turn out.

Commas in a Compound Sentence

A compound sentence is comprised of two or more independent clauses (two complete sentences). When these two clauses are joined by a coordinating conjunction, the conjunction should be preceded by a comma. (Solution number two for fixing a comma splice given above calls upon the writer to transform the splice into this sort of compound sentence.) The error is that writers sometimes fail to place the comma before the conjunction. Remember, the comma is there to signal the reader that another independent clause follows the coordinating conjunction. In other words, the comma is like a road sign, telling a driver what sort of road she is about to encounter. If the comma is missing, the reader does not expect to find the second half of a compound sentence and may be distracted from the text.

As the examples below indicate, the missing comma is especially a problem in longer sentences or in sentences in which other coordinating conjunctions appear:

INCORRECT: The senator promised to visit the hospital and investigate the problem and then he called the press conference to a close.

CORRECT: The senator promised to visit the hospital and investigate the problem, and then he called the press conference to a close.

INCORRECT: The water board can neither make policy nor enforce it nor can its members serve on auxiliary water committees.

CORRECT: The water board can neither make policy nor enforce it, nor can its members serve on auxiliary water committees.

An exception to this rule arises in shorter sentences, where the comma may not be necessary to make the meaning clear:

The mayor phoned and we thanked him for his support.

It is never wrong, however, to place a comma after the conjunction between the independent clauses. If you are the least bit unsure of your audience's notions about what makes for "proper" grammar, it is a good idea to take the conservative approach and use the comma:

The mayor phoned, and we thanked him for his support.

Commas with Restrictive and Nonrestrictive Elements

A nonrestrictive element is part of a sentence—a word, phrase, or clause—that adds information about another element in the sentence without restricting or limiting the meaning of that element. While this information may be useful, we do not have to have the nonrestrictive element for the sentence to make sense. To signal the inessential nature of the nonrestrictive element, we set it off from the rest of the sentence with commas.

Failure to use commas to indicate the nonrestrictive nature of an element can cause confusion. See, for example, how the presence or absence of commas affects our understanding of the following sentence:

The mayor was talking with the policeman, who won the outstanding service award last year.
The mayor was talking with the policeman who won the outstanding service award last year.

Can you see that the comma changes the meaning of the sentence? In the first version of the sentence, the comma makes the information that follows it incidental: *The mayor was talking with the policeman, who happens to have won the service award last year.* In the second version of the sentence, the information following the word policeman is important to the sense of the sentence; it tells us, specifically, which policeman—presumably there were more than one—the mayor was addressing. In this second version, the lack of a comma has transformed the material following the word *policeman* into a restrictive element, which means that it is necessary to our understanding of the sentence.

Be sure that in your paper you make a clear distinction between nonrestrictive and restrictive elements by setting off the nonrestrictive elements with commas.

Commas in a Series

A series is any two or more items of a similar nature that appear consecutively in a sentence. The items may be individual words, phrases, or clauses. In a series of three or more items, the items are separated by commas:

The senator, the mayor, and the police chief all attended the ceremony.
Because of the new zoning regulations, all trailer parks must be moved out of the neighborhood, all small businesses must apply for recertification and tax status, and the two local churches must repave their parking lots.

The final comma, the one before the *and*, is sometimes left out, especially in newspaper writing. This practice, however, can make for confusion, especially in longer, complicated sentences like the second example above. Here is the way that sentence would read without the final comma:

> Because of the new zoning regulations, all trailer parks must be moved out of the neighborhood, all small businesses must apply for recertification and tax status and the two local churches must repave their parking lots.

Notice that without a comma the division between the second and the third items in the series is not clear. This is the sort of ambiguous structure that can cause a reader to backtrack and lose concentration. You can avoid such confusion by always using that final comma. Remember, however, that if you do decide to include it, do so consistently; make sure it appears in every series in your paper.

3.2.5 Dangling Modifiers

A *modifier* is a word or group of words used to describe, or modify, another word in the sentence. A *dangling modifier* appears either at the beginning or ending of a sentence and seems to be describing some word other than the one the writer obviously intended. The modifier therefore "dangles," disconnected from its intended meaning. It is often hard for the writer to spot a dangling modifier, but readers can—and will—find them, and the result can be disastrous for the sentence, as the following examples demonstrate:

INCORRECT: Flying low over Washington, the White House was seen.

CORRECT: Flying low over Washington, we saw the White House.

INCORRECT: Worried at the cost of the program, sections of the bill were trimmed in committee.

CORRECT: Worried at the cost of the program, the committee trimmed sections of the bill.

CORRECT: The committee trimmed sections of the bill because they were worried at the cost of the program.

INCORRECT: To lobby for prison reform, a lot of effort went into the TV ads.

CORRECT: The lobby group put a lot of effort into the TV ads advocating prison reform.

INCORRECT: Stunned, the television broadcast the defeated senator's concession speech.

CORRECT: The television broadcast the stunned senator's concession speech.

You will note that in the first two incorrect sentences, the confusion is largely due to the use of passive-voice verbs: "the White House *was seen*," "sections of the bill *were trimmed*." Often, though not always, the cause of a dangling modifier is the fact that the actor in the sentence—*we* in the first sentence, *the committee* in the second—is either distanced from the modifier or obliterated by the passive-voice verb. It is a good idea to avoid passive voice unless you have a specific reason for using it.

One way to check for dangling modifiers is to examine all modifiers at the beginnings or endings of your sentences. Look especially for *to be* phrases ("to lobby") or for words ending in *-ing* or *-ed* at the start of the modifier. Then see if the modified word is close enough to the phrase to be properly connected.

3.2.6 Parallelism

Series of two or more words, phrases, or clauses within a sentence should be structured in the same grammatical way. Parallel structures can add power and balance to your writing by creating a strong rhetorical rhythm. Here is a famous example of parallelism from the Preamble to the U. S. Constitution. (The capitalization, preserved from the original document, follows eighteenth-century custom. Parallel structures have been italicized.)

> We the People of the United States, in Order to *form a more perfect Union, Establish Justice, insure Domestic Tranquility, provide for the common defence, promote the general Welfare, and secure the Blessings of Liberty to ourselves and our Posterity,* do *ordain* and *establish* this Constitution for the United States of America.

There are actually two series in this sentence, the first composed of several phrases that each completes the infinitive phrase beginning with the word *to* (*to form, [to] Establish, [to] insure, [to] provide, [to] promote, [to] secure*), the second consisting of two verbs (*ordain* and *establish*). These parallel series appeal to our love of balance and pattern, and they give an authoritative tone to the sentence. The writer, we feel, has thought long and carefully about the matter at hand and has taken firm control of it.

Because we find a special satisfaction in balanced structures, we are more likely to remember ideas phrased in parallelisms than in less highly ordered language. For this reason, as well as for the sense of authority and control that they suggest, parallel structures are common in political utterances:

> We hold these truths to be self-evident, that all men are created equal, that they are endowed by their Creator with certain unalienable Rights, that among these are Life, Liberty, and the pursuit of Happiness.
>
> The Declaration of Independence, 1776

> But, in a larger sense, we can not dedicate—we can not consecrate—we can not hallow—this ground. The brave men, living and dead, who struggled here, have consecrated it, far above our poor power to add or detract. The world will little note, nor long remember what we say here, but it can never forget what they did here.
>
> Abraham Lincoln, Gettysburg Address, 1863

> Ask not what your country can do for you, ask what you can do for your country.
>
> > John F. Kennedy, Inaugural Address, 1961

Faulty Parallelism

If the parallelism of a passage is not carefully maintained, the writing can seem sloppy and out of balance. Scan your writing to make sure that all series and lists have parallel structure. The following examples show how to correct faulty parallelisms:

INCORRECT: The mayor promises not only *to reform* the police department, but also *the giving of raises* to all city employees. [Connective structures such as *not only . . . but also*, and *both . . . and* introduce elements that should be parallel.]

CORRECT: The mayor promises not only *to reform* the police department, but also *to give* raises to all city employees.

INCORRECT: The cost *of doing nothing* is greater than the cost *to renovate* the apartment block.

CORRECT: The cost *of doing nothing* is greater than the cost *of renovating* the apartment block.

INCORRECT: Here are the items on the committee's agenda: (1) *to discuss* the new property tax, (2) *to revise* the wording of the city charter, (3) *a vote* on the city manager's request for an assistant.

CORRECT: Here are the items on the committee's agenda: (1) *to discuss* the new property tax, (2) *to revise* the wording of the city charter, (3) *to vote* on the city manager's request for an assistant.

3.2.7 Fused (Run-On) Sentences

A fused sentence is one in which two or more independent clauses (passages that can stand as complete sentences) have been run together without the aid of any suitable connecting word, phrase, or punctuation. There are several ways to correct a fused sentence:

INCORRECT: The council members were exhausted they had debated for two hours.

CORRECT: The council members were exhausted. They had debated for two hours. [The clauses have been separated into two sentences.]

CORRECT: The council members were exhausted; they had debated for two hours. [The clauses have been separated by a semicolon.]

CORRECT:	The council members were exhausted, having debated for two hours. [The second clause has been rephrased as a dependent clause.]
INCORRECT:	Our policy analysis impressed the committee it also convinced them to reconsider their action.
CORRECT:	Our policy analysis impressed the committee and also convinced them to reconsider their action. [The second clause has been rephrased as part of the first clause.]
CORRECT:	Our policy analysis impressed the committee, and it also convinced them to reconsider their action. [The clauses have been separated by a comma and a coordinating word.]

While a fused sentence is easily noticeable to the reader, it can be maddeningly difficult for the writer to catch in proofreading. Unpracticed writers tend to read through the fused spots, sometimes supplying the break that is usually heard when sentences are spoken. To check for fused sentences, read the independent clauses in your paper carefully, making sure that there are adequate breaks among all of them.

3.2.8 Pronoun Errors

Its versus It's

Do not make the mistake of trying to form the possessive of *it* in the same way that you form the possessive of most nouns. The pronoun *it* shows possession by simply adding an *s*:

The prosecuting attorney argued the case on *its* merits.

The word *it's* is a contraction, meaning *it is*:

It's the most expensive program ever launched by the council.

What makes the *its/it's* rule so confusing is that most nouns form the singular possessive by adding an apostrophe and an *s*:

The *jury's* verdict startled the crowd.

When proofreading, any time you come to the word it's, substitute the phrase it is while you read. If the phrase makes sense, you have used the correct form.

If you have used the word *it's*:

The newspaper article was misleading in *it's* analysis of the election.

Then read it as *it is:*

> The newspaper article was misleading in *it is* analysis of the election.

If the phrase makes no sense, substitute *its* for *it's:*

> The newspaper article was misleading in *its* analysis of the election.

Vague Pronoun Reference

Pronouns are words that stand in place of nouns or other pronouns that have already been mentioned in your writing. The most common pronouns include *he, she, it, they, them, those, which, who.* You must make sure that there is no confusion about the word to which each pronoun refers.

> The mayor said that *he* would support our bill if the city council would also back it.

The word that the pronoun replaces is called its *antecedent.* To check the accuracy of your pronoun references, ask yourself, *To what does the pronoun refer?* Then answer the question carefully, making sure that there is not more than one possible antecedent. Consider the following example:

> Several special interest groups decided to defeat the new health care bill. *This* became the turning point of the government's reform campaign.

To what does the word *This* refer? The immediate answer seems to be the word *bill* at the end of the previous sentence. It is more likely the writer was referring to the attempt of the special interest groups to defeat the bill, but there is no word in the first sentence that refers specifically to this action. The reference is thus unclear. One way to clarify the reference is to change the beginning of the second sentence:

> Several special interest groups decided to defeat the new health care bill. *Their attack on the bill* became the turning point of the government's reform campaign.

This point is further demonstrated by the following sentence:

> When John F. Kennedy appointed his brother Robert to the position of U.S. attorney general, he had little idea how widespread the corruption in the teamster's union was.

To whom does the word *he* refer? It is unclear whether the writer is referring to John or to Robert Kennedy. One way to clarify the reference is simply to repeat the antecedent instead of using a pronoun:

When President John F. Kennedy appointed his brother Robert to the position of U. S. attorney general, Robert had little idea how widespread the corruption in the teamster's union was.

Pronoun Agreement

A pronoun must agree with its antecedent in gender and in number, as the following examples demonstrate:

Mayor Smith said that *he* appreciated our club's support in the election.
One reporter asked the senator what *she* would do if the President offered *her* a cabinet post.
Having listened to our case, the judge decided to rule on *it* within the week.
Engineers working on the housing project said *they* were pleased with the renovation so far.

Certain words, however can become troublesome antecedents, because they may look like plural pronouns but are actually singular:

everybody	nobody	everyone	no one	somebody
each	someone	either	anyone	

A pronoun referring to one of these words in a sentence must be singular, too.

INCORRECT: *Each* of the women in the support group brought *their* children.

CORRECT: *Each* of the women in the support group brought *her* children.

INCORRECT: Has *everybody* received *their* ballot?

CORRECT: Has *everybody* received *his or her* ballot? [The two gender-specific pronouns are used to avoid sexist language.]

CORRECT: Have *all the delegates* received *their* ballots? [The singular antecedent has been changed to a plural one.]

A Shift in Person

It is important to avoid shifting unnecessarily among first person (*I, we*), second person (*you*), and third person (*she, he, it, one, they*). Such shifts can cause confusion:

INCORRECT: *Most people* [third person] who run for office find that if *you* [second person] tell the truth during *your* campaign, *you* will gain the voters' respect.

CORRECT: *Most people* who run for office find that if *they* tell the truth during *their* campaigns, *they* will win the voters' respect.

INCORRECT: *One* [first person]cannot tell whether *they* [third person]are cut out for public office until *they* decide to run.

CORRECT: *One* cannot tell whether *one* is cut out for public office until *one* decides to run.

3.2.9 Quotation Marks

It can be difficult to remember when to use quotation marks and where they go in relation to other marks of punctuation. When faced with these questions, unpracticed writers often try to rely on logic rather than on a rule book, but the rules governing quotation marks do not always seem to rely on logic. The only way to make sure of your use of quotation marks is to memorize the rules. Luckily, there are not many.

The Use of Quotation Marks

Use quotation marks to enclose direct quotations that are not longer than four typed lines:

> As one commentator explains, "The accumulation of capital and its unbalanced distribution during the 1920s resulted from swollen profits, huge dividends, and massive tax savings to the wealthy" (Leitch 1988, 2).

Notice that in brief quotations using the parenthetical referencing format, the parenthetical note that identifies the source occurs before the period that closes the sentence.

Longer quotes, which are called block quotes, are placed in a double-spaced block, *without quotation marks* and set off from the text by an indention on the left and by extra space above and below it. The block quote maintains the paragraphing of its original publication, meaning that if the first line of the quoted passage begins a paragraph in the original printing, then that line is indented further in the quote, but if the block quoted does not include the beginning of a paragraph, then the first line of the quote is not indented. For longer quotes, the parenthetical reference occurs after the period that ends the sentence:

> Lincoln explained his motive for continuing the Civil War clearly in his response to Horace Greeley's open letter:
>
> I would save the Union. I would save it the shortest way under the Constitution. The sooner the National authority can be restored, the nearer the Union will be the Union as it was. If there be those who would not save the Union unless they could at the same time save Slavery, I do not agree with

them. If there be those who would not save the Union unless they could at the same time destroy Slavery, I do not agree with them. (Lincoln 1946, 652)

Use single quotation marks to set off quotations within quotations:

"I intend," said the senator, "to use in my speech a line from Frost's poem, 'The Road Not Taken.'"

Note: When the interior quote occurs at the end of the sentence, both single and double quotation marks are placed outside the period.

Use quotation marks to set off titles of the following:

short poems (a poem that is not printed as a separate volume)
short stories
articles or essays
song titles
episodes of television or radio shows

Use quotation marks to set off words or phrases used in special ways.

1. To convey irony:

The "liberal" administration has done nothing but cater to big business.

2. To set off a technical term:

To "filibuster" is to delay legislation, usually through prolonged speech-making. The last notable filibuster occurred just last week in the Senate. [Once the term is defined, it is not placed in quotation marks again.]

Quotation Marks in Relation to Other Punctuation

Place commas and periods *inside* closing quotation marks:

"My fellow Americans," said the President, "there are tough times ahead of us."

Place colons and semicolons outside closing quotation marks:

In his speech on voting, the governor warned against "an encroaching indolence"; he was referring to the middle class.
There are several victims of the government's campaign to "Turn Back the Clock": the homeless, the elderly, the mentally impaired.

Use the context to determine whether to place question marks, exclamation points, and dashes inside or outside closing quotation marks. If the punctuation is part of the quotation, place it *inside* the quotation mark:

"When will Congress make up its mind?" asked the ambassador.
The demonstrators shouted, "Free the hostages!" and "No more slavery!"

If the punctuation is not part of the quotation, place it *outside* the quotation mark:

Which president said, "We have nothing to fear but fear itself"? [Although the quote was a complete sentence, you do not place a period after it. There can only be one piece of terminal punctuation, or punctuation that ends a sentence.]

Note: These rules concerning the placement of quotation marks in relation to other punctuation apply also to single quotation marks:

The title of Sherman's article was "'Fifty-Four Forty or Fight!': Sloganeering in Early America."

3.2.10 Semicolons

The semicolon is a little-used punctuation mark that you should learn to incorporate into your writing strategy because of its many potential applications. For example, a semicolon can be used to correct a comma splice:

INCORRECT: The union representatives left the meeting in good spirits, their demands were met.

CORRECT: The union representatives left the meeting in good spirits; their demands were met.

INCORRECT: Several guests at the fund-raiser had lost their invitations, however, we were able to seat them, anyway.

CORRECT: Several guests at the fund-raiser had lost their invitations; however, we were able to seat them, anyway.

As you can see from the second example, connecting the two independent clauses with a semicolon instead of a period strengthens their relationship.

Semicolons can also separate items in a series when the series items themselves contain commas:

The newspaper account of the rally stressed the march, which drew the biggest crowd; the mayor's speech, which drew tremendous applause; and the party afterwards in the park.

Avoid misusing semicolons. For example, use a comma, not a semicolon, to separate an independent clause from a dependent clause:

INCORRECT: Students from the college volunteered to answer phones during the pledge drive; which was set up to generate money for the new arts center.

CORRECT: Students from the college volunteered to answer phones during the pledge drive, which was set up to generate money for the new arts center.

Do not overuse semicolons. Although they are useful, too many semicolons in your writing can distract your reader's attention. Avoid monotony by using semicolons sparingly.

3.2.11 Sentence Fragments

A fragment is an incomplete part of a sentence that is punctuated and capitalized as if it were an entire sentence. It is an especially disruptive error, because it obscures the kinds of connections that the words of a sentence must make in order to complete the reader's understanding.

Students sometimes write fragments because they are concerned that a particular sentence is growing too long and needs to be shortened. Remember that cutting the length of a sentence merely by adding a period somewhere along its length often creates a fragment. When checking your writing for fragments, it is essential that you read each sentence carefully to determine whether it has (1) a complete subject and a verb, and (2) a subordinating word preceding the subject and verb, making the construction a subordinate clause rather than a complete sentence.

Types of Sentence Fragments

Some fragments lack a verb:

INCORRECT: The chairperson of our committee, having received a letter from the mayor. [The word *having*, which can be used as a verb, is here being used as a present participle introducing a participial phrase. Watch out for words that look like verbs but are being used in another way.]

CORRECT: The chairperson of our committee received a letter from the mayor.

Some fragments lack a subject:

INCORRECT: Our study shows that there is broad support for improvement in the health care system. And in the unemployment system.

CORRECT: Our study shows that there is broad support for improvement in the health care system and in the unemployment system.

Some fragments are subordinate clauses:

INCORRECT: After the latest edition of the newspaper came out. [This clause has the two major components of a complete sentence: a subject (*edition*) and a verb (*came*). Indeed, if the first word (*After*) were deleted, the clause would be a complete sentence. But that first word is a *subordinating word*, which acts to prevent the following clause from standing on its own as a complete sentence. Watch out for this kind of construction. It is called a *subordinate clause*, and it is not a sentence.]

CORRECT: After the latest edition of the newspaper came out, the mayor's press secretary was overwhelmed with phone calls. [A common method of revising a subordinate clause that has been punctuated as a complete sentence is to connect it to the complete sentence to which it is closest in meaning.]

INCORRECT: Several representatives asked for copies of the vice-president's position paper. Which called for reform of the Environmental Protection Agency.

CORRECT: Several representatives asked for copies of the vice-president's position paper, which called for reform of the Environmental Protection Agency.

3.3 Spelling

All of us have problems spelling certain words that we have not yet committed to memory. But most writers are not as bad at spelling as they believe they are. Usually it is a handful of words that an individual finds troubling. It is important to be as sensitive as possible to your own particular spelling problems—and to keep a dictionary handy. There is no excuse for failing to check spelling.

What follows are a list of commonly confused words and a list of commonly misspelled words. Read through the lists, looking for those words which tend to give you trouble. If you have any questions, *consult your dictionary.*

COMMONLY CONFUSED WORDS

accept/except	ascent/assent	cite/sight/site
advice/advise	bare/bear	complement/compli-
affect/effect	breath/breathe	ment
aisle/isle	brake/break	conscience/conscious
allusion/illusion	buy/by	corps/corpse
an/and	capital/capitol	council/counsel
angel/angle	choose/chose	dairy/diary

descent/dissent
desert/dessert
device/devise
die/dye
dominant/dominate
elicit/illicit
eminent/immanent/
imminent
envelop/envelope
every day/everyday
fair/fare
formally/formerly
forth/fourth
hear/here
heard/herd
hole/whole
human/humane
its/it's
know/no
later/latter
lay/lie

lead/led
lessen/lesson
loose/lose
may be/maybe
miner/minor
moral/morale
of/off
passed/past
patience/patients
peace/piece
personal/personnel
plain/plane
precede/proceed
presence/presents
principal/principle
quiet/quite
rain/reign/rein
raise/raze
reality/realty
respectfully/respectively
reverend/reverent

right/rite/write
road/rode
scene/seen
sense/since
stationary/stationery
straight/strait
taught/taut
than/then
their/there/they're
threw/through
too/to/two
track/tract
waist/waste
waive/wave
weak/week
weather/whether
were/where
which/witch
whose/who's
your/you're

COMMONLY MISSPELLED WORDS

a lot
acceptable
accessible
accommodate
accompany
accustomed
acquire
against
annihilate
apparent
arguing/argument
authentic
before
begin/beginning
believe
benefited
bulletin
business
cannot
category
condemn
committee

courteous
definitely
dependent
desperate
develop
different
disappear
disappoint
easily
efficient
equipped
exceed
existence
experience
environment
exercise
fascinate
finally
foresee
forty
fulfill
gauge

guaranteed
guard
harass
hero/heroes
humorous
hurried/hurriedly
hypocrite
ideally
immediately
immense
incredible
innocuous
intercede
interrupt
irrelevant
irresistible
irritate
knowledge
license
likelihood
maintenance
manageable

meanness
mischievous
missile
necessary
nevertheless
no one
noticeable
noticing
nuisance
occasion/occasionally
occurred/occurrences
omission
omit
opinion
opponent
parallel
parole
peaceable
performance
pertain
practical
preparation
probably
professor
prominent
pronunciation
process
psychology

publicly
pursue/pursuing
questionnaire
realize
receipt
received
recession
recommend
referring
religious
remembrance
reminisce
repetition
representative
rhythm
ridiculous
roommate
satellite
scarcity
scenery
secede/secession
science
secretary
senseless
separate
sergeant
shining
significant

sincerely
skiing
stubbornness
studying
succeed/success
successfully
susceptible
suspicious
technical
temporary
tendency
therefore
tragedy
truly
tyranny
unanimous
unconscious
undoubtedly
until
vacuum
valuable
various
vegetable
visible
without
women
writing

4 *Paper Formats*

4.1 General Page Format

Your history assignments should be typed or printed on 8 1/2-by-11-inch premium white bond paper, 20 pound or heavier. Do not try to impress your instructor with fancy colors or sizes, unless he or she gives specific instructions to do so. Do not use poor quality or draft paper. By the time you submit your assignment, you will have spent much of your recent life preparing it. Such an expenditure of your time deserves a top-quality presentation, and a few extra coins invested in good paper is money well spent.

Most, if not all, professors have received papers prepared on a typewriter whose ribbon was so old and faint that reading it resulted in eye strain and a headache. This does not make a good impression. If at all possible, use a laser printer to print the final draft. Another bad move is to submit a paper printed on tractor-feed computer paper whose pages are still connected top and bottom and still have the feeder holes on both sides! If your printer uses this technology, at least pull the pages apart and remove the edge strips before submitting it.

Always submit the original typed or computer-printed manuscript. Do not submit a photocopy. Make and retain copies for your files or to resubmit if, for some reason, the original is lost.

Margins, except for theses and dissertations, should be one inch on all sides of the paper. Unless otherwise instructed, all papers should be double-spaced in a 12-point word processing font or typewriter pica type. You may use typewriter elite type if another type is not available. Select a font that is plain and easy to read, such as Arial, Helvetica, Courier, Garamond, or Times Roman. Do not use script, stylized, or elaborate fonts. These will annoy, not impress.

Page numbers should appear in the upper-right-hand corner of each page, starting on the second page of text. No numbers should be placed on the title page or first page of text. For longer papers, the table of contents, tables of figures, lists of illustrations, and other "front matter" may be designated with lower case roman numerals (i, ii, iii, iv, v, vi, vii, and so on) placed at the center of the bottom of each page. All other page numbers thereafter must be placed one inch from the right side of the page and one-half inch from the top.

Individual instructors have different attitudes toward bindings. Ask yours what she or he prefers. Unless you are given specific directions to do so, do not use plastic covers with slide-on edges. They are a nuisance to handle in a large stack, and they come apart. Avoid using plastic spiral binding as well. Paper clips often come off or become attached to other papers in the same stack, and using them will prove to be an annoyance to your instructor. In most cases a staple placed neatly in the upper-left corner will get the job done unobtrusively and well. A paper submitted to a journal for consideration for publication should not be clipped, stapled, or bound in any form.

Many colleges and universities have official, specified formats for papers, particularly for theses and dissertations. Before you begin to prepare your final draft, determine whether your institution has such requirements. You do not want your work rejected simply because its margins were a few millimeters too small or large. As absurd as this may seem, it does happen. There may be an official university publication available to answer your questions about style. Whatever price you may have to pay to obtain such a document will be a worthwhile investment if it keeps you from having to retype your paper because of some small omission.

Keep in mind what we have been suggesting all through this manual: Your purpose for writing is communication, and you want nothing to stand in the way of this process! Your paper may be the most thoroughly researched, logically sound, and clearly presented example of scholarship that an instructor has ever received, but if it is submitted on poor-quality paper, printed in a cute, stylized script, and clipped together with a huge, gaudy, purple plastic paper clip, its worth will be diminished and your abilities questioned before your instructor reads your first word of text.

4.2 Title Page

As with all of our instructions, before you commit faithfully to one certain format, check with your particular institution to determine whether an official format exists for preparing title pages. In general, however, the following information should be included and centered on the page.

The order of these elements could vary, depending on the requirements of the college or the preferences of the individual instructor. Again, make sure you inquire! (We refuse to accept responsibility if your institution requires its own name on top and you place it in the middle just because we suggest it.)

```
                        title of the paper
                           your name
                 course name and section number


                           instructor
                       college or university
                             date
```

The title itself should be clear and to the point. If you have written an analysis of the activities of Confederate spies in the Tennessee theater of the American Civil War, you could entitle your paper, "Confederate Spies in Tennessee, 1863." Avoid titles that are too general or vague, such as "Civil War Spies," or "The Confederate Army." Also avoid titles that are long-winded and pretentious. If you present your instructor a paper with a title such as, "A Narrative Description and Comparative Analysis of Confederate Surveillance and Intelligence Operations from the Fall of Vicksburg to the Commencement of the Siege of Chattanooga, with Special Emphasis on the Plight of Spies Apprehended, Tried, and Convicted by the Union Army," you may send your teacher the message that you are trying to win favor with verbiage rather than with research and logical argument. Your title also should not be a cute play on words. The paper described above could be the best ever written on the subject, but if its solid text is heralded by a title such as, "To Spy or Not to Spy: That Was the Question in 1863," or (forbid it) "The Spies Who Came in for the Gold," its credibility will be severely damaged.

In most cases your name on the title page should match the official version that appears in your instructor's grade book. If the campus registrar has recorded your name as Jason Emanuel Smith, do not submit a paper with only J. Smith on it. This may lead to confusion and to your hard work being credited to another student. The course name always should be included, and the section number is a very good idea. Large institutions offer many sections of American History. If your paper should manage to declare its independence from the rest of its stack, the presence of the correct section number could help your professor return it to its comrades. Use your instructor's name as formally as possible without being pretentious. Even if your instructor goes by the name Liz, you probably should list her as Elizabeth. On the other hand, Dr. Edward Richard Henry IV could appear simply as Edward R. Henry. How would your instructor use her or his own name on a journal article? Use that form.

Many colleges and universities do not require the inclusion of the institutional name on title pages. Most do, however, and it is a good idea. Sometimes you may need to include the department name (British History, Liberal Arts) or the name of the specific college (Arts and Sciences, Graduate) within the university.

Unless you gain specific permission to do so, do not use fancy or unorthodox font or size on your title page. We realize that today's word processing programs come equipped with all kinds of ways to embellish your presentation. But
do not use them in an academic research paper. Unless you are permitted to do
so, refrain from using pictures or photographs on the title page. The following
page presents a sample title page

```
                    Mahlon Scott's Day on the Rhine
                                by
                         George C. Patton
                    History of World War II
                              HIS 4113
                    Dr. Bradley Eisenhower
                    EastWest University
                        January 1, 1998
```

4.3 Abstract

Sometimes, particularly in the case of graduate work, research papers may
need to be accompanied by an abstract. An abstract is a brief summary of a
paper, written primarily to allow potential readers to see if the paper contains
information of sufficient interest for them to read. You have probably had the
experience of lugging home a huge stack of books or of plunking coins into a
photocopier to reproduce journal articles, only to discover that some of those
books and articles are only of marginal use to your research project. People conducting research want specific kinds of information, and they often read dozens
of abstracts looking for papers that contain relevant data.

Your abstract page should have the designation "Abstract" centered near
the top of the page. Next is the title, also centered, followed by a paragraph that
precisely states the paper's topic, research and analysis methods, and results and
conclusions. The abstract paragraph should not exceed 150 words. Remember
that an abstract is not an introduction but a summary. Consider the following
actual example.

```
                 The Failure of the Canadian Identity
                         Walter F. Schnee
Canada's perennial constitutional and political crises are not, as common-
ly believed, an outgrowth of the flowering of modern Quebecois national-
```

```
ism in the 1960s. Rather, Canada is a troubled society because, for

reasons rooted in Canadian history, the French and the English have

differing views upon what it means to be Canadian and how their common

state is to be constituted. The Quebecois have constructed a national

identity which precludes their taking an active part in Canadian society

as Quebecois in a positive sense rather than in opposition to the rest of

Canadian society. The English, on the other hand, have proved incapable

of establishing an identity outside of the British Empire (an entity

which no longer exists) which at the same time welcomes the Quebecois as

full members of Canadian society.
```

4.4 Outline

A formal outline is usually not required when preparing a standard historical research paper. Some professors, however, may require one to be submitted along with your paper. Bear in mind that the type of outline we are talking about now is not the kind we discussed in Chapter 1, which serves as an invaluable aid to generating and organizing ideas in the preliminary stages of your project. That outline, written before you begin writing your first draft, helps you make crucial decisions regarding the direction of your paper. This formal outline, usually written after you have produced the final draft, helps your reader discern quickly the direction and shape of your argument. (Keep in mind, however, that a formal outline written at the end of the drafting process is also a good way for you to check the strengths and weaknesses of your final draft.)

You may be in a graduate writing seminar where you will need to furnish copies of your paper's outline to the other class members for the purpose of examining and critiquing each other's progress. The instructor may want you to present an outline to assist in the evaluation of the paper. Unless you are given specific instructions, you will not need to worry about creating an outline. If it becomes necessary, your instructor probably will provide exact specifications concerning content, style, format, and so forth. We cannot furnish you with detailed, concrete instructions, but we do offer some practical suggestions should you need to write an outline.

Depending upon your instructions, your outline will be one of the two broad categories we described in Chapter 1: a topic outline or a sentence outline. Here is an example.

```
Outline
I.      Homosexuality in Colonial times
        A.      Religious scruples
        B.      English law


II.     Jefferson's reaction to Henry's editing
        A.      Confusion at the Convention
        B.      Wording amended to delete reference to "sailors"
III.    Conclusion
```

4.5 Table of Contents

As is the case with abstracts and outlines, a table of contents is usually not required in students' papers, papers intended for presentation at professional meetings, and potential journal articles. If the paper is of sufficient length and organizational complexity to justify a table of contents, however, one may be included. Tables of contents are expected in books, theses, and dissertations. They should consist of chapter or main section titles, along with their page numbers. Obviously, if you prepare a table of contents, you should do so after the final draft has been written so you will know what those page numbers will be.

4.6 Lists of Tables, Figures, Illustrations, and Maps

If you are writing a twelve-page research paper for a general education or upper-division history class, your paper will probably not be intricate enough to require extensive use of tables, figures, illustrations, or maps. Even if you must use a few charts to illustrate voting patterns or a battlefield map or two to show the ebb and flow of a military encounter, you do not necessarily need to list these in the "front matter" of your paper. Generally speaking, you want your paper to be symmetrical, and four or five pages of preliminaries will not balance a twelve-page paper. On the other hand, a 150-page Master's thesis examining voting trends in Oregon in the Gilded Age may require the extensive use of charts and graphs. In order to give your readers the ability to refer to your illustrations as necessary, you will need to make a list of them near the beginning of the paper.

A list of tables or figures contains the titles of the tables or figures in the paper in the order in which they appear, along with their page numbers. You may list tables, illustrations, and figures together under the title "Figures." You may call them all "Figures" in the text, or, if you have more than a half-page of entries, you may have separate lists for tables, figures, illustrations, or maps and title them accordingly in the text. For most applications, unless you have received specific instructions, you may follow the example given below:

```
                            List of Figures

     1.    Population Growth in Five U.S. Cities 1980-1986  . . . . . . .1

     2.    Welfare Recipients by State, 1980 and 1990   . . . . . . . .3

     3.    Economic Indicators January to June 1991    . . . . . . . .6

     4.    Educational Reforms at the Tennessee Convention . . . . . .11

     5.    International Trade 1880-1890   . . . . . . . . . . . . . .21

     6.    Gross Domestic Product, Nova Scotia, 1900-1960   . . . . . .22

     7.    California Domestic Program Expenditures 1960-1980   . . . .35

     8.    Juvenile Recidivism in Illinois   . . . . . . . . . . . . .37

     9.    Albuquerque Arts and Humanities Expenditures 1978 . . . . .39

     10.   Railroad Retirement Payments after World War II . . . . . .40
```

4.7 Text

Make sure that when you receive your research assignment your instructor also tells you the paper's required length. Whether it is to be five, eight, twelve, or thirty pages, the text of the paper should conform to certain standards. The format of the text is discussed in Sections 4.1 and 4.2, and the actual writing of the material itself is detailed for you in Chapters 1 and 2. It is here where your ability to employ research data and to craft logical arguments will be used. Now you will use your newly enhanced talent to weave skillful, scintillating sentences into piquant, persuasive paragraphs.

4.8 Chapter Headings

Shorter papers should be presented without a formal array of headings and subheadings in the text. In general, papers that are not long enough to need a table of contents do not require text divisions either. Longer presentations, however, should be grouped logically into subsections. Even longer papers should include no more than the three following levels of headings:

- Primary headings, which should be centered, with each word except articles, prepositions, and conjunctions capitalized.
- Secondary headings, which begin at the left margin, also with each word except articles, prepositions, and conjunctions capitalized.
- Tertiary headings, which should be underlined and written in sentence style (with only the first word and proper nouns capitalized), with a period at the end.

The following illustration demonstrates the proper use of headings. You should notice a similarity between these levels and those of the outlining procedure described in Chapter 1.

```
                 A Twelfth-Century Renaissance in Europe


                          [title of paper]


                        Schools and Learning

                        [primary heading])

                 Monasteries and cathedrals.

                       [secondary heading]

                          Royal courts.

                        [tertiary heading]

                          Universities.

                        [tertiary heading]
```

4.9 Tables

Tables are used in the text to show relationships among data. Tables that show simple results or "raw" data should be placed in an appendix. Tables should not reiterate or rehash the content of the text; they should add something new. They should also stand on their own; that is, the reader should not have to read the text in order to interpret and understand the table. If communication is impaired by the use or misuse of tables, it would be better to omit them and explain the same ideas more carefully in the text.

To provide clarity, each table should be titled, with each of the words in the title capitalized (except for articles, prepositions, and conjunctions). You should label columns and rows within the table clearly. The source of the information

Figure 1   *American Population Growth, 1800–1900*

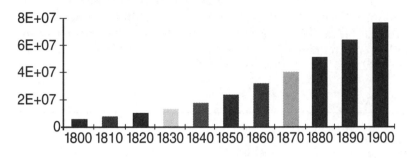

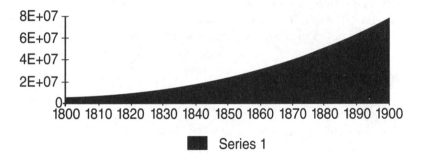

should be shown immediately below the table, not in a footnote or endnote. Look at the example tables. With no word of textual explanation here, you should be able to comprehend the table's meaning:

Table 1   *American Population Growth, 1800–1900*

Year	Population	Percent Increase (%)
1800	5,308,483	
1810	7,239,881	36.4%
1820	9,638,453	33.1
1830	12,866,020	33.5
1840	17,069,453	32.7
1850	23,191,876	35.9
1860	31,433,321	35.6
1870	39,818,449	26.6
1880	50,155,783	26.0
1890	62,947,714	25.5
1900	75,994,575	20.7

Source: Census Bureau, Statistical Abstract of the United States.

The same statistics listed in the table may be presented in the form of a chart or graph. These are sometimes helpful in explaining certain types of information. Whereas the table above provides helpful numbers, viewing the same information in chart or graph form will enable your reader to identify trends and, therefore, perceive a point that you may be trying to make.

4.10 Illustrations

For most standard history research papers, photographs, drawings, or other pictures are not necessary and tend to detract from the scholarly impression you are trying to make. College instructors can tell whether a student is trying to communicate or to dazzle. Allow your quality research and your carefully crafted argument to perform the task alone. If they cannot, perhaps you should rework the paper until you no longer need gimmicks.

Maps

Maps are employed in scholarly historical writing more than in any of the other social sciences. History happens in specific spatial locations, and it is often useful to be able to give readers a feel for these places. How often in your own reading or classroom experience have you appreciated being able to see on a page or hanging on a wall the extent of a particular empire? No matter how skillful you may be with the use of language, you cannot describe the route of Lewis and Clark or the assault on the Normandy beaches as well with words as you can with maps. Some maps, however, are more useful than others, and it is important to know how to use them well. Again, the goal is effective communication! You want your paper's maps to work in concert with your prose to deliver the message you intend. The general rules regarding map usage are the same as with tables, charts and graphs. You should title the map using the same rules, and you should supply the source of the map. Again, the map should stand alone; that is, the reader should not have to read the surrounding text in order to understand what the map shows. Also, the maps should supplement the text. If your reason for placing a map on a certain page is simply to fill space, you should consider placing it in an appendix instead.

Avoid drawing the map yourself. Photocopy an appropriate map from another published source if you can. (Remember to cite the source!) Do not tape, staple, paper clip, or paste your charts or maps onto the pages you will submit. Instead, leave enough blank space as you type the text where the map will appear, carefully tape the photocopied item (reduced or enlarged, if necessary) into the space on the hard copy, and then photocopy and submit the resulting composite.

4.11 Appendices

Appendices (appendixes) are reference materials provided at the back of the paper following the text for the edification and convenience of the reader.

An appendix provides information that supplements the important facts in the text. Typical kinds of information found in appendices include tables, charts, maps, or relevant documents. In the back of your American history texts, for example, you may have noticed the presence of the Declaration of Independence and the United States Constitution. There may be lists of presidents with their dates in office, their election opponents, or their vice-presidents. You may find charts dealing with population growth, admission dates of states, racial and ethnic mixes, or a variety of economic issues such as tariff rates, gross national product, or national debt. These materials are appropriate for the back of your history text; however, not all interesting lists of statistics belong in the back of your paper. A list of states with their order and dates of admission to the Union should not be included in a paper on the economic relationship between the United States and Israel in the 1960s. On the other hand, bar graphs showing import/export trade balances, U.S. aid to Israel, voting records in the U.S. Congress, or even the flow of immigration between the two countries would be entirely appropriate. These would supplement the information you present in the text without interrupting the flow of the narrative or argument. Place in an appendix only items that will answer questions raised by the text or are necessary to explain the text.

To format an appendix, follow the format guidelines for tables given above. At the top center of the page label your first appendix "Appendix A," your second appendix "Appendix B," and so forth. Keep these appended items relatively brief—individually and collectively. As we have indicated before, you should aim for a kind of balance in your presentation. Just as an eight-page paper should not be preceded by five pages of preliminaries, it should not be followed by six or seven pages of added materials. Do not append an entire government document, an entire journal article, or other publication. A fifteen-page paper on the origins of the Cold War should not have George Kennan's "The Sources of Soviet Conduct" included as an appendix. You may quote from it, but do not reprint it. The sources from which you derive your appendices, of course, should be acknowledged.

4.12 Works Cited, Bibliographies, and Other Reference Pages

It is very important that you be as careful in compiling and formatting your reference pages as you are in every other aspect of the paper. The next chapter describes two different referencing formats, the author-date system and the documentary-note system, both modeled on instructions given in the fourteenth edition of *The Chicago Manual of Style*.

5   *Citing Sources*

5.1 Preliminary Decisions

One of your most important jobs as a research writer is to document your use of source material carefully and clearly. Failure to do so will cause your reader confusion, damage the effectiveness of your presentation, and perhaps make you vulnerable to a charge of plagiarism. Proper documentation is more than just good form. It is also a powerful indicator of your own commitment to scholarship, and it underscores the sense of authority that you bring to your writing. Good documentation demonstrates your expertise as a researcher and increases your reader's trust in you and your work.

As anybody who has ever written a research paper knows, getting the documentation right can be a frustrating, confusing job, especially for the writer who is not familiar with citation systems. Positioning each element of a single reference citation accurately can require what seems like an inordinate amount of time looking through the style manual. Even before you begin to work on the specific citations, there are important questions of style and format to answer.

5.1.1 What to Document

Direct quotes must always be credited, as well as certain kinds of paraphrased material. Information that is basic—important dates, universally acknowledged facts or opinions—need not be cited. If, for example, you state in your paper that Franklin Roosevelt (FDR) was president of the United States during the Second World War, few (if any) readers will question that assertion. Information that is not widely known, whether fact or opinion, should receive documentation. What if you are unsure about whether a fact is widely known?

You are, after all, very probably a newcomer to the field in which you are conducting your research. If in doubt, supply the proper documentation. It is better to overdocument than to fail to do justice to a source.

Documentation also lends credibility to your research and to your thesis. As we have said, opinions are as common as water and less valuable. Everyone has opinions, and most are willing to share them whether we want them to or not. It would be easy to suggest, that FDR knew in advance that Pearl Harbor was about to be attacked and allowed it to happen to drag the United States into the war. To say so without the ballast of documentation, however, renders your statement as just another reckless accusation. On the other hand, if in your research you discover an unknown document—what now we often call a "smoking gun"—that reveals such a connection without question, chances are that readers will want to know the particulars about that document. If you can buttress your disclosure with careful and complete documentation of your source, the allegation will seem less preposterous and more believable.

5.1.2 The Choice of Style

As you probably already know, you have a number of choices concerning the way you cite sources. All of us have seen superscript (raised) reference numbers within or following paragraphs of text. Perhaps you have also seen parenthetical references inserted right into the text itself. If you have taken a course or two in the English department, you have probably become acquainted with the referencing system approved by the Modern Language Association (MLA). You may also have heard about or used *The Chicago Manual of Style.* Maybe your professor uses the name "Turabian"—the writer of a popular reference guide—as if quoting scripture. So which form are you supposed to use? After months of arduous research and weeks of prewriting, writing, and rewriting, the choice of where to place colons and commas in a single bibliographical entry may seem to you to be either a practical joke or a waste of your time.

In the interest of fairness and accuracy, each profession has certain goals to accomplish regarding the accurate transmission of reference material, and the documentation systems developed and practiced by each discipline do what needs to be done to reach those goals. At the time of this writing, there are no major historical or political science journals that actually use MLA; these two professions employ either the systems documented in *The Chicago Manual of Style* (*CMS*) or else use a system closely based on it. Our focus, therefore, will concern *CMS*—the style you will need to learn to produce standard history papers.

5.1.3 The Choice of Format

Another basic decision you must make concerns format. Are you going to credit the sources in your paper by using parenthetical references within the text or by using superscript numbers to refer to bibliographic notes placed either at the foot of the page (footnotes) or at the back of the paper (endnotes)? While the MLA style used in other disciplines within the liberal arts emphasizes parenthetical references, the history books and journals you read use footnotes or endnotes. Perhaps as a concession to modern times, the most recent edition of the *CMS* includes models for parenthetical references, referring to this format as the *author-date system* because the parenthetical references contain the author's last name and the source's date of publication. The *CMS* calls the superscript number format the *documentary-note system* or *the humanities system.* You have probably seen this system most often in your reading, and it is the one with which we in the history department are most familiar. It is very important to remember that both formats require a bibliography at the end of the paper.

The Importance of Consistency

Whichever style and format you use, the most important rule is to *be consistent.* Sloppy referencing undermines your reader's trust and does a disservice to the writers whose work you are incorporating into your own argument. And from a purely practical standpoint, inconsistent referencing can severely damage your paper's grade.

Using the Style Manual

Read through the following pages before trying to use them to structure your notes. Unpracticed student researchers tend to ignore this section of the style manual until the moment the first note has to be worked out, and then they skim through the examples looking for one that perfectly corresponds to the immediate case in hand. But most style manuals do not include every possible documentation model, so the writer must piece together a coherent reference out of elements from several models. Reading through all the models before using them gives you a feel for where to find different aspects of models and shows you how the referencing system works in general.

This manual offers examples for both the author-date system and the documentary-note system. With a few carefully noted exceptions, all models are based on those found in the fourteenth edition of *The Chicago Manual of Style* where helpful section numbers for relevant passages in the *CMS* appear in parentheses. For example, *CMS* (15.367) refers to section 367 of Chapter 15 of the *CMS*, a section which shows how to cite source material taken from the United States Constitution.

5.2 The Author-Date System: Parenthetical References

In the author-date system of citation, a note is placed in parentheses within the text, near the location where the source material appears. To minimize the reader's inevitable distraction from the text's narrative or argument, the reference must be as brief as possible, containing just enough information to refer the reader to the full citation in the bibliography following the text. The minimum information necessary is the author's name—meaning the name by which the source is alphabetized in the bibliography—and the date of the publication of the source. As indicated by the models that follow, this information can be supplied in a number of ways.

Note. Models of bibliographical entries that correspond to the parenthetical text references are given in the next section of this chapter.

Parenthetical Reference Models

Author, date, and page in parentheses

By 1910, West Virginia had twenty-one handplants employing 3,153 workers and accounting for nearly thirty percent of hand-blown window glass (Lookabill 1971, 56).

Note that, when it appears at the end of a sentence, the parenthetical reference is placed inside the period.

Page and chapter in notes

A text citation may refer to an entire article, in which case, you need not include page numbers, since they are given in the bibliography. However, you will sometimes need to cite specific page and chapter numbers, which follow the date and are preceded by a comma and, in the case of a chapter, the abbreviation "chap." Note that you do not use the abbreviation *p.* or *pp.* when referring to page numbers.

Page numbers

Bryson (1994, 242–244) recounts the development of the soft-drink industry America.

Chapter numbers

Bryson (1994, chap. 11) discusses the development of American eating habits.

Author and date in text

The following example focuses the reader's attention on Bryson's book: For a detailed presentation of the evolution of Coca-Cola as an American phenomenon, see Bryson 1994 (243).

Author in the text, date and page in parentheses

Here the emphasis is on the author, for only Bryson's name appears within the grammar of the sentence:

Bryson (1994, 243) tells interesting stories, such as how in 1887 an Atlanta pharmacist sold his recipe for Coca-Cola for $283.29.

Source with two authors

Note carefully the placement of the period in relation to the closing quotation marks and the parenthetical reference:

> Militarily, the United States was ill-prepared for war with Britain in 1812. "Some of the ranking generals were semisenile heirlooms from the Revolutionary War, resting on their laurels and lacking in vigor and vision" (Bailey and Kennedy 1994).

Source with three authors

> There were forty-four breakfast cereal companies in Battle Creek, Michigan, at the turn of the century (Bursk, Clark, and Hidy 1962).

Source with four or more authors

Place the Latin phrase *et al.,* meaning "and others," after the name of the first author. Note that the phrase appears in roman type, not italics, and is followed by a period:

> According to Herring et al. (1990, 42), five builders backed out of the project due to doubts about the local economy.

More than one source in a parenthetical reference

Note that the references are arranged alphabetically and separated by semicolons:

> Historians still debate the leadership qualities of Andrew Jackson (Bensen 1961; Hammond 1957; Pessen 1978).

Each of the sources will have its own entry in the bibliography following the paper. The entries will be alphabetized separately from the others that appeared in the parenthetical reference.

Two authors with the same last name

Use a first initial to differentiate two authors with the same last name:

> The resulting scandal, though kept out of most of the papers, nevertheless changed the way politicians reported their earnings (R. Brown 1971; T. S. Brown 1984).

Two works by the same author

If two references by the same author appear in the same note, place a comma between the publication dates:

> Jones (1943, 1947) argued for sweeping tax reform on the national level.

If the two works were published in the same year, differentiate them by adding lowercase letters to the publication date. Be sure to add the letters to the references in the bibliography, too.

> There were eight attempts during the course of the year to assassinate the duke's secretary (Emmons 1964a, 1964b).

Reprints

It is sometimes significant to note the date when an important text was first published, even if you are using a reprint of that work. In this case, the date of the first printing appears in brackets before the date of the reprint:

During that period, there were three advertising campaign strategies deemed potentially useful to political campaigners (Adams [1964] 1988, 12).

Modern editions of classic texts

You may use the author-date system to structure notes for classic texts, such as the Bible, standard translations of ancient works, or the *Federalist Papers*, by citing the date and page numbers of the edition you are using. Or you may refer to these texts by using the systems by which they are subdivided. Since all editions of a classic text employ the same standard subdivisions, this reference method has the advantage of allowing your reader to find the citation in any published version of the text. For example, you may cite a biblical passage by referring to the particular book, chapter, and verse, all in roman type, with the translation given after the verse number:

"And the angel said unto them, Fear not: for, behold, I bring you good tidings of great joy, which shall be to all people" (Luke 2:10 King James Version).

The Federalist Papers may be cited by their standard numbers:

Madison asserts that the formation of factions is inevitable but that it is possible to control their effects (*Federalist 10*).

Plays may be cited by act and scene numbers:

As Polonius says to Ophelia in *Hamlet*, "'Tis too much proved—that with devotion's visage/And pious action we do sugar o'er/The devil himself" (Act III, scene I).

Newspaper articles

According to the *CMS* (16.117), references to daily newspapers should be handled within the syntax of your sentence:

In an October 16, 1996, editorial in the *New York Times*, Maureen Dowd stated, "If Mr. Clinton is trivializing the campaign . . . he is only reflecting trivial yuppies used to a world not of heroic proportions but of Seinfeldian proportions, a world defined not by a battle between good and evil but a choice between skim or whole, caf or de, foam or no foam, carbonated or still, lemon or lime."

The *CMS* further states that references to newspaper items are not included in the bibliography. If you wish to include such references, however, there is a model of a bibliographic entry in the next section of this chapter.

Letters and other personal documents in published collections

According to the *CMS* (16.78), when you cite a letter, memo, or other communication that appears in a published work, identify the author, recipient, and date within the text of the sentence and refer to the author of the published work in parentheses:

> A dubious Roosevelt told Stimson in a letter of 2 May 1939, "I could carve a better-looking man out of a bar of soap" (Smeltson 1992).

Public Documents

You may cite public documents using the standard author-date technique. The *CMS* (15.322-411, 16. 148–79) gives detailed information on how to cite public documents published by the national, state, county, or city governments, as well as those published by foreign governments. Corresponding bibliographical entries appear in the next section.

Congressional journals

Parenthetical text references to either the *Senate Journal* or the *House Journal* start with the journal title in place of the author, the session year, and, if applicable, the page:

> Senator Jones endorsed the proposal as reworded by Senator Edward's committee (*Senate Journal* 1893, 24).

Congressional debates

Congressional debates are printed in the daily issues of the *Congressional Record*, which are bound biweekly and then collected and bound at the end of the session. Whenever possible, you should consult the bound yearly collection instead of the biweekly compilations. Your parenthetical reference should begin with the title *Congressional Record* (or *Cong. Rec.*) in place of the author's name and include the year of the congressional session, the volume and part of the *Congressional Record*, and, finally the page:

> Representatives Valentine and Beechnut addressed the question of funding for secondary education (*Cong. Rec.* 1930, 72, pt. 8: 9012).

Congressional reports and documents

References to congressional reports and documents, which are numbered sequentially in one- or two-year periods, include the name of the body generating the material, the year, and the page:

> Rep. Slavin promised from the floor to answer the charges against him within the next week (U.S. House 1993, 12).

NOTE: Any reference that begins with *U.S. Senate* or *U.S. House* may omit the *U.S.* if it is clear from the context that you are referring to the United States. Whichever form you use, be sure to use it *consistently* in both the notes and the bibliography.

Bills and resolutions

According to the *CMS* (15.347-48), bills and resolutions, which are published in pamphlets called "slip bills," on microfiche, and in the *Congressional Record*, are not always given a parenthetical reference and a corresponding bibliographic entry. Instead, the pertinent reference information appears in the text of the sentence. If, however, you wish to cite such information in a text reference, the form depends upon the source from which you took your information:

Citing to a slip bill

The ruling prohibited consular officials from rejecting visa requests out of hand (U.S. Senate 1992).
The ruling prohibited consular officials from rejecting visa requests out of hand (*Visa Formalization Act of 1992*).

You may cite either the body that authored the bill or the title of the work itself. Whichever method you choose for the parenthetical reference, remember to begin your bibliography entry with the same material.

Citing to the Congressional Record

The ruling prohibited consular officials from rejecting visa requests out of hand (U.S. Senate 1992, S7658).

The number following the date and preceded by an *S* (for Senate; *H* for House) is the page number in the *Congressional Record*.

Laws

As with bills and resolutions, laws (also called statutes) are not necessarily given a parenthetical text reference and bibliographic entry either. Instead, the identifying material is included in the text. If you wish to make a formal reference for a law, you must structure it according to the place where you found the law published. Initially published separately in pamphlets, as slip laws, laws are eventually collected and incorporated, first into a set of volumes called *U.S. Statutes at Large* and later into the *United States Code*, a multivolume set that is revised every six years. You should use the latest publication.

Citing to a slip law

You should either use U.S. Public Law, in roman type, and the number of the piece of legislation, or the title of the law:

Congress stipulates that any book deposited for copyright in the Library of Congress that suffers serious damage or deterioration due to age be rebound in library cloth (U.S. Public Law 678, 16-17).

or

Congress stipulates that any book deposited for copyright in the Library of Congress that suffers serious damage or deterioration due to age be rebound in library cloth (*Library of Congress Book Preservation Act of 1993*, 16-17).

Citing to the Statutes at Large

Include the page number after the year:

Congress stipulates that any book deposited for copyright in the Library of Congress that suffers serious damage or deterioration due to age be rebound in library cloth (*Statutes at Large* 1993, 466).

Citing to the United States Code

Congress stipulates that any book deposited for copyright in the Library of Congress that suffers serious damage or deterioration due to age be rebound in library cloth (*Library of Congress Book Preservation Act of 1993, U.S. Code.* Vol. 38, Sec. 1562).

United States Constitution

According to the *CMS* (15.367), references to the United States Constitution must include the number of the article or amendment, the section number, and the clause, if necessary:

The framers of the Constitution tried to give future generations of Americans the ability to deal with problems as they arise through the "elastic clause" (U. S. Constitution, art. 1, sec. 8, cl. 18).

Executive department documents

A reference to a report, bulletin, circular, or any other type of material issued by the executive department starts with the name of the agency issuing the document, although you may use the name of the author, if known.

By 1830, there were ten schools operating within the eastern Cherokee nation, educating 248 pupils per year; in the West, two schools taught eighty young Cherokees annually (Department of War, Indian Affairs 1831, 168).

Legal references

Supreme Court

As with laws, Supreme Court and lower court decisions are rarely given their own parenthetical reference and bibliographic entry but are instead identified in the text. If you wish to insert a more formal reference, however, you may place within the parentheses the title of the case, in italics, followed by the source, which is preceded by the volume number and followed by the page number. Before 1875, Supreme Court decisions were published under the names of official court reporters, and so the source for these cases will be the court reporter's name, as in the following example, where "Peters" is the name of the court reporter:

In his decision, Chief Justice Marshall ruled that the Cherokee Nation was a distinct community with recognized boundaries, over which the laws of the state of Georgia could have no force (*Cherokee Nation v. Georgia* 5 Peters 1 [1832]).

For cases after 1875 the name of the court reporter is replaced by a new source, the United States Supreme Court Reports, abbreviated U.S.

You should end the first reference to the case that appears in your paper with the date of the case, in brackets. You need not include the date in subsequent references.

Lower courts

Decisions of lower federal courts are published in the *Federal Reporter*. The note should give the volume of the *Federal Reporter* (*F.*), the series, if it is other than the first (*2d*, in the model below), the page, and, in brackets, an abbreviated reference to the specific court (the example below is to the Second Circuit Court) and the year:

One ruling takes into account the bias that often exists against the defendant in certain types of personal injury lawsuits (*United States v. Sizemore*, 183 F. 2d 201 [2d Cir. 1950]).

Corporate authors

Because government documents are often credited to a corporate author with a lengthy name, you may devise an acronym or a shortened form of the name and indicate in your first reference to the source that your devised name will be used in later citations:

(Office of Indian Affairs 1834, 942; *hereafter* OIA)
(*War of the Rebellion: A Compilation of the Official records of the Union and Confederate Armies 1862; hereafter OR*)
(United States Navy 1942; *hereafter* USN)

Interviews

According to the *CMS* (16.127, 130), citations to interviews should be handled within the syntax of the sentence rather than in parentheses. The *CMS* states that interviews need not be listed in the bibliography but may be included if you or your instructor wish. Model bibliography formats for such material appear in the bibliography section of this chapter.

Published interview

In an interview with Donald Frederic, Disraeli defended his immigration policy.

No parenthetical reference is necessary in the above example because sufficient information is given for the reader to find the complete citation, which will be alphabetized under Frederic's name in the bibliography.

Unpublished interview conducted by the writer of the paper

> In a 1981 interview with the author, James Crowder revealed his knowledge of the destruction in London of sensitive World War Two documents.

If you are citing material from an interview that you conducted, you should identify yourself as the author and give the date of the interview.

Manuscript Collections

A single item from a manuscript collection

Collections of original manuscripts—letters, diaries, private journals, and the like—are found in many libraries around the world and can be a rich source of information for the historian. According to the *CMS* (16.137), if in your paper you use only one manuscript from a special collection, place the name of the manuscript's author, if known, or else its title, if there is one, in the parenthetical reference, followed by the date, if given:

> Apparently, Sherman was upset that Grant had failed to respond to his request to attend the ceremony (Farquhar 1869).

This note refers to an 1869 memoir written by Major Edward Farquhar and housed in the Gillette Collection of Civil War Memorabilia, which is located at the Chambers Library of the University of Central Oklahoma. The next section of this chapter gives a bibliographic citation for this reference.

More than one item from a single manuscript collection

According to the *CMS* (16.135), when you use material from more than one manuscript located in a particular collection, you must identify the manuscript and the author within the text. You may also identify the specific collection within the text, but if you choose not to do so, you must identify the collection within a parenthetical reference:

> Clemens' letter to Howells of 10 June 1889 (Allen Papers) apparently did the trick: Howells was on the train the next day.

The collection identified in the parentheses above—not the individual manuscripts housed in it and referred to in your text—is then entered alphabetically in the bibliography. A bibliographic citation for this reference appears in the next section. See the CMS (15.277-92, 16.135-38) for more information about citing manuscript sources.

The Author-Date System: Bibliography

In a paper using the author-date system of referencing, the parenthetical text references point the reader to the full citation in the bibliography. This bibliography, which always follows the text, is arranged alphabetically according to the first element in each citation. This element is usually the last name of the author or editor, but in the absence of such information, the citation is alphabetized according to the title of the work, which is then the first element in the citation (*CMS* 16.41).

The bibliography is double-spaced throughout, even between entries. As with most alphabetically arranged bibliographies, there is a kind of reverse-indentation system: After the first line of a citation, all subsequent lines are indented five spaces.

Capitalization

Some disciplines use the "headline style" of capitalization for bibliographical citations. In this style, described in the *CMS* (15.104), all first and last words in a title, and all other words *except* articles (*a, an, the*), coordinating words (*and, but, or, for, nor*), and all prepositions (*in, at, on, over, below,* etc.) are capitalized. Other disciplines, however, use the "sentence style"—also known as the "down style"—of capitalization, in which, according to the *CMS* (15.73.3) you capitalize only the first word of the main title, the first word of the subtitle, and all proper nouns and proper adjectives. Check with your instructor to determine which capitalization style you should use. This manual will use headline capitalization in the following models.

Bibliographic Reference Models

Books

One author

> Bartlett, Jack. 1995. *Made in America: Industrialism in the Nineteenth Century.* Boston: Twayne.

First comes the author's name, inverted, then the date of publication, followed by the *italicized* title of the book, the place of publication (the city where the publisher's main editorial offices are located), and the name of the publishing house. *Note the reversed indention.* For place of publication, you need not identify the state or country unless the city is not well known or is not present elsewhere in the citation. Most readers will know in what state to find Oklahoma City or the University of Nebraska Press. If the state is not known, you may use standard, two-letter postal abbreviations, such as OK or NE:

> . . . Upper Saddle River, NJ: Prentice Hall.

According to the *CMS* (15.160-163), you may cite the full name of the publisher as it appears on the book's title page or you may use a suitable abbreviation, substituting *Univ.* for *University*, for example. Certain words, like an initial *The*, a final *Inc.*, or the phrases *and Company* and *and Sons* may be omitted. Be sure that your spelling and punctuation of the publisher's name are correct.

Periods are used to divide most of the elements in the citation, although a colon is used between the place of publication and publisher. Custom dictates that the main title and subtitle be separated by a colon, even though a colon may not appear in the title as printed on the title page of the book.

Two authors

Only the name of the first author is reversed, since it is the only one by which the citation is alphabetized:

> Bailey, Alice, and Allen Tomlinson. 1994. *The American Republic: Forebodings and Prognosis.* Lexington, MA: D. C. Heath.

Three authors

> Bursk, Arnold, Donald T. Revick, and Agnes White-Garnet. 1974. *The History of Business and the Business of History.* 2 vols. New York: Harcourt.

Four or more authors

> Herring, Ralph, et al. 1990. *Funding History Research.* Atlanta: Cayton Institute for Policy Development.

Editor, compiler, or translator as author

When no author is listed on the title page, the *CMS* (16.46) calls for you to begin the citation with the name of the editor, compiler, or translator:

> Trakas, Hayley, comp. 1995. *Listening to the Truth: Radio Accounts of the War in the Pacific.* New York: Heltzer.

Editor, compiler, or translator with author

Place the name of the editor, compiler, or translator after the title, prefaced, according to the *CMS* (16.47), by the appropriate phrase, in roman type: *Ed., Comp.,* or *Trans.*:

> Francis, Audrey. 1986. *France and Glory.* Trans. John Picard. Chicago: Jewell Press.

Untranslated book

If your source is in a foreign language, it is not necessary, according to the *CMS* (15.118), to translate the title into English. Use the capitalization format of the original language (see also *CMS* 9):

> Libæk, Ivar, and Øivind Stenersen 1992. *Die Geschichte Norwegens: Von der Eiszeit bis zum Erdöl-Zeitalter.* Oslo: Grøndahl and Dreyer.

> Picon-Salas, Mariano. 1950. *De la Conquesta a la Indépencia.* Mexico D.F.: Fondo de Cultura Económica.

If you wish to provide a translation of the title, do so in brackets or parentheses following the title. Set the translation in roman type and capitalize only the first word of the title and subtitle, proper nouns, and proper adjectives:

> Wharton, Edith. 1916. *Voyages au front* (Visits to the front). Paris: Plon.

Two or more works by the same author

According to the *CMS* (15.66, 16.28), the author's name in all citations after the first may be replaced, if you wish, by a three-em dash (six strokes) of the hyphen:

Abel, Annie Heloise. 1915. *The American Indian as Slaveholder and Secessionist.* Vol. 1 of *The Slaveholding Indians.* Cleveland: Arthur H. Cook.

————. 1919. *The American Indian as Participant in the Civil War.* Vol. 2 of *The Slaveholding Indians.* Cleveland: Arthur H. Cook.

Chapter in a multiauthor collection

MacMullen, Ramsay. 1978. "Militarism in the Late Empire." In *The End of the Roman Empire: Decline or Transformation?* ed. Donald Kagan. 2nd ed. Lexington, MA: D. C. Heath.

Note in this example that when a title ends with a question mark, the regular documentary punctuation—a comma in this case—is omitted. The same is true for an exclamation point.

If the author and the editor are the same person, you must repeat the name:

Farmer, Susan A. 1992. Educated farmers and illiterate nobility. In *This Strange Land: A Tour of Medieval Freedonia,* ed. Susan A. Farmer. Austin: Gadzooks.

Author of a foreword or introduction

There is no need, according to the *CMS* (16.51), to cite the author of a foreword or introduction in your bibliography, unless you have used material from that author's contribution to the volume. In that case, the bibliography entry is listed under the name of the author of the foreword or introduction. Place the name of the author of the work itself after the title of the work:

Farris, Helga. 1995. Foreword to *Marital Stress among the Puritans: A Case Study,* by Basil Givan. New York: Galapagos.

The parenthetical text reference cites the name of the author of the foreword or introduction, not the author of the book:

(Farris 1995)

Subsequent editions

If you are using an edition of a book other than the first, you must cite the number of the edition or the status, such as *Rev. ed.* for *Revised edition,* if there is no edition number:

Hales, Sarah. 1993. *Water Wars in the 1880s.* 2d ed. El Paso: Del Norte Press.

Multivolume work

If you are citing a multivolume work in its entirety, use the following format:

Graybosch, Charles. 1988-89. *The Rise of the Unions.* 3 vols. New York: Starkfield.

If you are citing only one of the volumes in a multivolume work, use the following format:

>   Ronsard, Madeleine. 1992. *Monopolies.* Vol. 2 of *A History of Capitalism.* Ed.
>   Joseph M. Sayles. Boston: Renfrow.

Reprints

>   Russell, William Howard [1864] 1988. *My Diary North and South.* Ed.
>   Eugene H. Berwanger. New York: Alfred A. Knopf.

Modern editions of classic works

It is not necessary to provide the date of original publication of a classic work:

>   Burke, Edmond. 1987. *Reflections on the Revolution in France.* Ed. J.G.A.
>   Pocock. Indianapolis: Hackett.

Remember, if the classic text is divided into short, numbered sections (such as act and scene numbers in plays or book, chapter, and verse divisions of the Bible), you do not need to include the work in your bibliography unless you wish to specify a particular edition.

Periodicals

Journal articles

Journals are periodicals, usually published either monthly or quarterly, that specialize in serious scholarly articles in a particular field. In Chapter 7 of this book, we present a list of the most commonly consulted journals in the discipline of history.

Journal with continuous pagination

Most journals are paginated so that each issue of a volume continues the numbering of the previous issue. The reason for such numbering is that most journals are bound in libraries as complete volumes of several issues; continuous pagination makes it easier to consult these large compilations:

>   Haywood, C. Robert. 1988. " 'No Less a Man': Blacks in Cow Town Dodge
>   City, 1876-1886." *Western Historical Quarterly* 19:161-182.

Note that the italicized name of the journal is followed without punctuation by the volume number, a colon, and the page numbers on which the article appears. There should be no space between the colon and the page numbers, which are inclusive. Do not use *p.* or *pp.* to introduce the page numbers.

Journal in which each issue is paginated separately

>   Sherman, Browning. 1991. " 'Fifty-Four Forty or Fight!': Sloganeering in
>   Early America." *American History Digest* 28(3): 25-34.

The issue number appears in parentheses immediately following the volume number. Place one space between the colon and the page numbers.

Magazine articles

Magazines, which are usually published weekly, bimonthly, or monthly, appeal to the popular audience and generally have a wider circulation than journals. *Newsweek* and *Reader's Digest* are examples of magazines.

Monthly magazine

The name of the magazine is separated from the month of publication by a comma. In a magazine reference, inclusive page numbers are not necessary.

> Stapleton, Bonnie. 1981. "How It Was: On the Campaign Trail with Ike." *Lifetime Magazine*, April.

Weekly or bimonthly magazine

The day of the issue's publication appears before the month:

> Bruck, Connie. 1993. "The World of Business: A Mogul's Farewell." *The New Yorker*, 18 October, 12-15.

If an article begins in the front of the magazine and finishes at the back, the *CMS* (15.232) states that there is no point in recording inclusive page numbers in the bibliography entry. The specific pages used in your paper, however, must still be cited in the parenthetical note in the text.

Newspaper articles

The *CMS* (16.117) says that bibliographies usually do not include entries for articles from daily newspapers. If you wish to include such material, however, here are two possible formats for the same editorial:

> *New York Times*. 1996. Editorial, 10 October.
> Dowd, Maureen. 1996. "The Man in the Mirror." *New York Times*, 10 October.

Note that "The" is omitted from the newspaper's title, as it is for all English language newspapers (*CMS* 15.242). If the name of the city in which an American newspaper is published does not appear in the paper's title, it should be appended, in italics. If the city is not well known, the name of the state is supplied, in parentheses:

> Fine, Austin. 1992. "Hoag on Trial." *Carrollton (Texas) Tribune*, 24 November.

The *CMS* (15.234-42) offers additional suggestions for citations of newspaper articles.

Public Documents

Congressional documents

References to either the *Senate Journal* or the *House Journal* begin with the journal's title and include the years of the session, the number of the Congress and session, and the month and day of the entry:

> *U.S. Senate Journal.* 1993. 103rd Cong., 1st sess., 10 December.

The ordinal numbers *second* and *third* may be represented as *d* (52d) or as *nd* and *rd*, respectively (52nd, 53rd).

Congressional debates

> *Congressional Record.* 1930. 71st Cong., 2d sess., Vol. 72, pt. 8.

Congressional reports and documents

> U.S. House. 1993. *Report on Government Efficiency As Perceived by the Public.* 103d Cong., 2d sess., H. Doc. 225.

The abbreviation *H. Doc.* refers to *House Document.* Likewise, *S. Doc.* refers to *Senate Document.*

Bills and resolutions

> *Citing to a slip bill*

> U.S. Senate. 1992. *Visa Formalization Act of 1992.* 103d Cong. 1st sess. S. R. 1437.

or

> Visa Formalization Act of 1992. *See* U.S. Senate. 1992.

The abbreviation *S. R.* in the first model above stands for *Senate Resolutions,* and the number following is the bill or resolution number. For references to House bills, the abbreviation is *H. R.* Notice that the second model refers the reader to the more complete entry above. The choice of formats depends upon the one you used in the parenthetical text reference.

> *Citing to the* Congressional Record

> Senate. 1993. *Visa Formalization Act of 1993.* 103d Cong., 1st sess., S. R. 1437. *Congressional Record* 135, no. 137, daily ed. (10 December): S7341.

Laws

> *Citing to a slip law*

> U.S. Public Law 678. 103d Cong., 1st sess., 4 December 1993. *Library of Congress Book Preservation Act of 1993.*

or

> *Library of Congress Book Preservation Act of 1993.* U.S. Public Law 678. 103d Cong., 1st sess., 4 December 1993.

> *Citing to the Statutes at Large*

> Statutes at Large. 1994. Vol. 82, p. 466. *Library of Congress Book Preservation Act of 1993.*

or

> *Library of Congress Book Preservation Act of 1993. Statutes at Large* 82:466.

Citing to the United States Code

Library of Congress Book Preservation Act, 1993. U.S. Code. Vol. 38, sec. 1562.

United States Constitution

According to the *CMS* (16.172), the Constitution is not listed in the bibliography.

Executive department documents

A reference to a report, bulletin, circular, or any other type of material issued by the executive department starts with the name of the agency issuing the document, although you may use the name of the author, if known:

Department of War. 1831. *Report of the Commissioner of Indian Affairs for the Year 1830.* Washington, DC: GPO.

The abbreviation for the publisher in this model, *GPO*, stands for the *Government Printing Office*, which prints and distributes most government publications. According to the *CMS* (15.327), you may use any of the following formats to refer to the GPO:

Washington, DC: U.S. Government Printing Office, 1984.
Washington, DC: Government Printing Office, 1984.
Washington, DC: GPO, 1984.
Washington, 1984.
Washington 1984.

Remember to be consistent in using the form you choose.

Legal references

Supreme Court

According to the *CMS* (16.174), Supreme Court decisions are only rarely listed in bibliographies. If you do wish to include such an entry, here is a suitable format to use for cases before 1875, when cases were published under the names of official court reporters (in this case, William Cranch):

Marbury v. Madison. 1803. 1 Cranch 137.

For cases after 1875, use the following format, in which the abbreviation *U.S.* stands for the *United States Supreme Court Reports*, with the volume number preceding and the page number following:

State of Nevada v. Goldie Warren. 1969. 324 U.S. 123.

Electronic Sources

On-Line Sources

See the discussion of electronic sources in the section of this chapter dealing with the author-date bibliographical style. Until such time as an authoritative citation system for the Internet is available, we suggest the following simple formats, based in part on the work of other researchers currently available on the Internet.

A site on the World Wide Web

Place the following information in this order, separating most of the elements with periods. Name of author (if known), reversed. Title of Document (in quotation marks). Edition, revision, or version information. Date of document. Site address, starting on the next line and enclosed in v-brackets (< and >), followed by the date upon which you last accessed the cite (in parentheses)

> Page, Melvin E. "A Brief Citation Guide for Internet Sources in History and the Humanities. Ver. 2.1 20 February 1996.
> <http://www.nmmc.com/libweb/employee/citguide.him>   (13   April 1997).

The two symbols < and > which surround the site address are not part of the address; they serve merely to differentiate the address from the rest of the citation. It is important not to break the often lengthy information string that constitutes the site address, hence the relatively short second line of the citation. Note that there is no period between the > and the access date, in parentheses.

Bibliographical reference for an FTP Site

> Dodd, Sue A. "Bibliographic References for Computer Files in the Social Sciences: A Discussion Paper." Rev. May 1990.

> <ftp://ftp.msstate.edu/pub/docs/history/netuse/electronic.biblio.cite> (13 April 1997).

Remember, the one thing that is absolutely required in order to find a site on the Internet is the site address, so make sure that you copy it accurately.

Bibliographical reference for a CD-ROM

A CD-ROM's publisher can usually be identified in the same way as a book's publisher. The following model is for a source with an unascertainable author. Note that it is still necessary to include, in parentheses, the latest date on which you accessed the database.

> *Dissertation Abstracts Ondisc.* 1861–1994. CD-ROM: UMI/Dissertation Abstracts Ondisc. (15 December 1996).

Bibliographical reference for an e-mail document.

Due to the ephemeral nature of e-mail sources, most researchers recommend not including citations to e-mail in the bibliography. Instead, you may handle e-mail documentation within the text of the paper.

> In an e-mail dated 22 March 1997, Bennett assured the author that the negotiations would continue.

If however, you would like to include an e-mail citation in your references section, here is a possible format:

Bothey, Suzanne, <sbb@mtsu.edue). 15 March 1997. RE: Progress on education reform petition [E-mail to Courtney Cline <clinecl@usc.cola.edu>].

The name of the author of the e-mail message is placed first, followed by the author's e-mail address and the date of the message. Next comes a brief statement of the subject of the message, followed finally by the name of the person who originally received the message and that person's e-mail address.

Interviews

According to the *CMS* (16.130), interviews need not be included in the bibliography, but if you or your instructor wants to list such entries, here are possible formats.

Published interviews

Untitled interview in a book

Norvich, Helena. 1995. Interview by Alan McAskill. In *Survivors of the Wreck.* Ed. Alan McAskill, 62-86. Richmond: Dynasty Press.

Titled interview in a periodical

Simon, Ralph. 1993. "Picking the Record Apart: An Interview with Ralph Simon." By Brett Fox. *Weekly Watch*, 14 March, 40-54.

Interview on television

Snopes, Edward. 1994. Interview by Todd Guinn. *Oklahoma Politicians.* WWY Television, 4 June.

Unpublished interview

Crowder, James. 1981. Interview by author. Tape recording. Edmond, OK, 23 April.

Unpublished Sources

Theses and Dissertations

Bahos, Charles Lee. 1968. "John Ross: Unionist or Secessionist in 1861?" Master's thesis. University of Tulsa.
Englund, Donald R. 1973. "A Demographic Study of the Cherokee Nation." Ph.D. diss. University of Tulsa.

Paper presented at a meeting

Hellstern, Mark. 1992. "Divide and Be Conquered: The Influence of Christian Missionaries Within the Cherokee Nation Before the Civil War." Paper presented at the annual meeting of the Conference on Faith and History, Santa Barbara, CA.

Manuscript in the author's possession

> Thomas, Paula L. "Mexican-American Border Conflicts, 1915-1970." University of Texas at El Paso. Photocopy.

The entry includes the institution with which the author is affiliated and ends with a description of the format of the work (typescript, photocopy, etc.).

Manuscript collections

A single item from a manuscript collection

According to the *CMS* (16.137), the bibliographical entry begins with name of the author of the manuscript, if known, or else its title, followed by the date of the manuscript, then the name of the manuscript collection, the repository where the collection is housed, and the location of the repository:

> Farquhar, Edward. 1869. Memoir, entry for 14 May. Gillette Collection of Civil War Memorabilia, Chambers Library, Univ. of Central Oklahoma.

More than one item from a single manuscript collection

When you use material from more than one manuscript in a collection, the *CMS* (16.135) tells you to place identifying information for the specific manuscript within the text and name the collection in the parenthetical reference. Place the name of the collection and its location in the bibliographical reference:

> Allen, John C. Papers. East Hampton Athenaeum.

More information on the handling of manuscript collections is given in the *CMS* (15.277-92, 16.136-138).

Listing manuscript collections

The information in the following section does not come from the *CMS* but refers to a practice that has become a staple of history research. If you are preparing a standard research paper, it may not be necessary to separate and list each manuscript source according to its repository location. If you are writing a thesis or a dissertation, on the other hand, you will need to do so. If you are using the author-date referencing system, your list of manuscript collections and repositories will constitute a separate section of your bibliography, following your other citations. Categorize manuscript collections first by library and then by collection.

Microform collections

Many manuscript sources are now preserved in microform collections—either on microfiche or microfilm. Although the *CMS* does not discuss the separate listing of microform collections, as a rule, you should cite dates and reel numbers for the microform documents you use:

NATIONAL ARCHIVES

Letters Received by the Office of Indian Affairs, 1824-1881, M 234.

THOMAS GILCREASE INSTITUTE OF AMERICAN HISTORY AND ART,

Tulsa, Oklahoma

 John Drew Papers

 Cherokee Papers

 Samuel Worcester Papers

 Grant Foreman Collection

WESTERN HISTORY COLLECTION, University of Oklahoma, Norman, Oklahoma

 Cherokee Nation Papers

 Doris Duke Collection, American Indian Oral History

ARKANSAS HISTORY COMMISSION, Little Rock, Arkansas

 Dwight Mission Papers

 Cephas Washburn Papers

TENNESSEE STATE LIBRARY AND ARCHIVES, Nashville, Tennessee

 Gideon Morgan Letters

 Cherokee Collection

HOUGHTON LIBRARY, Harvard University, Cambridge, Massachusetts

 Cherokee Mission Papers

Letters Sent by the Office of Indian Affairs, 1824-1881, M 21.
Cherokee Old Settlers Census, T 985.
Records of the Cherokee Indian Agency in Tennessee, 1801-1935, M 208.

5.3 The Documentary-Note System: Numbered References

In the documentary-note system, instead of putting text references in parentheses, you place a superscript (raised) number after the passage that includes source material. The number refers to a full bibliographic citation given either at the foot of the page (a footnote) or in a list at the end of the paper (an endnote). Most major scholarly historical journals employ this system.

Numbering System

Number the notes consecutively throughout the paper, starting with [1]. In other words, do not begin again with [1] at the beginning of each new page, as seen in some published works. If you are writing a longer, multichaptered work such as a master's thesis or doctoral dissertation, you have the option of starting the numbering over again with [1] at the beginning of each new chapter or maintaining continuous numbering from the first note in the work to the last, but be warned: If you choose this method for a longer work, you may accumulate superscript note numbers in the hundreds. If you average even four notes per page in a 250-page thesis or dissertation, you will exceed [1000] (one thousand) notes.

Placement of Superscript Numerals

Whenever possible, the superscript numeral should go at the end of the sentence:

> By 1912, just four years after Ford's introduction of the Model T, it comprised three-quarters of all the cars on American roads.32

If it is necessary to place the reference within a sentence instead of at the end, position the numeral at the end of the pertinent clause:

> In his speech of 13 August, Bismark had intended to denounce the press[23]—and thousands of his countrymen felt the same way.

Notice in the example above that the superscript numeral occurs *before* the dash. With all other pieces of punctuation—comma, semicolon, period, exclamation mark, question mark—the superscript numeral *follows* the punctuation. The superscript numeral also follows the terminal quotation mark of a direct quote:

> Sharing Washington's view "that the Indian [was] fully the equivalent of the European in his physical and mental capacities,"[19] Jefferson, through his Secretary of War Henry Dearborn, continued the policy of converting Indians into independent landowners.

Multiple references in a single note

When a passage refers to more than one source, do not place more than one superscript numeral after the passage. Instead use only one numeral and combine all the references into a single footnote or endnote:

> Separate studies by Lovett, Morrison, and Collins all corroborate the research team's findings.[16]

The next section of this chapter gives a bibliographical model for this kind of multiple notation.

Models for Documentary Notes and Bibliography Citations

In each pair of models below, the first example is for a documentary note, and the second is for the corresponding bibliographic entry. A note may appear either as a *footnote*, placed at the bottom of the page of text on which the reference occurs, or as an *endnote*, placed, in numerical order, in a list following the text of the paper. The bibliography is usually the final element in the paper. Because its entries are arranged alphabetically, the order of entries in the bibliography will differ from the order of the endnotes, which are arranged according to the appearance of the reference within the text.

Pay attention to the basic differences between the note format and the bibliography format. Notes are numbered; bibliographical entries are not. The first line of a note is indented; all lines in a bibliography are indented *except* the first. While the author's name is printed in normal order in a note, the order is reversed in the bibliography to facilitate alphabetizing. There are also other variations within the individual references.

In your text, you may refer to a source dozens of times, while that source will appear in your bibliography only once. It is likely, therefore, that the number of endnotes you generate will be much larger than the number of bibliographic entries. If the numbers are the same (and this happens with many students' papers), you may be doing something wrong.

If the note refers to a book or an article in its entirety, you need not cite page numbers in it. If, however, you wish to cite material on a specific page or pages, give those in the note. Bibliography citations for periodicals usually give the inclusive page numbers for the articles cited.

Books

One author

Note

1. Jack Bartlett, *Made in America: Industrialism in the Nineteenth Century* (Boston: Twayne, 1995), 242-244.

Bibliography

Bartlett, Jack. *Made in America: Industrialism in the Nineteenth Century.* Boston: Twayne, 1995.

Two authors

Note

14. Alice Bailey and Allen Tomlinson, *The American Republic: Forebodings and Prognosis* (Lexington, MA: D. C. Heath, 1994), 57.

Bibliography

Bailey, Alice, and Allen Tomlinson. *The American Republic: Forebodings and Prognosis.* Lexington, MA: D. C. Heath, 1994.

Three authors

Note

2. Arnold Bursk, Donald T. Revick, and Agnes White-Garnet, *The History of Business and the Business of History,* 2 vols. (New York: Harcourt, 1974).

Bibliography

Bursk, Arnold, Donald T. Revick, and Agnes White-Garnet. *The History of Business and the Business of History.* 2 vols. New York: Harcourt, 1974.

Four or more authors

The Latin phrase *et al,* meaning "and others," appears in roman type, after the first author's name:

Note

3. Ralph Herring, et al., *Funding History Research* (Atlanta: Cayton Institute for Policy Development, 1990), 42.

Bibliography

Herring, Ralph, et al. *Funding History Research.* Atlanta: Cayton Institute for Policy Development, 1990.

Editor, compiler, or translator as author

Note

6. Hayley Trakas, comp., *Listening to the Truth: Radio Accounts of the War in the Pacific* (New York: Heltzer, 1995), 139-140.

Bibliography

Trakas, Hayley, comp. *Listening to the Truth: Radio Accounts of the War in the Pacific.* New York: Heltzer, 1995.

Editor, compiler, or translator with author

Note

37. Audrey Francis, *France and Glory,* trans. John Picard (Chicago: Jewell Press, 1986), 135-136.

Bibliography

Francis, Audrey. *France and Glory.* Trans. John Picard. Chicago: Jewell Press, 1986.

Untranslated book

Note

8. Ivar Libæk and Øivind Stenersen, *Die Geschichte Norwegens: Von der Eiszeit bis zum Erdöl-Zeitalter* (Oslo: Grøndahl and Dreyer, 1992), 67.

Bibliography

Libæk, Ivar, and Øivind Stenersen. *Die Geschichte Norwegens: Von der Eiszeit bis zum Erdöl-Zeitalter.* Oslo: Grøndahl and Dreyer, 1992.

Translated book

Note

12. Edith Wharton, *Voyages au front* (Visits to the Front) (Paris: Plon, 1916).

Bibliography

Wharton, Edith. *Voyages au front* (Visits to the Front). Paris: Plon, 1916.

Two or more works by the same author

In the notes, subsequent works by the same author are handled exactly as the first work. In the bibliography, those works are listed alphabetically, with the author's name replaced, in all entries after the first, by a three-em dash (six strokes of the hyphen):

Bibliography

Abel, Annie Heloise. *The American Indian as Slaveholder and Secessionist.* Vol.1 of *The Slaveholding Indians.* Cleveland: Arthur H. Cook, 1915.
————. *The American Indian as Participant in the Civil War.* Vol. 2 of *The Slaveholding Indians.* Cleveland: Arthur H. Cook, 1919.

Chapter in a multiauthor collection

Note

9. Ramsay MacMullen, "Militarism in the Late Empire," in *The End of the Roman Empire: Decline or Transformation?* ed. Donald Kagan, 2d ed. (Lexington, MA: D.C. Heath, 1978), 114-132.

Bibliography

MacMullen, Ramsay. "Militarism in the Late Empire." *In The End of the Roman Empire: Decline or Transformation?* Ed. Donald Kagan. 2d ed. Lexington, MA: D.C. Heath, 1978.

Note in these examples that when a title ends with a question mark, the regular documentary punctuation—a comma in the case of the note, a period in the bibliography—is omitted. The same is true for an exclamation point.

You may, if you wish, place the inclusive page numbers either in the note, following the publication information, or in the bibliography entry, following the name of the editor. If the author of the article is also the editor of the book, you must place his or her name in both locations. If the entire book is written by the same author, do not specify the chapter in the bibliography reference.

Author of a foreword or introduction

Note

70. Helga Farris, Foreword to *Marital Stress among the Puritans: A Case Study,* by Basil Givan (New York: Galapagos, 1995), 41.

Bibliography

Farris, Helga. Foreword to *Marital Stress among the Puritans: A Case Study,* by Basil Givan. New York: Galapagos, 1995.

It is not necessary to cite the author of a foreword or introduction in the bibliography unless you have used material from that author's contribution to the volume.

Subsequent editions

If you are using an edition of a book other than the first, you must cite the number of the edition or the status, such as *Rev. ed.* for *Revised edition,* if there is no edition number:

Note

45. Sarah Hales, *Water Wars in the 1880s,* 2d ed. (El Paso: Del Norte Press, 1993), 72.

Bibliography

Hales, Sarah. *Water Wars in the 1880s.* 2d ed. El Paso: Del Norte Press, 1993.

Multivolume work

If you are citing the multivolume work in its entirety, use the following format:

Note

3. Charles Graybosch, *The Rise of the Unions,* 3 vols. (New York: Starkfield, 1988-89).

Bibliography

Graybosch, Charles. *The Rise of the Unions.* 3 vols. New York: Starkfield, 1988-89.

If you are citing only one of the volumes in a multivolume work, use the following format:

Note

29. Madeleine Ronsard, *Monopolies,* vol. 2 of *A History of Capitalism,* ed. Joseph M. Sayles (Boston: Renfrow, 1992), 302.

Bibliography

Ronsard, Madeleine. *Monopolies.* Vol. 2 of *A History of Capitalism.* Ed. Joseph M. Sayles. Boston: Renfrow, 1992.

Reprints

Note

16. William Howard Russell, *My Diary North and South,* ed. Eugene H. Berwanger (1864; reprint, New York: Alfred A. Knopf, 1988).

Bibliography

Russell, William Howard. *My Diary North and South.* Ed. Eugene H. Berwanger. 1864. Reprint, New York: Alfred A. Knopf, 1988.

Modern editions of classics

It is not necessary to provide the original publication date of a classic work:

Note

10. Edmond Burke, *Reflections on the Revolution in France*, ed. J.G.A. Pocock (Indianapolis: Hackett, 1987).

Bibliography

Burke, Edmond. *Reflections on the Revolution in France.* Ed. J.G.A. Pocock. Indianapolis: Hackett, 1987.

Remember, if the classic text is divided into short, numbered sections (such as act and scene numbers in plays or book, chapter, and verse divisions of the Bible), you do not need to include the work in your bibliography unless you wish to specify a particular edition.

Periodicals

Journal Articles

Journals are periodicals, usually published either monthly or quarterly, that specialize in serious scholarly articles in a particular field. One significant distinction between the note format and the bibliography format for a journal article is that in the note you cite only those pages from which you took material, while in the bibliography you report the inclusive pages of the article. Chapter 7 presents a list of the most commonly consulted journals in the discipline of history.

Journal with continuous pagination

Most journals are paginated so that each issue of a volume continues the numbering of the previous issue. The reason for such pagination is that most journals are bound in libraries as complete volumes of several issues; continuous pagination makes it easier to consult these large compilations:

Note

31. C. Robert Haywood, "'No Less a Man': Blacks in Cow Town Dodge City, 1876-1886," *Western Historical Quarterly* 19 (1988): 175, 178.

Bibliography

Haywood, C. Robert. "'No Less a Man': Blacks in Cow Town Dodge City, 1876-1886." *Western Historical Quarterly* 19 (1988):161-182.

Note that the italicized name of the journal is followed without punctuation by the volume number, the year of publication, in parentheses, a colon, and the page numbers on which the article appears. Do not use p. or *pp.* to introduce the page numbers.

In this example, the title of the article contains material in quotes. Since the title of a journal article already appears in quotation marks, the quote-within-a-quote must be enclosed by single quotation marks. Notice also that the colon after the main title is placed after the second single quotation mark.

Journal in which each issue is paginated separately

Note

32. Browning Sherman, "'Fifty-Four Forty or Fight!': Sloganeering in Early America," *American History Digest* 28, no. 3 (1991): 27, 29.

Bibliography

Sherman, Browning. "'Fifty-Four Forty or Fight!': Sloganeering in Early America." *American History Digest* 28, no. 3 (1991): 25-34.

The issue number follows the volume number, introduced by *no.* It is also permissible to enclose the issue number in parentheses, without the *no.*, moving the year to the end of the entry and placing it in a second parentheses:

. . . *American History Digest* 28 (3): 25-34 (1991).

Magazine articles

Magazines, which are usually published weekly, bimonthly, or monthly, appeal to the popular audience and generally have a wider circulation than journals. *Newsweek* and *Reader's Digest* are examples of magazines.

Monthly magazine

Note

9. Bonnie Stapleton, "How It Was: On the Campaign Trail with Ike," *Lifetime Magazine*, April 1981, 22-25.

Bibliography

Stapleton, Bonnie. "How It Was: On the Campaign Trail with Ike." *Lifetime Magazine*, April 1981, 19-30.

Weekly or bimonthly magazine

The day of the issue's publication appears before the month:

Note

34. Connie Bruck, "The World of Business: A Mogul's Farewell," *The New Yorker*, 18 October 1993, 13.

Bibliography

Bruck, Connie. "The World of Business: A Mogul's Farewell." *The New Yorker*, 18 October 1993, 12-15.

If an article begins in the front of the magazine and finishes at the back, the *CMS* (15.232) states that there is no point in recording inclusive page numbers in the bibliography entry. The specific pages used in your paper, however, must still be cited in the note.

Newspaper articles

   Notes

      11. Editorial, *New York Times,* 10 October 1996.
      4. Austin Fine, "Hoag on Trial," *Carrollton (Texas) Tribune,* 24 November 1992.

Note that The is omitted from the newspaper's title, as it is for all English language newspapers (CMS 15.242). If the name of the city in which an American newspaper is published does not appear in the paper's title, it should be appended, in italics. If the city is not well known, the name of the state is supplied, in italics, in parentheses, as in the models above.

      While the *CMS* (15.235) maintains that news stories from daily papers are rarely included in a bibliography, it does suggest that you may, if you wish, give the name of the paper and the relevant dates in the bibliography:

   Carrollton (Texas) Tribune, 24 November 1992.

The *CMS* (15.234-42) offers additional suggestions for citations of newspaper material.

Public documents

Congressional documents

      References to either the *Senate Journal* or the *House Journal* begin with the journal's title and include the years of the session, the number of the Congress and session, and the day of the entry.

   Note

      19. *Senate Journal.* 103d Cong., 1st sess., 10 December 1993, 46-47.

   Bibliography

   Senate Journal. 103d Cong., 1st sess., 10 December 1993.

or

      U.S. Congress. *U.S. Senate Journal.* 103d Cong., 1st sess., 10 December 1993.

You may dispense with the *U.S.* at the beginning of an entry if it is clear from the context that you are talking about the United States Congress, Senate, or House. Again, be consistent in your use of format.

      The ordinal numbers *second* and *third* may be represented as *d* (52d) or as *nd* and *rd*, respectively (52nd, 53rd).

Congressional debates

      The debates are printed in the daily issues of the *Congressional Record,* which are bound biweekly and then collected and bound at the end of the session. Whenever possible, you should consult the bound yearly collection of the journal instead of the biweekly compilations.

The number following the year is the volume, followed by the part and page numbers:

Note

    20. *Congressional Record,* 71st Cong., 2d sess., 1930, 72, pt.8: 9012.

Bibliography

Congressional Record. 71st Cong., 2d sess., 1930. Vol. 72, pt. 8.

Congressional reports and documents

Note

    55. House, *Report on Government Efficiency As Perceived by the Public,* 103d Cong., 2d sess., 1993, H. Doc. 225, 12.

Bibliography

House. *Report on Government Efficiency As Perceived by the Public.* 103d Cong., 2d sess., 1993. H. Doc. 225, 12.

The abbreviation *H. Doc.* refers to *House Document.* Likewise, *S. Doc.* refers to *Senate Document.*

Bills and resolutions

Bills and resolutions are published in pamphlets called slip bills, on microfiche, and in the *Congressional Record.* According to the *CMS* (15.347-48), bills and resolutions are not always given a note and a corresponding bibliographic entry. Instead, the pertinent reference information appears in the text of the sentence. If, however, you wish to cite such information in your referencing system, the models you use depend upon the source from which you took your information:

Citing to a slip bill

Note

    21. Senate, *Visa Formalization Act of 1992,* 103d Cong., 1st sess., S.R. 1437.

or

    21. *Visa Formalization Act of 1992,* 103d Cong., 1st sess., S.R. 1437.

Bibliography

Senate. *Visa Formalization Act of 1992.* 103d Cong., 1st sess., S.R. 1437.

or

Visa Formalization Act of 1992. 103d Cong., 1st sess., S.R. 1437.

The abbreviation *S.R.* in the models above stands for *Senate Resolutions,* and the number following is the bill or resolution number. For references to House bills, the abbreviation is *H.R.*

Citing to the Congressional Record

Note

52. Senate, *Visa Formalization Act of 1992*, 103d Cong., 1st sess., S.R. 1437, *Congressional Record* 135, no. 137, daily ed. (10 December 1992): S7341.

Bibliography

Senate. *Visa Formalization Act of 1992.* 103d Cong., 1st sess., S.R. 1437. *Congressional Record* 135, no. 137, daily ed. (10 December 1992): S7341.

Laws

If you wish to make a formal reference for a law (also called a statute), you must structure it according to the place where you found the law published. Initially published separately in pamphlets, as slip laws, statutes are eventually collected and incorporated, first into a set of volumes called *U.S. Statutes at Large* and later into the *United States Code*, a multivolume set that is revised every six years. You should use the latest publication.

Citing to a slip law

Note

31. Public Law 678, 103d Cong., 1st sess. (4 December 1993), 16-17.

or

31. Public Law 678, 103d Cong., 1st sess. (4 December 1993*), Library of Congress Book Preservation Act of 1993*, 16-17.

or

31. *Library of Congress Book Preservation Act of 1993*, Public Law 678, 103d Cong., 1st sess. (4 December 1993), 16-17.

Bibliography

U.S. Public Law 678. 103d Cong., 1st sess., 4 December 1993.

or

U.S. Public Law 678. 103d Cong., 1st sess., 4 December 1993. *Library of Congress Book Preservation Act of 1993.*

or

Library of Congress Book Preservation Act of 1993. U.S. Public Law 678. 103d Cong., 1st sess., 4 December 1993.

Citing to the Statutes at Large

Note

10. *Statutes at Large* 82 (1993): 466.

or

10. *Library of Congress Book Preservation Act of 1993, Statutes at Large* 82 (1993): 466.

Bibliography

Statutes at Large 82 (1993): 466.

or

Library of Congress Book Preservation Act of 1993. Statutes at Large 82 (1993): 466.

Citing to *the United States Code*

Note

42. *Library of Congress Book Preservation Act of 1993, U.S. Code,* vol. 38, sec. 1562 (1993).

Bibliography

Library of Congress Book Preservation Act of 1993. U.S. Code. Vol. 38, sec. 1562 (1993).

United States Constitution

In the documentary-note format, according to the *CMS* (15.367), the Constitution is cited by article or amendment, section, and, if relevant, clause. The Constitution is not listed in the bibliography.

Note

23. U.S. Constitution, art.1, sec. 8, cl. 18.

Executive Department documents

A reference to a report, bulletin, circular, or any other type of material issued by the executive department starts with the name of the agency issuing the document, although you may use the name of the author, if known:

Note

24. Department of War. *Report of the Commissioner of Indian Affairs for the Year 1830* (Washington: GPO, 1831), 168.

Bibliography

U.S. Department of War. *Report of the Commissioner of Indian Affairs for the Year 1830.* Washington, DC: GPO, 1831.

The abbreviation for the publisher in this model, *GPO,* stands for *the Government Printing Office,* which prints and distributes most government publications. According to the *CMS* (15.327), you may use any of the following formats to refer to the GPO:

Washington, DC: U.S. Government Printing Office, 1984.
Washington, DC: Government Printing Office, 1984.
Washington, DC: GPO, 1984.
Washington, 1984.
Washington 1984.

Remember to be consistent in using the form you choose.

Legal references

Supreme Court

Before 1875, Supreme Court decisions were published under the names of official court reporters. The following reference is to William Cranch, *Reports of Cases Argued and Adjudged in the Supreme Court of the United States, 1801-15*, 9 vols. (Washington, DC, 1804-17). The number preceding the clerk's name is the volume number; following the clerk's name is the page number and year, in parentheses:

Note

25. *Marbury v. Madison*, 1 Cranch 137 (1803).

After 1875, Supreme Court decisions have been published in a series of volumes entitled *United States Supreme Court Reports*, which is represented in the following note by the abbreviation *U.S.* Preceding the *U.S.* is the volume number; following is the page number and year, in parentheses.

Note

26. *State of Nevada v. Goldie Warren*, 324 U.S. 123 (1969).

As we have stated before, Supreme Court decisions are rarely listed in bibliographies.

Electronic Sources

On-Line Sources

See the discussion of electronic sources in the section of this chapter dealing with the author-date bibliographical style. In the absence of an established, authoritative citation system for electronic sources, we suggest the following formats, based in part on the work of other researchers currently available on the Internet.

A Site on the World Wide Web

Note

32. Melvin E. Page. "A Brief Citation Guide for Internet Sources in History and the Humanities." Ver. 2.1. 20 February 1996. <http://www.nmmc.com/libweb/employee/citguide.him> (13 April 1997).

Place the following information in this order, separating most of the elements with periods: name of author (if known), reversed; title of document (in quotation marks); edition, revision, or version information; date of document; site address, starting on the next line and enclosed in v-brackets (< and >), followed by the date upon which you last accessed the cite (in parentheses).

Bibliography

Page, Melvin E. "A Brief Citation Guide for Internet Sources in History and the Humanities." Ver. 2.1. 20 February 1996.
<http://www.nmmc.com/libweb/employee/citguide.him> (13 April 1997).

The two symbols < and > which surround the site address are not part of the address; they serve merely to differentiate the address from the rest of the citation. It is important not to break the often lengthy information string that constitutes the site address, hence the relatively short second line of the citation. Note that there is no period between the > and the access date, in parentheses.

Bibliographical reference for an FTP Site

Note

4. Sue A. Dodd. "Bibliographic References for Computer Files in the Social Sciences: A Discussion Paper.: Rev. May 1990.
<ftp://ftp.msstate.edu/pub/docs/history/netuse/electronic.biblio.cite> (13 April 1997).

Bibliography

Dodd, Sue A. "Bibliographic References for Computer Files in the Social Sciences: A Discussion Paper." Rev. May 1990.
<ftp://ftp.msstate.edu/pub/docs/history/netuse/electronic.biblio.cite> (13 April 1997).

Remember, the one thing that is absolutely required in order to find a site on the Internet is the site address, so make sure that you copy it accurately.

Bibliographical reference for a CD-ROM

A CD-ROM's publisher can usually be identified in the same way as a book's publisher. The following model is for a source with an unascertainable author. Note that it is still necessary to include, in parentheses, the latest date on which you accessed the database:

Note

9. *Dissertation Abstracts Ondisc.* 1861-1994. CD-ROM: UMI/Dissertation Abstracts Ondisc. (15 December 1996).

Bibliography

Dissertation Abstracts Ondisc. 1861-1994. CD-ROM: UMI/Dissertation Abstracts Ondisc. (15 December 1996).

Bibliographical reference for an E-mail document

Due to the ephemeral nature of e-mail sources, most researchers recommend not including citations to e-mail in the bibliography. Instead, you may handle e-mail documentation within the text of the paper.

In an e-mail dated 22 March 1997, Bennett assured the author that the negotiations would continue.

If, however, you would like to include an e-mail citation in your references section, here is a possible format:

Note

17. Bothey, Suzanne. <sbb@mtsu.edu>. 15 March 1997. RE: Progress on education reform petition [E-mail to Courtney Cline <clinecl@usc.cola.edu>].

Bibliography

Bothey, Suzanne. <sbb@mtsu.edu>, 15 March 1997. RE: Progress on education reform petition [e-mail to Courtney Cline <clinecl@usc.cola.edu>].

The name of the author of the e-mail message is placed first, followed by the author's e-mail address and the date of the message. Next comes a brief statement of the subject of the message, followed finally by the name of the person who originally received the message and that person's e-mail address.

Interviews

According to the *CMS* (16.130), interviews need not be included in the bibliography, but if you or your instructor wants to list such entries, here are possible formats:

Published interview

Untitled interview in a book

Note

15. Helena Norvich, interview by Alan McAskill, in *Survivors of the Wreck*, ed. Alan McAskill (Richmond: Dynasty Press, 1995), 68.

Bibliography

Norvich, Helena. Interview by Alan McAskill. In *Survivors of the Wreck*. Ed. Alan McAskill, 62-86. Richmond: Dynasty Press, 1994.

Titled interview in a periodical

Note

5. Ralph Simon, "Picking the Record Apart: An Interview with Ralph Simon," interview by Brett Fox, *Weekly Watch,* 14 March 1993, 43-44.

Bibliography

Simon, Ralph. "Picking the Record Apart: An Interview with Ralph Simon." By Brett Fox. *Weekly Watch,* 14 March 1993, 40-54.

Interview on television

Note

67. Edward Snopes, interview by Todd Guinn, *Oklahoma Politicians*, WKY Television, 4 June 1994.

Bibliography

Snopes, Edward. Interview by Todd Guinn. *Oklahoma Politicians*. WKY Television, 4 June 1994.

Unpublished interview

Note

27. James Crowder, interview by author, tape recording Edmond, OK, 23 April 1981.

Bibliography

Crowder, James. Interview by author. Tape recording. Edmond, OK, 23 April 1981.

Unpublished sources

Theses and Dissertations

Note

28. Charles Lee Bahos, "John Ross: Unionist or Secessionist in 1861?" (Master's thesis, University of Tulsa, 1968), 23-25.

Bibliography

Bahos, Charles Lee. "John Ross: Unionist or Secessionist in 1861?" Master's thesis, University of Tulsa, 1968.

Note

29. Donald R. Englund, "A Demographic Study of the Cherokee Nation." (Ph.D. diss., University of Oklahoma, 1973), 69-75.

Bibliography

Englund, Donald R. "A Demographic Study of the Cherokee Nation." Ph.D. diss., University of Oklahoma, 1973.

Paper presented at a meeting

Note

30. Mark Hellstern, "Divide and be Conquered: The Influence of Christian Missionaries Within the Cherokee Nation Before the Civil War"

(presented at the annual meeting of the Conference on Faith and History, Santa Barbara, CA, April 1992), 10,11.

Bibliography

Hellstern, Mark. "Divide and Be Conquered: The Influence of Christian Missionaries Within the Cherokee Nation Before the Civil War." Presented at the annual meeting of the Conference on Faith and History, Santa Barbara, CA, April 1992.

Manuscript collections

A single item from a manuscript collection

According to the *CMS* (15.279) the note for a letter, diary entry, or other such item housed in a manuscript collection begins with a description of the item discussed in the text, including the names of the writer and recipient. For a letter, you should next report the place where it was written (if known) and then its date. You need not use the word "letter," but you should specify other types of documents, such as diary, telegram, or memorandum:

Note

43. Ebenezer Allen to Douglas Grant, 12 February 1902, Douglas Grant Papers, Olustee Municipal Library.

Note

51. Edward Farquhar, Memoir, 14 May 1869, Gillette Collection of Civil War Memorabilia, Chambers Library, Univ. of Central Oklahoma.

The order of items in the bibliographical entry begins with name of the author of the manuscript collection or with the title of the collection, followed by the name of the repository housing the collection and its location.

Bibliography

Grant, Douglas. Papers. Olustee Municipal Library. Olustee, OK.

Bibliography

Farquhar, Edward. Memoir. Gillette Collection of Civil War Memorabilia. Chambers Library, Univ. of Central Oklahoma, Edmond, OK.

More information on the handling of manuscript collections is given in the *CMS* (15.277-92).

Listing manuscript collections

These instructions are not specific to the *CMS* and are located above, in the Author-Date section of this chapter.

Multiple references in a single note

When one superscript numeral in the text refers to more than one source, handle the note in the following way:

23. Alicia Lovett, "Cromwell's Bloody Business: The Murder of the King," *Review of English History* 14 (1983): 67-89; Daniel Morrison, *God Save the King: The Life and Death of Charles I* (New York: Musgrave, 1990), 379-392; Barbara Starns, "Dastardly Deeds: The Repercussions of the Murder of Charles I," *English History in Review* 4 (1992): 31-40.

In the bibliography handle each source separately, alphabetizing as usual.

Subsequent or shortened references in notes

After you have given a complete citation for a source in a note, it is possible, if the citation is lengthy, to shorten later references to the source. One convenient method of shortening subsequent references, described in the *CMS* (15.249), is to give only the last name of the author, followed by a comma and the page number of the reference:

One work by an author in notes

First reference

35. James Oaks, *The Ruling Race: A History of American Slaveholders* (New York: Alfred A. Knopf, 1982), 35-37.

Later reference

40. Oaks, 45.

More than one work by an author in notes

First references

36. William G. McLoughlin, *Cherokees and Missionaries, 1789-1839* (New Haven: Yale University Press, 1984), 135.
39. William G. McLoughlin, *Cherokee Renaissance in the New Republic* (New Haven: Yale University Press, 1986), 47-49.

Later references

40. McLoughlin, *Cherokees and Missionaries*, 141.
43. McLoughlin, *Cherokee Renaissance*, 51.

Government documents

Methods for shortening references to government documents vary, depending on the type of source. One rule is to make sure there is sufficient information in the shortened reference to point the reader clearly to the full citation in the bibliography.

Statute cited to a slip law

First reference

16. Public Law 678, 103d Cong., 1st sess. (4 December 1993), *Library of Congress Book Preservation Act of 1993*, 16-17.

Later reference

    19. Public Law 678, 17.

or

    19. PL 678, 17.

Court decisions

First reference

    63. *United States v. Sizemore*, 183 F. 2d 201 (2d Cir. 1950).

Later reference

    67. *United States v. Sizemore*, 203.

Use of Ibid.

Ibid., an abbreviation for the Latin term *ibidem*, meaning "in the same place," can be used to shorten a note that refers to the source in the immediately preceding note:

First reference

    37. Patricia Nelson Limerick, *The Legacy of Conquest: The Unbroken Past of the American West* (New York: W.M. Norton and Company, 1987), 33.

Following reference

    38. Ibid., 34.

NOTE: Many of the sources used as models in this chapter are not references to actual publications.

5.4 The Student Citation System (SCS)

As an alternative to the author-date and documentary-note citation systems, you may want to use the Student Citation System (SCS). Be sure to get your instructor's approval before using the SCS system. Why, you may ask, would anyone want another citation system, especially since so many disciplines have their own systems (MLA, APA, etc.) already? It is precisely because college students are currently required to use several different citation systems that the SCS was created. The SCS is the first system specifically designed for use in all undergraduate college courses. Students who use it will be able to use the same system in their English, psychology, sociology, math, science, history, political science, and other courses.

How is the SCS different from other citation systems? In addition to the fact that it is designed to be used in courses in all disciplines, the SCS has several other distinctive features:

• The SCS is made for students, not academicians. It is more simple, has less rules to learn, and is easier to type than other systems.

• SCS uses the punctuation and syntax of a new grammar that students are quickly learning around the world: the universal language of the Internet. The Internet is rapidly becoming the foremost means of a wide range of research and communication activities. SCS symbols are familiar to anyone who has used the Internet: / @ + . They allow citations to be constructed with a minimum of space, effort, and confusion.

5.4.1 Rules for Notes

Like other citation systems, the SCS requires that each source citation include (1) a note in the text in which the reference to the source cited occurs, and (2) an entry in a reference page. Notes in the text always appear at the end of the sentence in which the reference is made. Study the models that accompany the following list of rules for notes.

RULE	EXAMPLE
1. Notes in the text always contain, in this order: —a forward slash (/) —a source reference numeral (1, 2, 3, etc.) —a dot (.) that ends the sentence.	Reagan waved to the convention /1. (Notice in the above example that there is a space before the /, but no spaces between the / and the 1 or between the 1 and the dot.)
2. Direct quotes and references to materials on a specific page both require a page number.	Reagan waved to the convention /1.23. (Note that no space appears between the dots and the page number.)
3. You may indicate a range of pages or a page and a range of pages.	Reagan waved to the convention /1.23-25. Reagan waved to the convention /1.19.23-25.
4. Indicate chapters, sections, parts, and volumes in the note with appropriate abbreviations. Note that there is no dot between the abbreviation and the number of the chapter, section, part, or volume.	Reagan waved to the convention /1.c3. Reagan waved to the convention /1.s3. Reagan waved to the convention /1.pt3. Reagan waved to the convention /1.v3.
5. You may cite more than one source in a single note. Separate sources using a /, without spaces between any of the characters.	Reagan waved to the convention 1.v3.23/4/13c6. (This note refers to source 1, volume 3, page 23; source 4; and source 13, chapter 6.)
6. Once used, reference numbers always refer to the same source. They may be used again to refer to a quote or idea from that same source.	Reagan waved to the convention /1.19. Nancy, who had had a severe headache the evening before, came to join him /5/7. One source reported that they had argued about the color suit he was to wear /1.33.

RULE	EXAMPLE
	(The second note in this passage refers the reader to two difference sources, numbers 5 and 7. The third note is another reference to the first source used in the paper.)
7. Refer to constitutions of nations or states with article and section number.	Bill Clinton fulfilled his obligation to address the state of the nation /18.3.
8. Refer to passages in the Bible, the Koran, and other ancient texts that are divided into standard verses with the verse citation in the note.	Jake forgot that "the seventh day shall be your Holy day" /6.Exodus 35.2. (This example refers to the book of Exodus, chapter 35, verse 2. The 6 indicates that this is the sixth source cited in the paper. There is a dot between the source number and the verse citation.)

5.4.2 Rules for References Page

General Format Rules

The reference list is usually the final element in the paper. It is entitled "References." Its entries are arranged in the order that citations appear in the paper. The references page has standard page margins. All lines are double spaced. Model reference pages appear at the end of this chapter.

Rules of Punctuation and Abbreviation

1. Punctuation imitates the format used on the Internet.
2. No spaces appear between entry elements (author, date, and so on) or punctuation marks (/ . + @ ").
3. Dots (.) always follow entry elements with exceptions for punctuation rules 5-6.
4. The source number is always followed immediately by a dot.
5. Dots are also used to separate volume and edition numbers in journals.
6. Additional authors are denoted by a plus (+) sign.
7. Subtitles of books and articles are separated from main titles by a colon and a single space: "Crushing Doubt: Pascal's Bleak Epiphany."
8. Book chapters and periodical articles are enclosed in quotation marks (" ").
9. The following abbreviations are used:

c	chapter
comp	compiler
ed	editor
NY	New York (Use postal abbreviations for all states. Note that NY is unique in that when it is used alone it always means New York City. Cite other New York state locations in this

form: "Oswego NY." Cite cities in other states similarly: "Chicago IL" "Los Angeles CA" "Boston MA.")

pt	part
s	section
sess	session
tr	translator
v	volume
S	September (Months: Ja F Mr Ap My Je Jl Au S Oc N D)
C	College
I	Institute
U	University

10. Full names instead of initials of authors are used whenever they are used in the original source. When listing publishers, you may use the commonly used names instead of full titles. For example, use "Yale" for "Yale University Press"; use "Holt" for Holt, Rinehart and Winston." Use Internet abbreviations when known, such as "Prenhall" for "Prentice Hall." When abbreviating universities in dissertation and thesis citations, place no dot between the names of the state or city and the university. For example, use "MaIT" for the Massachusetts Institute of Technology and "UMa" for the University of Massachusetts. Always use the second letter of the state abbreviation, in lower case, to avoid the following type of confusion: "OSU" could be a university in Ohio, Oklahoma, or Oregon.

Rules of Order

Elements are always entered in the order shown in the following list of examples. Not all elements are available for every citation. For example, authors are sometimes not provided in source documents. Also, an element may be inappropriate for a certain type of citation. Cities of publication, for instance, are not required for magazines. Carefully examine the order of elements in the following list.

Source	Citation Elements and Examples
Books	
One author	3.Edna Applegate.1995.My Life on Earth.4th ed.Howard Press.St. Louis MO.
	Note the order of elements:
	—Reference number of note (1, 2, 3, etc.), followed by a dot
	—Author's name
	—Year of publication
	—Title of book
	—Number of edition, if other than the first
	—Name of publisher
	—City of publication
	—State of publication (not necessary for New York City)
Two to three authors	10.William Grimes+Joan Smith+Alice Bailey. 1996. Philosophy and Fire.Harvard.Cambridge MA.
More than three authors	42.Lois Mills+others.1989.Revolution in Thought.Agnew.NY.

Source	Citation Elements and Examples
Editor, compiler, or translator in place of as author	1.Michael Schendler ed.1992.Kant's Cosmology.Bloom.NY. (Remember that the citation for New York City does not require a state abbreviation.)
Editor, compiler, or translator with author	9.Elena White.1997.Nietzsche Was Right.Alexander Nebbs tr.Spartan.Biloxi MS.
No author, editor, compiler, or translator	5.The Book of Universal Wisdom.1993.4th ed.Northfield Publications.Indianapolis IN. (Reverse the placement of the date and title of the book, beginning the entry with the title.)
Separately authored foreword, afterword, or preface as source	17.Beulah Garvin.1992.Preface.Down in the Hole by James Myerson.Philosopher's Stone Press.Boston MA.
Separately authored chapter, essay, or poem as source	5.Jack Wittey.1994."Chickens and People."Animal Rights Anthology.3rd ed.Gene Cayton comp.Palo Duro Press.Canyon TX.73-90.
One volume in a multivolume work	9.Astrid Schultz+others.1991.The Myth of the West.v3 of The Development of European Thought.8 vols.Muriel Hodgson ed.University of Rutland Press.Rutland ME.

Encyclopedias

Citation from an encyclopedia that is regularly updated	24.Ronald Millgate.1985."Mill, John Stuart."Encyclopedia Americana. (The date refers to the edition of the encyclopedia. Cite the name of the article exactly as it appears in the encyclopedia.)
When no name is given for the article's author	2. "Mill, John Stuart."1946.Hargreave's Encyclopedia.

Ancient Texts

Bible, Koran, etc.	24.Holy Bible.New International Version. (Because the book, chapter, and verse numbers are given in the textual reference, it is not necessary to repeat them here. Remember to cite the traditional divisions of the work instead of the page number and publication information of the specific edition you used.)

Periodicals
Journal articles

Article with author or authors named	30.Ellis Michaels+Andrea Long.1996."How We Know: An Exercise in Cartesian Logic."Philosopher's Stone.12.4.213-227. (This citation refers to an article published in a journal entitled *Philosopher's Stone*, volume 12, number 4, pages 213-227.)
Article with no author named	7."Odds and Ends."1995.Philosopher's Stone.12.4.198-199.

Magazine articles

Article in a weekly or bi-weekly magazine	11.Lorraine Bond.1994."The Last Epicurean."Mental Health.6Jn.34-41. (This citation refers to an article published in the June 6, 1994, issue of *Mental Health*.)
Article in a monthly magazine	3.Allan Hull.1996."My Secret Struggle."Pathology Digest.Mr.17-30. (The difference between a citation for a monthly magazine and one for a weekly or bi-weekly magazine is that the former does not include a reference to the specific day of publication.)

Source	Citation Elements and Examples
Newspapers Article with named author	10.Anne Bleaker.1995."Breakthrough in Artificial Intelligence."New York Times.10My.14. (The word *The* is omitted from the newspaper's title.)
Article with unnamed author	22."Peirce Anniversary Celebration Set."1996.Kansas City Times-Democrat.1Ap.14.
When city is not named in newspaper title	13.Boyd Finnell.1996."Stoic Elected Mayor."(Eugenia TX) Daily Equivocator.30D.1. (Place the name of the city, and the abbreviation for the state if the city is not well known, in parentheses before the name of the paper.)
Government Documents Agency publications	28.U.S. Department of Commerce.1996.Economic Projections: 1995-2004.GPO. (Note that, when no author's name is given, the government department is considered the author. Because the Government Printing Office [GPO], the government's primary publisher, is located in Washington, DC, you need not list the city of publication.)
Legislative journals	31.Senate Journal.1993.103Cong.sess1.D10. (This citation refers to the record, published in the *Senate Journal*, of the first session of the 103rd Congress, held on December 10, 1993.) 8.Congressional Record.71 Cong.sess.2.72.8. (This citation refers to the account of the second session [sess.2] of the 71st Congress, published in volume 72, part 8, of the *Congressional Record*.)
Bills in Congress	13.U.S. Senate.1997.Visa Formalization Act of 1997.105Cong.sess1.SR.1437. (This citation refers to Senate Resolution 1437, originated in the first session of the 105th Congress. Bills originating in the House of Representatives are designed by the abbreviation HR.)
Laws	17.U.S. Public Law 678.1993.Library of Congress Book Preservation Act of 1993.U.S.Code.38.1562. (The law referred to in this citation is recorded in section 1562 of volume 38 of the *U.S. Code*.)
Constitutions	31.U.S.Constitution. 8.MO.Constitution. (This citation refers to the Missouri State Constitution.)
Internet Documents	4.Akiko Kasahara and K-lab,Inc.1995.ArtScape of the Far East: Seminar on the Philosophy of Art.Shinshu.University Nagano.Japan.@http://Pckiso3.cs.Shinshuu.ac.jp/artscape/index.html.Oct27.96. (The last two items in an Internet citation are always the website at which the document was found, followed by the date upon which the site was accessed by the researcher.)
Unpublished Materials Interview	12.Lily Frailey.1994.Interview with Clarence Parker.Santa Fe NM.10Ag.
Thesis or Dissertation	21.Gregory Scott.1973.Mysticism and Politics in the Thought of Bertrand Russell.MA thesis.UVa.

Source	Citation Elements and Examples
Paper presented at a meeting	5.Celia Hicks.1995."What Whitehead Would Say."Conference on the Western Imagination.14Ja.Boston MA. (The citation includes the name of the conference and the date on which the paper was presented, and ends with the city where the conference took place.)
Manuscript housed in a collection	32.Jose Sanchez.1953?-1982.Journal.Southwest Collection.Arial Library.Chisum Academy.Canyon TX. (Unpublished manuscripts are sometimes left unnamed and undated by their authors. Use any relevant information supplied by the repository catalogue to complete the citation. When a date is hypothesized, as in the above example, place a question mark after it.)
Manuscript in the author's possession	14.Jane Fried.1996.Life in California.UTx.Photocopy. (The citation includes the institution with which the author is affiliated and ends with a description of the format of the work: typescript, photocopy, and so on).

Sample References

1.Amanda Collingwood.1993.Architecture and Philosophy.Carlington Press.Detroit MI.

2.Tom Barker+Betty Clay, eds.1987.Swamps of Louisiana.Holt.NY.

3.Joan Garth+Allen Sanford.1963."The Hills of Wyoming."Critical Perspectives on Landscape.Prentice Hall.Upper Saddle River NJ.49-75.

4.Hayley Trakas, ed.1994.Russell on Space.3rd ed.Harmony Press.El Paso.TX

5.Philippe Ariès.1962.Centuries of Childhood: A Social History of Family Life in the Northeastern Region of Kentucky.Robert Baldock tr.Knopf.NY.

6.Jesus Gonzolez.1995."The Making of the Federales."Mexican Stories Revisited.Jules Frank ed.Comanche Press.San Antonio TX.54-79.

7.Carla Harris.1994.Foreword.Marital Stress and the Philosophers: A Case Study by Basil Givan.Galapagos.NY.

8.Jasper Craig.1993."The Flight from the Center of the Cities."Time.10S.67-69.

9.Matthew Moen.1996."Evolving Politics of the Christian Right."PS:Political Science and Politics.29.3.461-464.

10.Patrick Swick.1996."Jumping the Gun on the Federal Reserve."New York Times.10My.78.

11.Frances Muggeridge.1993."The Truth is Nowhere."Conundrum Digest.Mr.40-54.

12.Alan McAskill.1994."Interview with Mary Jordan."Hospice Pioneers of New Mexico.Dynasty Press.Enid.OK.62-86.

13.Jane Smith.1997.Interview with Jerry Brown.San Francisco CA.15Oc.

14.Jacob Lynd.1973.Perfidy in Academe: Patterns of Rationalization in College Administrations.Ph.D. diss.UVA.

15.Holy Bible.New King James Version.

16.Paula Thomas.1970-1976.Diary.Museum of the Plains.Fabens TX.

17.U.S. Department of Labor.1931.Urban Growth and Population Projections:1930-1939.GPO.

18.Senate Journal.1993.103Cong.sess1.D10.

19.U.S.Senate.1997.Visa Formalization Act of 1997.105Cong. sess1.SR.1437.

21.Peter Bolen.1995."Creating Designs in Social Systems."The Internet Journal of Sociological Welfare.14.6.http://www.carmelpeak.com.

22. U.S.Public Law 678.1993.Library of Congress Book Preservation Act of 1993.U.S.Code.38.1562.

23.U.S.Constitution.

5.5 Ethical Use of Source Materials

You want to use your source material in your paper as effectively as possible. This will sometimes mean that you should quote from a source directly, while at other times you will want to express such information in your own words. At all times, you should work to integrate the source material into the flow of your written argument.

Your main purpose in writing is to present a logical, believable case. To accomplish this, you want your argument to be as credible as possible. As we have said, undocumented opinions are as common as water and worthless. An established authority might be able to get away with writing a paper without notes. If Arthur Schlesinger, for example, wrote a magazine article about the legacy of Andrew Jackson, he would not necessarily need to document his thoughts to be believed. If Henry Kissinger wrote a piece on America's role on the post-Cold War world stage, his work would be read and considered, even though he quoted no one. It may be a few years before you achieve the reputation of a

Schlesinger or Kissinger; therefore, you should bolster your opinions with evidence.

5.5.1 When to Quote

By the time you have organized the fruits of your research and are prepared to begin writing, you may be so impressed by the weight of the evidence you have gathered that you will be tempted to present it verbatim. Many students submit papers that are, in effect, anthologies of quotations by other authors. The quotes may be taken from appropriate sources and may be very carefully documented, but your job as a writer of history is not to glue together strings of lengthy quotes with a few lines of your own prose here and there. Some professors discourage the use of block quotations at all, claiming that most readers actually skip over these anyway. This is to be your paper, not that of a committee of learned authors.

Most of the time, you can buttress your assertions with references to the sources you have accumulated without quoting them directly. This is particularly true if you are using a narrative style of historical exposition. Consider the following example, a paragraph and corresponding footnote reference, taken from an article by Robert Oppenheimer that appeared in the October 1985 issue of *The Western Historical Quarterly.*

> Through the 1920s, few Mexicans in Kansas graduated from high school. The first to graduate were in the late 1920s or early 1930s. In Topeka they graduated from Catholic Hayden High School and later from public schools. In Emporia from 1932 to 1941 only fifteen Mexican students (five males and ten females) graduated from high school. Seven of these graduated in 1941. By 1950 only eighteen Mexican-Americans had graduated from Garden City High School. Lucille Ramirez was the first female in 1934, and Frank Rodriguez was the first male in 1950.[37]
>
> 37. *Topeka Capital Journal,* December 19, 1961; Rutter, "Mexican Americans in Kansas," 134-36; Swan, "Ethnic Heritage of Topeka," 151; Ramirez, "Mexicans in Emporia," 24; and List of High School Graduates, 1900-50, Garden City School District.

Pay attention to this example; while it does not use the specific referencing format that we describe earlier in this chapter, its listing of multiple sources is a practice widely accepted in historical journals. The author has named five different sources in his footnote, even though he did not quote directly from any of them. Why then are they listed at all? Because they perform the task mentioned above; they lend credence—the weight of evidence—to the point Oppenheimer makes in the topic sentence of this paragraph. You, the reader, are inclined to believe the author's assertion that "through the 1920s few Mexicans in Kansas graduated from high school." The use of multiple references in a single footnote at the end of an entire paragraph will substantiate all the information presented in that paragraph.

You should quote directly from a source when the original language is distinctive enough to enhance your argument or when rewording the passage would lessen its impact. In the interest of fairness, you should also quote a passage to which you will take exception. Rarely, however, should you quote a source at great length (longer than two or three paragraphs). The more language you take from the writings of others, the more these quotations will disrupt the rhetorical flow of your own words. Too much quoting creates a choppy patchwork of varying styles and borrowed purposes in which your sense of your own control over your material is lost.

5.5.2 *Quote Carefully and Accurately*

The passage devoted to quotations in Chapter 3 will show you how to place quotations accurately within your paper according to the fourteenth edition of *The Chicago Manual of Style.* Failure to signal the presence of a quotation skillfully can lead to confusion or choppiness, as in the following example:

> The famous Webster/Hayne debate ended with his ringing phrase, "Liberty and Union, now and forever, one and inseparable!"

Unless your readers just happen to know of this famous moment, they will not know whether it was Webster or Hayne who uttered the quoted phrase. Make sure that your quote is clearly matched with its speaker or writer, just as you clearly pair a pronoun with the correct antecedent.

If your transcription of a quotation introduces careless variants of any kind, you are misrepresenting your source. Proofread your quotations very carefully, paying close attention to such surface features as spelling, capitalization, italics, and the use of numerals.

Occasionally, in order either to make a quotation fit smoothly into a passage, to clarify a reference, or to delete unnecessary material, you may need to change the original wording slightly. You must, however, signal any such change to your reader. Some alterations may be noted by brackets or by ellipses. In the following quotation, the bracketed material identifies the subject of the quote, and the three ellipsis indicate that a passage of the original has been deleted:

> As *The New Yorker* explains, "His [Richardson's] Picasso is an honorable man and . . . He does not feel quite comfortable unless he always has his Picasso the artist clearly lined up with the classics" (Gopnik 1996, 95).

Note: If the passage preceding the three ellipsis dots is grammatically complete, the three ellipsis dots are preceded by a period:

> "The Republicans, upon taking control of Congress . . . for the first time in forty years, proved to be even more intemperate than the Democrats. . . . They strutted about in triumph" (Klein 1996, 54).

A complete explanation of the uses of ellipsis dots appears in section 10 of the fourteenth edition of *The Chicago Manual of Style.*

5.5.3 Paraphrasing

Your writing has its own rhetorical attributes, its own rhythms, and structural coherence. Inserting several quotations into one section of your paper can disrupt the patterns of your prose and diminish its effectiveness. Paraphrasing, or recasting source material in your own words, is one way to avoid the choppiness that can result from a series of quotations.

Remember that a paraphrase is to be written in your language; it is not a near copy of the source writer's language. Merely changing a few words of the original does justice to no one's prose and frequently produces stilted passages. This sort of borrowing is actually a form of plagiarism. To integrate another's material into your own writing fully, use your own language.

Paraphrasing may actually increase your comprehension of source material, because in recasting a passage you will have to think very carefully about its meaning, more carefully, perhaps, than if you had merely copied it word for word.

5.5.4 Avoiding Plagiarism

Paraphrases require the same sort of documentation as direct quotes. The words of a paraphrase may be yours, but the idea belongs to someone else. Failure to give that person credit, in the form of references within the text, in a foot or endnote, and in the bibliography, may make you vulnerable to a charge of plagiarism.

Plagiarism is the use of someone else's words or ideas without proper credit. While some plagiarism is deliberate, produced by writers who understand that they are guilty of a kind of academic thievery, much of it is unconscious, committed by writers who are not aware of the varieties of plagiarism or who are careless in recording their borrowings from sources. Plagiarism includes

- Quoting directly without acknowledging the source
- Paraphrasing without acknowledging the source
- Constructing a paraphrase that closely resembles the original in language and syntax

One way to guard against plagiarism is to keep careful notes of when you have directly quoted course material and when you have paraphrased, making sure that the wording of the paraphrases is yours. Make sure that all direct quotes in your final draft are properly set off from your prose, either with quotation marks or in indented blocks.

What kind of paraphrased material must be acknowledged? Basic material that you find in several sources need not be documented by a reference. For example, most students are familiar with the fact that Mary Tudor was the first-born child of Henry VIII. If you state this fact in your paper, you do not need to justify the "assertion" with a reference. On the other hand, if you write that Mary conspired to ruin the subsequent five marriages of her father, this will raise some readers' eyebrows. They will want to know how you arrived at this conclusion. A situation such as this demands a reference both for your own credibility and for the sake of giving proper credit to those sources from which you derived your information. In other words, any information that is not widely known, whether factual or open to dispute, should be documented. This includes statistics, graphs, tables, and charts taken from sources other than your own primary research.

6 *Organizing the Research Process*

6.1 Gaining Control of the Research Process

Most of the writing we do as historians involves research. When we write about the history of a person, event, trend, or phenomenon, we must base our analyses and assertions on something more substantial than pet theories. An opinion is worthless unless it is an informed opinion. Researchers in all fields work to make themselves knowledgeable enough to be able to give informed opinions. This is what you are setting out to do in your research paper: You are working to earn the right to give informed opinions to your readers.

The research paper is where all your skills as an interpreter of details, an organizer of facts and theories, and a writer of clear prose come together. Building logical arguments on the basis of fact is the way things are done in history, and the most successful historians are those who master the art of research as well as writing. Would you rather enroll in a British history course being taught by a part-time instructor, moonlighting to pay a few bills, or by a professor who has researched and written in the area of British history? The part-timer may be a better, more entertaining public speaker, but the professor will offer more reliable information. (The ideal situation, of course, would provide a person who is both an expert and a joy to hear!)

Students new to the job of writing research papers sometimes find themselves intimidated by the job ahead of them. After all, the research paper adds what seems to be an extra set of complications and complexities to the writing process. As any other expository or persuasive paper does, a research paper must offer an original thesis using a carefully organized and logical argument. But a research paper also investigates a topic that is generally outside the writer's own experience. This means that writers must locate and evaluate information that is new to them, in effect educating themselves as they explore their topics. A beginning researcher sometimes feels overwhelmed by the basic requirements of the assignment or by the authority of the source material being investigated.

As you begin a research project, it may be difficult to establish a sense of control over the different tasks you are undertaking. You may have little notion of where to search for a thesis or even for the most helpful information. If you do not carefully monitor your own work habits, you may find yourself unwittingly abdicating responsibility for the paper's argument by borrowing it wholesale from one or more of your sources.

Who is in control of your paper? The answer, of course, must be you—not the instructor who assigned the paper, and certainly not the published writers whom you consult as sources. If your paper does no more than to paste together the writings of others, it is of little or no use. It is up to you to locate and investigate as much relevant source information as possible and then to synthesize an original idea from a judicious evaluation of your material. At the beginning of the research phase of your paper, you may not have a thesis. You will probably discover also that as soon as you begin to form one it may be challenged or changed through further research. Even before your thesis or argument takes shape, however, you can establish a measure of control over the process you will go through to complete the paper. And if you work regularly and systematically, keeping yourself open to new ideas as they present themselves, your sense of control will grow. Here are a few suggestions to help you establish and maintain control of your paper.

1. *Understand your assignment.* It is possible for a research assignment to go badly simply because the student did not read the assignment carefully. Professors can tell you sad stories about students from the past who invested hours upon hours in research and writing, only to learn to their horror that they had failed to apprehend the true intent, direction, or details of their assignment. Considering how much time and effort you are about to spend on your project, it is a very good idea to make sure you have a clear understanding of what your instructor wants you to do. Be sure to ask your instructor about any aspect of the assignment that is unclear to you, but only after you have read it carefully. Recopying the assignment in your own handwriting is a good way to start, even though your instructor may have already given it to you in writing. Make sure, before you dive into the project, that you have considered the questions listed below.

2. *What is your topic?* The assignment itself may give you a great deal of specific information about your topic, or you may be allowed considerable freedom in establishing one for yourself. In a class on the history of American foreign policy, chances are that you will not get to write a paper on the Crusades, no matter how interested in them you may be. In such a class, your professor might want you to examine American military adventures in Latin America in the nineteenth century, or you may be permitted to focus on any aspect of American foreign policy that interests you. You need to understand the terms, set up in the assignment, by which you will design your project.

3. *What is your purpose?* Whatever the degree of latitude you are given in the matter of your topic, pay close attention to the way in which your instructor has phrased the assignment. Is your primary job to *describe* a certain historical situation or to *take a stand* on it? Are you to *compare* two people, events, or trends? Are you to *classify, persuade, survey, analyze?* Look for such descriptive terms in the assignment to determine the purpose of your project.

4. *Who is your audience?* Your own orientation to the paper is profoundly affected by your conception of the audience for whom you are writing. Granted, your main reader is your instructor, but who else would be interested in your paper? The other members of your graduate seminar? The editors of a local historical journal?

5. *What kind of research will you be doing?* Your project will require one if not both of the following kinds of research:

> *Primary research,* which requires you to locate and sift through first-hand accounts of a particular event or idea. In primary research, you are collecting and examining raw data which have often not been interpreted by researchers. This raw data may be the opinions of experts or people on the street, historical documents, the published letters of famous politicians, or material collected from other researchers. It is important to set up carefully the methods by which you collect your data. Your aim is to gather the most accurate information possible, from which sound observations may be made later, either by you or by other writers using the material you have uncovered.

> *Secondary research,* which uses published interpretations by other scholars who have investigated similar topics. While primary research collects, analyzes, and makes available raw data, secondary research focuses on other researchers' interpretations of raw data. Most of your college history papers will be based on your use of secondary sources.

SECONDARY SOURCES	PRIMARY SOURCES
Don Fehrenbacher's *The Era of Expansion*	the journal of Lewis and Clark
David McCulloch's *Mornings on Horseback*	the letters of Theodore Roosevelt
Danney Goble's *Progressive Oklahoma*	a box of 1920s Ku Klux Klan materials found in a Tulsa attic
Phillip Davidson's *Vietnam at War*	*Dear America: Letters Home from Vietnam*

6. *Keep your perspective.* Whichever type of research you perform, you must keep your results in perspective. There is no way in which you, as a primary researcher, can be completely objective in your findings. If you are conducting secondary research, you must remember that the articles and books you are reading are shaped by the aims of their writers, who are interpreting primary materials for their own ends. The farther you are removed from a primary

source, the greater the possibility for distortion. Your job as a researcher is to be as accurate as possible, which means keeping in view the limitations of your methods and their ends.

6.2 Effective and Efficient Research Methods

In any research project there will be moments of confusion, but you can prevent this confusion from overwhelming you by establishing an effective research procedure. You need to design a schedule that is as systematic as possible yet flexible enough so that you do not feel trapped by it. A schedule will keep you from running into dead ends by always showing you what to do next. It will also help to keep you from forgetting important or time-sensitive steps. At the same time, the schedule helps you retain the focus necessary to spot new ideas and strategies as you work.

6.2.1 Give Yourself Plenty of Time

You may feel like delaying your research for many reasons: unfamiliarity with a big, imposing library; the procrastination we all face when confronted with a huge task; anxiety over the sea of information to be consulted; the press of other assignments and responsibilities; or (everyone's favorite) a deadline that seems comfortably far away. But you cannot allow such factors to deter you. Those of us who are do-it-yourselfers are all too aware that the best-planned schedules for accomplishing a particular goal usually prove to be insufficient. Weekend projects often require twice the time (and money) than we had allowed when we began. Library work tends to speed up the clock. That hour you had planned to devote to locating a particular source will subtly grow to two hours—or an entire afternoon. You must allow yourself the time needed not only to find material but also to read it, assimilate it, and set it in the context of your own thoughts.

If you delay starting your research, you may well find yourself distracted by the deadline, having to keep an eye on the clock while trying to make sense of a writer's complicated arguments. In the end, it is a sure bet that you will not produce a quality project. No matter how confident you may be in your talent for glossing over problems, your paper will look like what it is: a rush job.

The following schedule lists the steps of a research project in the order in which they are generally accomplished. Remember that each step is dependent upon the others, and it is quite possible to revise earlier decisions in the light of later discoveries. After some early background reading, for example, your notion of the paper's purpose may change, a fact that may in turn alter other steps. One of the strengths of any good schedule is flexibility. Note that the schedule lists tasks for both primary and secondary research; you should use only those steps that are relevant to your project.

RESEARCH SCHEDULE	
TASK	**DATE OF COMPLETION**
Determine topic, purpose, and audience	_____
Do background reading in reference books	_____
Narrow your topic; establish a tentative hypothesis	_____
Develop a working bibliography	_____
Write for any needed information	_____
Read and evaluate secondary sources, taking notes	_____
Locate relevant primary sources	_____
Consult and evaluate primary sources	_____
Envision an outline and organize notes accordingly	_____
Develop a thesis	_____
Write a first draft	_____
Obtain feedback (show draft to instructor, if possible)	_____
Do more research, if necessary	_____
Revise the draft, using corrected bibliographical format	_____
Proofread	_____
Deadline for final draft	_____
Do background reading	_____

Suppose you have enrolled in a course that is only of marginal interest to you. Suppose further that the instructor has offered the class a fairly broad range of topics for a research paper, yet none of the topics on her list are familiar to you. Now the task of choosing a topic has become truly daunting. The library which your instructor talks about navigating with such ease is a foreboding chasm to you, and you begin to wonder when the drop/add period for this class closes! Before you sprint to the Registrar's office to change classes, give it a chance. Often some quick, basic reading will supply a sufficient reservoir of knowledge to allow you to face your task knowledgeably.

Archaeological investigations often begin with remote sensing techniques from aircraft or even satellites far above the surface of the earth. From this beginning, the scope of the work becomes more and more focused and restricted. The tools become increasingly smaller, from tractors and backhoes to shovels and spades to hand trowels and small brushes. When we conduct historical research, we also are "excavating" down through layers of the material that has been written on the subject. Do not be afraid, therefore, to begin your examination of a topic with what you may think is very superficial source material, then dig into deeper layers with each step of the research process.

Before you start pulling card catalog drawers or typing key search words on your school's library computer system, try looking for a basic article in a print encyclopedia, such as the *World Book, Colliers,* or *Britanica,* or a CD-ROM encyclopedia, such as *Encarta.* You will find that even a quick examination of the essentials of the topic will make you conversant enough about it to establish necessary parameters in your mind. By the time you finish reading the article, you may have begun to identify certain aspects of the topic that interest you more than others, thus beginning the narrowing process. Look for "Related Articles," and read the ones that interest you most. This will broaden your knowledge base and offer additional vantage points from which to view your original topic. Perhaps one of these could provide just the "angle" you have been seeking to open the topic for you.

6.2.2 Narrow Your Topic and Establish a Working Thesis

You will find that most encyclopedia articles contain not only ideas for related articles to read but also a brief bibliography or suggestions for further reading. These works are usually the most widely recognized books on that subject. You may notice that some of these center on narrow aspects of the topic that have piqued your interest. Make note of these works, and find them in the library and examine them briefly. By the time you have examined the relevant portions of these books, you will be armed with even more information, and you will probably have refined your topic and your ideas even further. These reference works will also provide useful bibliographies that you can use to probe into the next, deeper phase of your research. You will find that each step you take in the process will reveal several additional steps you may take in several different directions. You may find that as your research begins to deepen, your topic may actually narrow itself. Consider the following example.

GENERAL TOPIC:	Feudalism
FIRST SOURCE:	"Feudalism," Microsoft *Encarta*
SECOND LAYER:	Marc Bloch, *Feudal Society*, 1966. David Herlihy, ed. *The History of Feudalism*, 1979
THIRD LAYER:	Georges Duby, *The Three Orders: Feudal Society Imagined*, 1980. Sidney Painter, *French Chivalry: Chivalric Ideas and Practices in Medieval France*, 1957. Margaret Wade Labarge, *A Small Sound of the Trumpet: Women in Medieval Life*, 1986.

Notice the trend in these articles and books. The encyclopedia provided some basic information about life in the Middle Ages. The next stage of the investigation began to eliminate military and political affairs and to center on social aspects of medieval life. By the time the search reached the third layer, the focus narrowed toward a study of gender roles in Medieval France. What began with a very general perusal of an encyclopedia article became more specific, by subject and geography, and already much more manageable and much less intimidating!

6.2.3 Develop a Working Bibliography

As you delve deeper into your research, keep track of the sources you have consulted. Whether you derive this list from your school's library catalog or from bibliographies in other works, it will serve your interests in the long haul if you can begin to organize your sources now. In your paper's final draft, you will need to present these sources in a prescribed order in the paper's own bibliography. This order is detailed for you in Chapter 5. For now, however, you may wish to organize your sources according to the role they play in unfolding the paper's story, regardless of whether they are books, articles, newspaper accounts, or government documents.

It is from your working bibliography that you will select the items you will actually use to help build and support the ideas in your paper. Early in your research you will not know which of the sources will help you and which will not, but it is important to keep an accurate description of each entry in your working bibliography so you will be able to tell clearly which items you have investigated and which you will need to consult again. Establishing the working bibliography also allows you to practice using the bibliographical format you are required to follow in your final draft. As you make your list of potential sources, be sure to include all the information about each one in the proper bibliographical format, using the proper punctuation. (See Chapter 5 for ways to handle these decisions.)

There are two important reasons why you will want all relevant bibliographic information available at all times. First, it is frustrating when you know that you have seen a very important piece of information but cannot remember where it was—what chapter, what book, or even what library. Second, it is perhaps even more frustrating to type quotes from a particular source into the final draft of your paper, begin to prepare the corresponding citation, then realize that a critical piece of the citation—a volume number, a publication date, or a page number—is still on some library's shelf! You must make a decision at this point. Do you make yet another trip to the library to find the missing information, or do you leave it out of the reference, hoping that the instructor will not notice? Rather than face this dilemma, do yourself a great favor early in the research phase of the paper's production and jot down all parts of the citation you may need later.

6.2.4 Write for Needed Information

In the course of your research you may need to consult a source that is not immediately available to you. Not every researcher is blessed with easy access to the Vatican Archives, the British Museum, or the Library of Congress. If your research takes you beyond the borders of your hometown, you can plan to drive or fly somewhere to find what you need. Or you could take advantage of the United States Postal Service or the interlibrary loan system. Many large corporations and most government agencies have persons or entire departments whose job is to furnish information to the public. Do not hesitate to contact such persons. Likewise, the person in charge of acquiring materials through interlibrary loan at your university library is very knowledgeable about how to acquire distant materials and will be delighted to lend you a hand in doing so.

If you ask for materials through the mail, make sure that your request is as specific as possible, so that the person who receives your inquiry will be able to give you the most satisfying assistance. It is a good idea to outline your project in a few sentences to help the respondent determine the types of information that will be useful to you.

In this age of electronic marvels, it is easier than ever to track and obtain materials from distant places. Still, these methods take time, not because of lagging technology, but often because of the humans who must operate it. Give them (and yourself) a cushion of time. If you need to write a letter to obtain something, do so in January when you first realize you need it, not in April, three weeks before your paper is due. Do not make your job harder than it needs to be by being timid or by procrastinating.

6.2.5 Evaluate Written Sources

Fewer research experiences are more frustrating than trying to recall information found in a source you can no longer identify. You must establish an efficient method of examining and evaluating the sources in your working bibliography. Here are some suggestions for compiling an accurate record of your written sources.

6.2.6 Determine Quickly the Potential Usefulness of a Source

In order to determine whether a book might be of help to your project, you should read the front material (the introduction, foreword, and preface), looking for the thesis and an overview of the book's argument; you can also examine chapter headings, dust jackets, and indexes. A journal article should announce its intention in its introduction, which in most cases will be a page or less in length. This sort of preliminary examination should tell you whether a more intensive examination is worthwhile. Whatever you decide about the source, photocopy its title page, making sure that all important publication information (including title, date, author, volume number, and page numbers) is present. If any of these items are missing, make sure you take time to write in everything necessary for future reference. Without such a record, later in your research you may forget that you have consulted a text, in which case you may find yourself repeating your work.

When you have determined that a potential source is worth closer inspection, explore it carefully. If it is a book, determine whether you should invest the time needed to read it in its entirety. Whatever the source, make sure you understand not only its overall thesis, but also each part of the argument that the writer sets up to illustrate or prove the thesis.

As you read, try also to get a feel for the larger argument in which the source takes its place. Its references to the works of other writers will show you where to look for additional material and indicate the general shape of scholarly opinion concerning your subject. If you can see the source you are reading as only one element of an ongoing dialogue instead of the last word on the subject, then you can place its argument in perspective.

6.2.7 Use Photocopies

Periodicals and most reference works cannot be checked out of the library. Before the widespread availability of photocopy machines, students could use these materials only in the library, jotting down information on note cards. While there are advantages to using the note card system (see the next section), photocopying saves you time in the library and allows you to take the original information home, where you can decide how to use it at your own convenience.

If you decide to copy source material, you should observe the following:

- Be sure to follow all copyright laws.
- Before your visit to the library, obtain enough correct change (a roll, perhaps, of nickels or dimes) so that you do not have to rely on battle-scarred and cantankerous change machines.
- Record all necessary bibliographical information on the photocopy! If you forget to do this, you may find yourself with a stack of unmarked photocopies, whose information you would dearly love to employ in your paper, but whose missing details will make it impossible without an extra trip back to the library just to track down a missing publication date or page number.

Photocopying a source is not the same as examining it. It is not enough merely to have the information close at hand or even to have read it once or twice. You must understand it thoroughly. Be sure to give yourself time for this kind of evaluation.

The Note Card: A Thing of the Past?

In many ways, the note cards we were taught to use in high school are now an old-fashioned method of recording source material, and for unpracticed researchers, they may seem unwieldy and unnecessary, since the information jotted on them—one fact per card—will eventually have to be transferred again into the research paper. It seems to be a much more efficient use of time to drop some coins into a machine, place the resulting stack of photocopied pages into your briefcase, and be on you way back home. Before you decide, however, to abolish the note card system once and for all, consider these advantages.

1. Using note cards is a way of forcing yourself to think productively as you read. In translating the language of the source into the language of your notes, you are assimilating the material more completely than you would merely by reading it.
2. Note cards give you a handy way to arrange and rearrange your facts, looking for the best possible organization for your paper. Not even a computer gives you the flexibility of a pack of cards as you try to order your paper.
3. Any single photocopied page will probably contain more than one bit of information that you will want to employ in your paper, and the order in which you will use the pieces of information may not correspond to the order in which they appear in the photocopy. Moving backward and for-

ward through a stack of photocopies could become confusing and cumbersome. You can order individual note cards any way you like.

6.2.8 Locate, Consult, and Evaluate Primary Sources

As your research deepens, you will discover that most secondary works are built, in part, on primary sources—those that would be considered eye-witness accounts of a time or event. A book's bibliography will include these. Some libraries have specially cataloged collections of such sources. You will find examining primary sources to be some of the greatest fun in doing historical research. Our colleagues in the other social sciences (political science or psychology, for example) must find joy in public opinion surveys and three-year studies of laboratory animals. We historians, however, may hold in our hands books, treaties, and other documents which may be, in some cases, several hundred years old! If you are preparing a biographical account of the life of a certain individual, how thrilling it is to examine correspondence, financial records, and other daily business written not about that person but by him or her!

Using primary sources, on the other hand, requires some special considerations, such as the following:

- Not every primary source must be read in manuscript form. Many such sources have been edited and published and are widely available. These include the personal papers of most famous public figures, U. S. presidents and other government leaders, explorers such as Lewis and Clark, and so forth. One need not hold the actual pages themselves to discover what Napoleon had to say when he wrote to Josephine. Do not abandon the hope, therefore, of using such source. They may not be as far away as you might think; they could be on the shelves of your school's library.

- If a source is not on a library shelf near you, it may be available in a microform version. Your library may have a set of these. Others may be obtained through interlibrary loan. Again, do not think that you must budget hundreds of dollars for travel to an exotic repository in order to examine a primary source. Nor should you abandon the use of a document just because it is not close at hand.

- When you do plan to visit a library to examine a rare source, remember that some public and private libraries have certain restrictions governing the use of special collections. In some cases these documents are reserved for use only by graduate students and professional historians. Often you must arrange an appointment to use materials. Some places might require a fee. Most libraries restrict access to rare manuscripts and will absolutely forbid photocopying fragile, light-sensitive pages. It is always best to write or to call ahead to determine availability, accessibility, and procedures before you invest time and money in a trip to see the special collections of a distant or special library.

6.2.9 Draft a Thesis and Outline

No matter how thoroughly you may hunt for secondary and primary sources or how fast you read, you will not be able to find and assimilate every piece of written material pertaining to your subject, and you should not prolong your research unduly. At some point, the research phase of your project must come to an end—though you always have the option of resuming it if the need arises—and you must begin to shape both the material you have gathered and your thoughts about it into a paper. During the research phase, you have been thinking about your working thesis, testing it against the material you discovered and considering ways to improve or alter it. Now you must formulate a thesis that sets out an interesting and useful task that can be satisfactorily managed within the limits of your assignment and that effectively employs much, if not all, of the material you have gathered.

Once you have developed your thesis, it is a very good idea to make an outline of the paper. Your writing needs structure; otherwise, your well-crafted prose will not be sufficient by itself to make your paper interesting and worth reading. It may seem like a waste of time to construct an outline, but taking the time now to organize your material into a logical exposition will, in the long run, make your writing task easier and your finished product better.

In helping you to determine a structure for your writing, the outline is also testing your thesis, prompting you to discover the kinds of work your paper will have to do to complete the task set out by the main idea. Chapter 1 discusses the structural requirements of the formal and informal outline. (If you have used note cards, you may want to start outlining by organizing the cards according to the headings you have given them and looking for logical connections among the different groups of cards. Experimenting with various structures in this way may lead you to discoveries that will further improve your thesis.)

No thesis or outline is chiseled in stone. There is still time to improve the structure and purpose of your paper even after you have begun to write your first draft or, for that matter, your final draft. Some writers actually prefer to write a first draft before outlining, and then study the draft's structure to determine what revisions need to be made. Stay flexible, always looking for a better connection, a sharper wording of your thesis. All the time you are writing, the testing of your ideas continues.

6.2.10 Write a First Draft

Despite all the preliminary work you have done on your paper, you may feel a resistance to beginning your first draft. Integrating all your material and your ideas into a smoothly flowing argument is indeed a complicated task. It may help to think of your first attempt as only a rough draft, which can be changed as necessary. Another strategy for reducing reluctance to starting is to begin with the part of the draft that you feel most confident about, instead of the introduction. (The introduction to this book was written last!) You may write sections of the draft in any order, piecing the parts together later. But however you decide to start writing—Start.

6.2.11 Obtain Feedback

It is not enough that you understand your argument; others have to understand it, too. If your instructor is willing to look at your rough draft, you should take advantage of the opportunity and pay careful attention to any suggestions for improvement. Other readers may also be of help, although having a friend or a relative read your draft may not be as helpful as having it read by someone who is knowledgeable in your field. In any event, be sure to evaluate carefully any suggestions. Remember that the final responsibility for the paper rests with you.

Revision and Proofreading

Before submitting your final draft, it is important that you make sure it is as well organized, skillfully phrased, and error free as it can be. Chapter 2 gives suggestions for the revision, editing, and proofreading necessary to assure a fine paper and a good grade.

7 *Information in the Library*

Students making their first research trip to their university library often find it an intimidating journey. The stacks, the reference area, the card catalogs, or banks of terminals can all seem pretty overwhelming at first. Many inexperienced student researchers, confused or worried about seeming inexperienced, sail past the information desk—where professional librarians are waiting to help them—and begin to wander back through the stacks, hoping to stumble across material that could be useful to their paper. Before you spend hours of time wandering, it would be a good idea for you to acquaint yourself with the way in which your library is organized. There really is a reason for every item's niche.

7.1 A Library's Departments

You may never need many of a library's specialized services, such as its business office, its community information service, the personnel office, or the purchasing offices. It may be sufficient now for you simply to know that they are there. For your research purposes, however, you should be familiar with those departments which house the library's basic categories of information. Not all libraries will have all these departments. There are smaller libraries whose budget limitations require consolidation of several functions. Then there are larger research libraries and those at major universities with many special collections, often housed in separate buildings on different areas of the campus or even different campuses. A law library, for example, may be located in a particular building in one area of a campus, while the fine arts collections may be a half-mile away on the opposite side. Both of these might be separate from the general library, normally (we hope) near the center of the campus. On the other hand, a small municipal library holding just the particular manuscript collection you need to see might be found in a single, old, restored historic building on a shady street.

On the following pages, you will find a description of the most helpful departments of most libraries. You will need to know how to find journal articles, newspaper accounts, certain reference materials, government documents, and manuscript sources. We will begin our list, however, with what is probably the most basic of all library materials—books.

7.2 Classification Systems for Books

It is probably not news to you to learn that the thousands of books displayed on your library's shelves are not arranged by size, color, or jacket design. There are classification systems that tell library personnel and visitors alike where to find general areas of interest and specific books. It would be a good idea for you to acquaint yourself with both major systems.

7.2.1 The Dewey Decimal System

This method of classification is the older of the two that you will need to know, yet many institutions, public and private, large and small, still use it. Knowledge is divided into ten major categories, each of which is given a 100-number span. These are listed as follows:

000-099	General Works (encyclopedias, newspapers, and periodicals)
100-199	Philosophy/Psychology
200-299	Religion/Mythology
300-399	Social Sciences
400-499	Language
500-599	Pure Science
600-699	Technology
700-799	The Arts (including Sports and Recreation)
800-899	Literature
900-999	History/Geography/Biography/Travel

A library book is shelved according to its call number. Here is a Dewey call number for a copy of Booker T. Washington's *Up from Slavery*:

378.111092	(Social Science Classification)
W 27a	(Author's name begins with "W")
1901	(Year of authorship)
1967	(Year of this edition, if different)

Here is another call number, this one for Arthur M. Schlesinger's *The Age of Jackson*:

973.560924	(We historians spend most of our time in the 900s)
J 13sc	
1945	

7.2.2 The Library of Congress System

Devised by the staff of the Library of Congress in Washington, DC, the LC System divides human knowledge into twenty-one large classes, indicated by the following capital letters:

A	General Works
B	Philosophy/Religion
C	History/Auxiliary Sciences
D	Universal History
E, F	American History
G	Geography/Anthropology
H	Social Sciences
J	Political Science
K	Law
L	Education
M	Music
N	Fine Arts
P	Language and Literature
Q	Science
R	Medicine
S	Agriculture
T	Technology
U	Military Science
V	Naval Science
Z	Bibliography and Library Science

Within these categories, books are arranged from broad, general topics to specific, narrow applications. Some specific topics are designated by combinations of capital letters and/or by 3-digit numbers. The Library of Congress system is an improvement over the Dewey system, because the possible combinations of a few letters and a few numbers eliminate the need for long, hard-to-remember, numerical designations. Within the E (History) classification, for example, books numbered 1–99 in the LC System concern pre-Columbian America. Numbers 100 through 199 deal with social, cultural, political, and racial aspects of general American history. The 200's begin a period-by-period breakdown, beginning with Colonial America (200–299). Here are how the Washington and Schlesinger books appear on a shelf using the Library of Congress system.

E (American history)	E (American History)
185.97 (racial history)	381 (the 1830s)
W 3163 (Washington's name begins with "W")	.S 38 ("S" as in Schlesinger)
1011257	1000940

You may find the Dewey system in use at public or municipal libraries. Many institutions, however, have made the switch from Dewey to the newer

Library of Congress method. Because of the flexibility of the LC System, it is better suited to the demands of larger libraries in general and research libraries in particular.

7.3 Types of Information Sources in the Library

7.3.1 Periodicals

As the name implies, periodicals are serial works published regularly over time, such as newspapers, magazines, and journals. Each of these types has a specific purpose, and we will discuss each separately. A library's periodicals are usually found in a separate location, its own floor of a building, for example, and often on microfilm or microfiche instead of in print.

7.3.2 Newspapers

Every library subscribes to at least some newspapers. Even a small-town library will hold back issues of its own local newspaper as well as a major daily paper. Larger libraries receive regular issues of many major newspapers, even those from foreign nations. On the display racks of a typical university you are likely to find copies of most of the major American dailies, such as the *New York Times*, the *Wall Street Journal*, *USA Today*, and the *Christian Science Monitor*, as well as the *Chicago Tribune*, *Dallas Morning News*, the *Los Angeles Times*, and the *Washington Post* and many others. You also may find London's *Times*, *The Guardian*, or the *Daily Telegraph*. If you prefer to read French, you might consult *Le Figaro* or *Le Monde*. German readers could peruse *Frankfurter Allgemeine*, *Süddeutche Zeitung*, *Die Zeit*, or *Die Welt*. If you need your news in Italian, you could try *La Stampa* or *Corriere della Sera*. You also might find *Al Ahram* (Cairo), *Pravda* (Moscow), *La Nación* (Buenos Aires), or *Asahi Shimbun* (Tokyo). Many trades publish their own newspapers, as do labor unions and a variety of other public and private organizations. Political organizations from mainstream to the far left and the far right also issue their views of current events.

For the historian, the latest issues of the world's major dailies will not be of as much interest as newspapers published in the past. Most larger papers such as the *New York Times* maintain indexes of past issues. Larger libraries and state historical societies often maintain complete collections of that state's past newspapers on microfilm rolls. The Oklahoma State Historical Society, for example, holds microform versions of every newspaper published in the state as well as many published before statehood by various native American nations. These rolls are organized county by county and, within these, alphabetically by title. The shelves of drawers of microfilm rolls fill a rather large room, and the microfilm readers that line the walls are in constant use, morning until night. And Oklahoma has been a state only since 1907! Older, more populous states will have collections many times larger. In 1850 one hundred and thirty-three

German-language papers were in circulation across the country. By 1935, Yiddish-speaking New Yorkers could chose from among twelve different publications, and Norwegians could read the news in at least forty different Norwegian newspapers across the upper Midwest and the Plains.

7.3.3 Magazines

You already are familiar with these. In many a doctor's waiting room you have tried to amuse yourself by thumbing through issues of *People, Reader's Digest,* or *Popular Mechanics.* (These waiting-room issues are so old, of course, that they are historical relics all by themselves.) Magazines have become a huge industry in America. Virtually every activity with its own group of followers, from wind surfing to mountain biking, from log home construction to computer software, is represented in a magazine.

Many magazines are historical, but while some of these are top-notch, scholarly, and worthwhile, many delve more into fantasy—what might be called "pulp"—and should be avoided. Excellent articles have appeared in publications such as *American History Illustrated, Civil War Times Illustrated,* and *American Heritage.* The magazines *Archaeology* and *Biblical Archaeology* offer solid, well-documented articles related not only to current trends in the field but also to the results of archaeological investigation. But while some magazines successfully combine academic rigor with broad appeal, remember that the distinction between scholarly and popular aims is important. Make sure that any article you use for your paper is written for historical purposes and not merely for entertainment.

7.3.4 Journals

These serial publications are generally more substantial than magazines. Their articles are written by recognized scholars and edited by professional historians who screen submissions for their veracity and contribution to the profession and to our body of historical knowledge. Most of them do not have slick, eye-catching covers but rather plain, nonnondescript ones, often with the contents of the issues printed right on top. Each issue usually will contain four or five scholarly articles, a number of book reviews, some book notices, and often news from the organization that publishes the journal. There are many of these. Here is a partial list of some of the more widely read titles:

Africa Quarterly	*Capitol Studies*
American Historical Review	*Civil War History*
American History	*Comparative Studies in Society and History*
American Neptune	*Congress and the Presidency*
Asian Quarterly	*Diplomatic History*
Australian Journal of Politics and History	*East European Quarterly*
British Journal of Political Science	*Economic History Review*

English Historical Review
European Journal of Political Science
European Studies Review
Fides et Historia
Foreign Affairs
German Political Studies
Great Plains Historical Review
Historian
Historical Journal
History
History and Theory
History of Political Thought
History Teacher
International Affairs
International Review of Social History
International Studies
International Studies Quarterly
Journal of African Studies
Journal of American History
Journal of Asian Studies
Journal of Constitutional and
    Parliamentary Studies
Journal of Contemporary History
Journal of Economic History
Journal of International Affairs
Journal of Japanese Studies
Journal of Law and Politics
Journal of Medieval History
Journal of Modern African History
Journal of Modern History
Journal of Political and Military Sociology
Journal of Political Science
Journal of Politics
Journal of Social History
Journal of Social, Political, and Economic
    Studies
Journal of Southern History
Journal of Strategic Studies
Journal of the History of Ideas
Journal of the West
Journal of Urban History

Legislative Studies Quarterly
Local Historian
Mankind
Middle East Journal
Middle Eastern Studies
New Statesman
North American Review
Pacific Affairs
Pacific Historical Review
Parliamentary Affairs
Past and Present
Policy Studies Journal
Political Quarterly
Political Science
Political Science Quarterly
Political Science Review
Political Theory
Politics
Presidential Studies Quarterly
Prologue
Public Finance
Public Opinion Quarterly
Public Policy
Railroad History
Renaissance News
Review of International Studies
Reviews in American History
Scandinavian Political Studies
Slavic Review
Social History
Social Science Journal
Social Science Quarterly
Social Science Research
Societas
Soviet Studies
Strategic Review
War and Society
West European Politics
Western Historical Quarterly
Western Political Quarterly
Women and Politics

In addition to these, every state and many regions and localities of the country have their own historical societies, and they publish scholarly journals pertaining to the history of that state or region.

7.3.5 Periodical Indexes

With over two hundred scholarly and popular publications to consult, you may find the task of trying to find specific information about your topic taking on gargantuan proportions. In all the articles in all the issues of all the journals that have been published, you know there exists information you can use in your paper. But how do you begin to locate the journal articles you need? One answer is to consult periodical indexes, those books—or multivolume collections— which list articles, usually by subject, and give publication information for them. The index you will see most often in your undergraduate career is called the *Reader's Guide to Periodical Literature*. This well-known and easy-to-use source will help you with much of your search through serial publications. There are, how-ever, more specific indexes. Here is a brief list.

America: History and Life
American Humanities Index
Bibliographic Index
Biography Index
Book Review Index
Book Reviews in Historical Periodicals
Combined Retrospective Index Set to
    Journals in Political Science, 1886-
    1974. 6 vols.
Historical Abstracts
Humanities Index

Index to Book Reviews in the Humanities
Index to U. S. Government Periodicals
New York Times Biographical Service
PAIS International in print
Public Affairs Information Service PAIS
Social Sciences Index
Sociological Abstracts
Ulrich's International Periodicals
    Directory, 1993-94. 5 vols.
United States Political Science Documents

As we have said, periodicals are usually grouped together in one section or floor of a library, and there often will be periodical specialists on staff to help you. Go ahead. Make their day. Ask them for help if you need it.

7.3.6 Government Documents

Most libraries of any size will have at least some U. S. Government docu-ments in their collection. The *Congressional Record*, for example, has document-ed the daily activities of both houses of Congress for two centuries. If you want-ed to examine the speeches of the "Great Triumvirate" (Henry Clay, Daniel Webster, and John C. Calhoun), you could do so with this publication. There is even an index to help you locate specific pieces of information. Most larger libraries also hold *The Official Records of the War of the Rebellion*, a 127-volume com-pendium of all official civil and military correspondence sent and received dur-ing the American Civil War. You will find this often in a microform version.

Do you need to find what James K. Polk had to say about the possibility of his seeking a second term in office in 1848? The personal papers of presidents and other historical persons may be found in edited, bound versions, often many volumes long. These important primary sources are usually located among the other historical works in the main bookshelves.

Some libraries have been designated as official repositories of government documents. Each year, the departments of all three branches of government publish literally millions of pages of documents that are supposed to be a matter of public record and availability. The volume of paper is so overwhelming that it would be impractical, if not impossible, for every library to be furnished with a complete set. (For the government to print such an output of information would triple the national debt.) The number of libraries that receive it are therefore necessarily limited by size and geographical distribution. If you attend a fairly large public or private university, your school library may be one of these repositories. If it is, and if your historical interests take you into the realm of U.S. public policy or political history, you should develop a close friendship with the librarians in charge of the government document section. In some of these departments, even though the documents are public record, they are closely watched. You cannot wander through these stacks as you would the main shelves of the library. Sometimes you must make an appointment and submit a formal request to examine specific documents.

If you think that the sheer weight of available government documents would make it a monumental task to research them, you are right. If you think there are indexes around that will make the task easier, you are right again. Here are some.

Barone, Michael, and Grant Ujifusa. *The Almanac of American Politics*

Congress A to Z: A Ready Reference Encyclopedia

Congressional Quarterly Almanac

Congressional Quarterly's Guide to U. S. Elections

Congressional Quarterly's Guide to the U.S. Supreme Court

Federal Regulatory Directory

Gimlin, Hoyt, ed. *Historic Documents*

Graham, Judith, ed. *Current Biography Yearbook*

Kay, Ernest. *Dictionary of International Biography*

Levy, Felice, comp. *Obituaries on File*

Malone, Dumas. *Dictionary of American Biography*

Marcus, Sharon J., ed. *The National Directory of State Agencies*

Morris, Dan, and Inez Morris. *Who Was Who in American Politics*

Office of the Federal Register. *The United States Government Manual*

Office of Management and Budget. *Catalog of Federal Domestic Assistance*

Orvedahl, Jerry A., ed. *Washington Information Directory*

Public Papers of the Presidents

Robinson, Judith Shiek. *Tapping the Government Grapevine: The User-Friendly Guide to U.S. Government Information Sources*

Who Was Who in America, with World Notables

Yearbook of the United Nations

7.3.7 Published Primary Sources

For most of us, our historical research will aim toward primary sources, first-hand, eye-witness accounts that give credibility to our work. It is one thing to read in a research paper that "Franklin Roosevelt was a conservative, not a liberal." Anyone could make such an assertion. To see subsequent, actual quotations from FDR's public speeches and personal correspondence, however, would tend to convince a reader that the assertion has merit and should be considered.

Not all primary sources must be unearthed from the dusty, back-room shelves of major repositories. You will find that the known writings—public and private, important and mundane—of many individuals have been collected and published in indexed, bound volumes. In a way, this takes a little of the fun out of the research process. On the other hand, this procedure widens the availability and accessibility of important sources. Now it is possible to comb the letters of Napoleon without planning a trip to France. (Too bad!) You may search the voluminous correspondence of Thomas Jefferson in your hometown library. The handwriting of many historical persons is, shall we say, "historical," and often the deterioration of ink or paper though time has rendered the original manuscript illegible. These considerations will make you glad that some scholar has spent years deciphering those ancient manuscripts and preserving them in a more readable format.

7.3.8 Manuscript Collections

The things that people in the past actually wrote themselves—their personal letters, their diaries, their financial receipts and bills of sale—are known as manuscripts. So are the records of businesses and organizations. These documents may be found in the basement vaults of major university libraries, in the file cabinets and cardboard boxes of smalltown historical societies, and many locations in between. Few activities in academia match the thrill of spending weeks researching the life of a person and then actually holding in your own hands the same slips of paper that he or she once held more than one hundred years ago! It is one thing to read about the Magna Carta; it is quite another to stand in the Chapter House at Salisbury Cathedral and read in Latin one of the four extant copies.

Part of the trick in using manuscripts is knowing where to find them in the first place. Another is knowing how to go about using them. As you read through the books and articles you have found, pay attention to the authors' bibliographies. Many times, these will refer not only to the source but also to its location. In a footnote you may see, for example,

> Contract of John Astor and Ephraim Santford, 28 September 1789, John Astor Papers, Baker Library, Harvard University, microfilm reel 10.

If you are doing research on aspects of early nineteenth-century American business practices, or on the fur trade in particular, you have just learned the whereabouts of at least some, if not most, of the personal papers of John Jacob Astor. Most major American universities have extensive manuscript collections of whose existence the average student is unaware.

Every university and every historical society has rules and regulations governing the use of its manuscript collections. Some will allow you to select boxes of material right from their selves. Others will require you to request materials from the manuscript librarian, who will disappear for several minutes and emerge with the specific documents you want. Some private universities may not allow you to use their materials at all unless you are one of their students.

We cannot hope to tell you here exactly what procedures you will need to follow in each library situation. The diversity of practices across the nation and the world is a strong argument in favor of getting an early start on your research. You may need time to write letters, make phone calls, or even make a personal visit to a repository within reasonable geographic proximity. If several letters, calls, or visits are required, this increases your research time and delays the point at which you can begin to piece your materials together into a rough draft.

If the collection you need to consult is near and you have the time to make a visit, write or call the library ahead of time. You may discover that the institution does not permit use by outsiders, and you will have saved yourself a trip. Or you may learn that the library is closed during special days or hours. Some manuscript collections are housed in their own buildings with their own rules and hours of operation. It would be frustrating to drive to a nearby state only to discover that the library you need to visit is closed on the very Tuesday you arrive. Some places may allow you to photocopy their materials, while others may not. Knowing it in advance will tell you whether to take along a roll of coins or a notebook (or note cards) and a very comfortable pen.

7.3.9 Interlibrary Loan

Every college, large or small, has procedures for acquiring materials from distant locations. This interlibrary loan program may be run by a department with a host of employees or it may be one of the jobs performed by the campus librarian. Not even the largest university has a copy of everything you might need, so you should become familiar with this important method of obtaining materials. Using interlibrary loan, you can borrow anything from books to photocopied articles and manuscripts. Get to know your school's interlibrary loan officer.

7.3.10 The Vertical File

There are several other kinds of library materials available that do not fit any of the categories mentioned above. Maps, pamphlets, and brochures, and handbills, for example, are published all the time by private corporations, utility companies, and so forth. These cannot be shelved with books or with serial publications. You usually will find this sort of material in file drawers. Unless the library has a very efficient method of organization, you may find sifting through these drawers to be time-consuming. What you may discover there, however, may prove invaluable to your research, so do not neglect this possibility.

8 *History on the World Wide Web*

8.1 A Whirlwind Introductory Tour of the Internet

To understand the Internet and how to use it, we need to begin with the basics. Follow along on our whirlwind tour of the Internet. Let's let this symbol 🖳 represent a computer. Two or more computers linked together by a telephone line, fiber optic line, radio wave, or satellite beam compose a network:

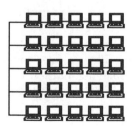

Let's call this dot [.] a symbol for a network composed of ten thousand computers and place a dot on a map of the world for every ten thousand computers.

The map would probably look like the one on page 146 which represents the *Internet,* a network of thousands of computer networks linked together by communications lines and using a common computer language to communicate with each other. The Internet was conceived in the late 1960s when the Advanced Research Projects Agency of the U.S. Department of Defense, working

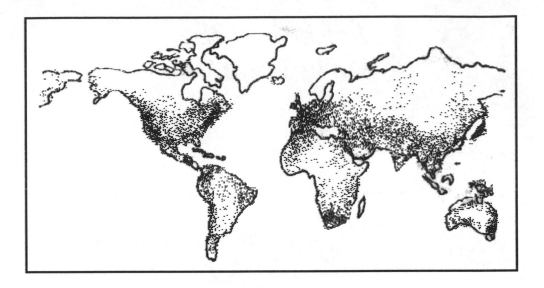

to develop military communications systems capable of surviving a nuclear war, produced ARPANET, a network of computers which at first linked military research labs and universities but later added many more computer systems.

Two decades later the National Science Foundation initiated a project called NSFNET, the purpose of which was to connect American supercomputer centers. Throughout the world similar networks were being established, and by the late 1980s connections among these networks came to be known as the Internet, which is now growing at a phenomenal rate. In 1991 there were about 700,000 people using the Internet. By 1996 that number was approaching 40 million, with 160,000 new users each month.

The World Wide Web (WWW) is an organized system for accessing the information on the Internet. Tim Berners-Lee of CERN, the European Laboratory for Particle Physics in Geneva, Switzerland, launched the WWW when he successfully created a method for using a single means of access to the networks on the Internet. The WWW is now the primary vehicle for access to information on the Internet.

8.2 How Do I Access the Internet and the World Wide Web?

The best way to connect with, or "access," the Internet is to sit down at a new computer with the latest communications software and follow the directions included in the software. Before long you will be "surfing the Net" to your heart's content. In the pages that follow we will examine briefly each stage of the process by which you can access the Internet. To do so you need four things:

- a computer
- a modem
- a service provider
- a browser

First, you need two pieces of "hardware": a computer and a modem. We will assume that you know what a computer is, but you may not be aware that your local magazine stand or bookstore carries a wide variety of periodicals that review and rate computers. When the time comes for you to purchase one, you will make a much more informed choice if you read the articles in such magazines as *Consumer Reports* and the *Computer Shopper.* It is very important to buy a computer with the largest memory and hard-drive disk capacity that you can afford. The Internet is getting more sophisticated every day, and many of the materials that you will want to "download" (electronically transmit) from the Internet to your computer will require substantial space on your computer's hard drive.

A *modem* is a device which connects your computer to a telephone line or other line of communication. Because it can take time to download files, and because many Internet access programs charge their customers for the time they spend hooked up to the Internet, it is important that your modem be capable of running at a fast rate of speed. Both computers and modems require software containing operations instructions.

Next, you will need an Internet service, a commercial business that connects you to the Internet and charges you a monthly fee that varies with the service and the amount of time you spend using it. Some of the most popular Internet services, with telephone numbers you can use to contact them, are

- America Online 1-800-827-3338
- Compuserve 1-800-848-8990
- Earthlink Network 1-213-644-9500
- Global Network Navigator (GNN) 1-800-819-6112
- Microsoft Network (MSN) 1-800-386-5550
- Prodigy 1-800-776-3449

Many smaller companies also provide Internet service, and you may be able to get rates more suited to your own pattern of Internet use from them. You will find these services listed in the yellow pages of your phone book. If you buy a new computer from a major manufacturer, you may find Internet service product brochures and software included with your computer. In addition to connecting you to the World Wide Web, some services also provide you with news, communications and other services.

Finally, you need a *browser,* a software program that allows you to search for information on the Internet. In 1993 the National Center for Supercomputing Applications (NCSA) introduced Mosaic, a browser that greatly facilitated searching for information on the WWW and encouraged many people to gain access to the Internet, but since that time other commercial browsers have become more popular. At the moment this book is being written, *Netscape Navigator* is the most popular browser, but Microsoft's *Internet Explorer* is challenging Navigator's dominance with some success. If you contract with MSN for Internet service, you will be able to download MSN's browser, *Internet Explorer,* for free, and from time to time Netscape makes a special offer of its *Navigator* for free.

You will experience a browser as a window, or *dialog box,* on your computer screen that assists you in finding information on the Internet. Once you have opened the *home page* (the starting page for a web site) of your browser you will notice that it offers you a number of *search engines,* programs that allow you to search the Internet using key words or phrases. Your browser will also provide a space in which you can type Internet addresses to access search engines and other Internet sites. Some of the most commonly used search engines and their Internet addresses are

- AltaVista: http://altavista.digital.com
- EXCITE: http://www.excite.com
- LYCOS: http://www.lycos.com
- Webcrawler: http://webcrawler.com
- YAHOO!: http://www.yahoo.com

Let's suppose you use the Yahoo search engine. In the search engine's dialog box you type in the word "history." The search engine will then make several clickable links appear on the screen. A *clickable link* (or simply *link*)is an icon or line of text highlighted and programmed so that when you click your mouse button on it, you immediately go to a new Internet address.

8.3 History Resources on the Internet

Let's take a sample Internet tour. Our history instructor has given us a writing topic, the Vietnam War, and we are going to surf the Net looking for sources. Every major Internet service will lead you to one of the search engines listed above, and many more. All the major search engines are different from each other, but each provides directions on how to use it. Reading the directions for using a search engine will save you time and effort.

To reach the Yahoo! search engine we type the Yahoo! address (http://www.yahoo.com/) in the address box provided by our Internet service's home page. At the Yahoo! home page we find a search engine box in which we can type in key words. We also find a menu that includes the following items:

Arts and Humanities Architecture, Photography, Literature . . .

Business and Economy [Xtra!] Companies, Investments, Classifieds . . .

Computers and Internet [Xtra!] Internet, WWW, Software, Multimedia . . .

Education Universities, K-12, College Entrance . . .

Entertainment [Xtra!] Cool Links, Movies, Music, Humor . . .

Government 96 Elections, Politics [Xtra!], Law . . .

Health [Xtra!] Medicine, Drugs, Diseases, Fitness . . .

News and Media [Xtra!] Current Events, Magazines, TV, Newspapers . . .

Recreation and Sports [Xtra!] Sports, Games, Travel, Autos, Outdoors . . .

Reference Libraries, Dictionaries, Phone Numbers . . .

Regional Countries, Regions, U.S. States . . .

Science CS, Biology, Astronomy, Engineering . . .

Social Science Anthropology, Sociology, Economics . . .

Society and Culture People, Environment, Religion . . .

If we click on the line that says "Arts and Humanities Architecture, Photography, Literature . . . ," we find instantly appearing a new Internet site (http://www.yahoo. com/Arts/), which gives us a new list of links, each with a number next to it indicating the number of resources we will find if we go to the page indicated by the link. For example, if we select *Artists*, we will find a list of 952 resources that have to do with artists. Here is the complete list of links we see at this stage in our voyage through the Internet:

Directories (18)	Design Arts (1609)	Organizations (208)
Indices (60)	Education (220)	Performing Arts (1729)
Sub Category Listing	Events (175)	Publications (21)
Art History (461)	Forums (13)	Real-Time Chat (4)
Artists (952)	Humanities (8261)	Television Shows@
Arts Therapy@	Institutes (41)	Thematic (14)
Children (40)	Libraries (14)	Tour Operators@
Companies@	Magazines (198)	Visual Arts (3085)
Countries and Cultures (37)	Museums and Galleries (411)	

If from the above list we select *Humanities,* we will go to another list (http://www.yahoo. com/Arts/ Humanities/) which provides the following choices:

Indices (9)	History (2939)	Literature (4471)
Classics (80)	Institutes (44)	Organizations (13)
Courses (11)	Journals (14)	Philosophy (663)
Events (2)	Linguistics and Human	Theology@
General Resources (4)	Languages@	Usenet (2)

From the above list we select *History*, which takes us to a Yahoo! page (http://www.yahoo.com/Arts/Humanities/History/) giving us the following choices:

Regional	History of Business (7)	Science and Technology
Indices (19)	Institutes (99)	(39)
17th Century (7)	Journals (34)	Sports@
18th Century (7)	Judaism@	Today in History (29)
19th Century (19)	Magazines (3)	Tour Operators@
20th Century (425)	Maps (3)	U.S. History (914)
Ancient History (21)	Maritime History (57)	Women's History@
Archives (46)	Medicine@	Usenet (6)
Art@	Medieval Studies (214)	Gateway to World
Aviation@	Military History (67)	History—Internet
Books@	Movies and Films@	resources for the study
Business@	Museums (56)	of world history and in
Christianity@	Music@	support of the struggle
Classics@	Oral History (13)	for social progress.
Costume@	Organizations (44)	History Channel, The@
Courses (16)	People (28)	History Place, The
Disasters (1)	Preservation (19)	HyperHistory Online
European History@	Radio@	Project
Genealogy (689)	Renaissance (23)	Links to the Past
Historic Buildings@	Roman History (8)	Moment in Time, A

From the above list we select *Organizations* (http://www.yahoo.com/Arts/ Humanities /History/Organizations/), and this link takes us to another Yahoo! menu with the following choices:

Aviation@

Living History (21)

Medieval Studies@

Reenactment Organizations@

Renaissance@

International Churchill Societies

American Cultural Resources Association

American Historical Association

Beckenham & Bromley Branch of the Historical Association

International Association of Labour History Institutions (IALHI)

International Students of History Association

Korean Historical Connection

Lancaster County Historical Society— genealogical and historical infor-mation in Lancaster County, Pennsylvania.

Leiden Historical Student Society H.P.G. Quack

Organization of American Historians

Point Richmond History Association

Scottish Military Historical Society

SHARP Web—from the Society for the History of Authorship, Reading & Publishing.

Sons and Daughters of the American Revolution@

Tippecanoe County Historical Association—documents the history of Lafayette, Indiana and the surrounding area.

US Newspaper Program@

Victorian Society in America

Volusia Anthropological Society

From the above list we select *American Historical Association*, which leads us to the American Historical Association home page (http://www.gmu.edu/ chnm/AHA/). Here we find the following options:

The AHA Directory of Affiliated Societies

The AHA Annual Meetings

The AHA Calendar of Historical Events—From Perspectives

The AHA General Information about the AHA

The AHA Issues, information and links for K–12 teaching

The AHA Membership information

The AHA Perspectives Online

The AHA Public Policy issues

The AHA Publications of the AHA

From this list we select *The AHA Perspectives Online* (http://www.gmu.edu/ chnmAHA/persp/) and here we find AHA's online journal, which provides its own search engine for articles and the following options:

AHA Activities

From the Director's Desk

Professional Issues

Teaching Innovations

Computers and Software

Public History

Film and Media

Archives and Research

Viewpoints

Museums and Interpretive Programs

Advertising

Submission Guidelines

Calendar of Historic Events

Announcements

Searching Perspectives Online

Next we use the "back" button on our browser—a button which, each time we depress it, returns us to the previous screen—to return to http://www.yahoo. com/Arts/Humanities /History/. From the list that appears before us on this page we select *Military History*, a selection which takes us to a Yahoo! page (http://www.yahoo.com/Arts/Humanities /History/Military_History/) listing the following options:

Indices (6)	De re militari Association Resources
Art of War (8)	Germ Warfare—Hall of Shame
Costume (13)	Jim's USS Liberty Page
Korean War@	L'Arma dei Carabinieri—"The
Museums (7)	Meritorious Corps".
Persian Gulf War@	Mil-Hist
Philippine-American War of 1899-	Militaria Magazine
1902@	Military History
Products@	Military History on the Net
Specialty Bookstores@	Resources on Military Uniforms
Civil War@	Save our Sara
Revolutionary War@	Scots at War
Vietnam War@	Team Redstone Hypermedia
World War I@	Historical Information
World War II@	The Tankers' Military History and
French and Indian War	Wargaming
African-American Warriors	Submarine Accident
Coastal Fortification on the Gulf of	US Army Center of Military History
Mexico	War Times Journal
Countdown to '95	Usenet

We select *Vietnam War@*, and go to a page (http://www.yahoo.com/Arts/ Humanities /History/20th_Century/Vietnam_War/) which gives us the following options:

Indices (2)	Sixties Project & Vietnam Generation
Books@	Timeline of the Counter-Culture
Combat Photographers (2)	Vietnam—Yesterday and Today
Documents (2)	Vietnam Casualty Search
Museums and Memorials (8)	Vietnam Combat Art
Personal Accounts (5)	Vietnam Era FTP Server
Units@	Vietnam Experience
Veterans@	Vietnam Interactive Portfolio
Bibliography of the Vietnam War	Vietnam War Usenet Newsgroup
Medal of Honor Citations	Homepage
Resources on the Vietnam Conflict	Usenet

From the above list we select *Personal Accounts* (http://www.yahoo.com/ Arts/ Humanities/History/20th_Century/Vietnam_War/Personal_Accounts/), which gives us the following choices:

Images of My War—A (then) young infantry officer's view of the Vietnam War

One Day In Vietnam—written by combat artist, Jim Pollock

Operation Homecoming—tells of the release of the American POWs from Vietnam in 1973

Re: Vietnam—Stories Since the War Vietnam Memoirs

From this list we select *Images of My War*, and go to a page (http://www.ionet. net/~uheller/vnbktoc.shtml) that gives us a personal account of the Vietnam war:

```
                           IMAGES OF MY WAR

                 by Ulf R. Heller, RVN Jul 68 - Jan 70 1994

     Table of Contents (Last Revision 10/19/96)

        •      Photo Album

        •      Introduction

        •      The 1st 22 Years

        •      The Years Leading Up to My Military Service

        •      Jungle School—What it was like to go through Jungle Warfare

               Training in Panama.

        •      A Brave New World—Impressions on Arrival in Viet Nam.

        •      Admin Company—My first taste of battle with the "Remmington

               Raiders" We don't retreat, we just backspace.

        •      The Red Swinging Doors—My introduction to the inscrutable

               orient.

        •      Fort Apache—I finally join the Infantry.

        •      Ambush—Techniques, tactics and some not-so-typical ambushes.

        •      The Dead Man in the O-Club—The warrior at leisure. •Recon

               Platoon—I become Reconnaissance (Recon) Platoon Leader.

        •      Darkness Alpha Six—I take over a Rifle Company (Yet

               Unwritten).

        •      Days at Phu Hoa Dong A Village Seal Operation.

        •      Company C—I get put back in the barrel.

        •      Discipline and Morale—Observations on discipline, morale and

               leadership.

        •      The Last Days—Back to the World.

        •      Appendix 1—Chronology •Appendix 2—Extra Duty.
```

From the above choices we select *Ambush*, and on the page this link leads us to (http://www.ionet.net/~uheller/vnbk06.html) we find a remarkable narrative of several pages which includes the following paragraph:

> A favorite ambush was one where nobody got hurt, in fact, our intended victim literally felt no pain. New Year's Eve, 1968, found us on the inevitable ambush, this time near a small village. My men laid out the ambush with practiced dispatch and we settled in for the night. Around midnight, I heard some singing. We could see fairly well, perhaps because of the moon. I don't remember. The singing grew louder and louder. We were all awake and ready to kill. In a few minutes, a skinny old man on a bicycle weaved his way into sight. He was taking swigs on a bottle he was carrying and singing. My finger tightened on the clacker of my claymore. As he reached the center of our kill zone, he fell off of his bicycle. He sat there laughing and singing. He tried to get back on his bike only to fall again. He kept laughing and singing. I heard other laughter around me as my men couldn't hold it back at the comical sight. Pretty soon we were all laughing. I didn't have the heart to kill him. The next morning several men came up to me and said they were glad I let him go. So was I. Hell! He was probably the local party secretary.

The lists above are only the tip of the Internet history resources iceberg. The purpose of this chapter is to pique your curiosity and help you get started on your own exploration of the Internet. Once you have begun, you will discover thousands of sites and dozens of types of information that we have not mentioned in this chapter. Some of the things you will find will be

- *Mailing Lists.* You can join a mailing list and receive by E-mail or in printed form publications of a wide variety of organizations.
- *Bibliographies.* Numerous extensive bibliographies of historical information already appear on the net.
- *Publishers and Bookstores.* You will find publishers offering to sell you virtually any title in history, and you will find bookstores that offer not only new books, but old, outdated, and rare editions of many texts.
- *History Projects.* Many history research and discussion projects have home pages on the Net, and sometimes you can join in the research and discussions.
- *History Resource Guides.* Guides to all these resources and more are on the net, with clickable links which take you directly to the sources they cite.
- *News Groups.* News groups are Internet pages in which people exchange information on current events.

9 *Book Reviews*

9.1 The Purpose of a Book Review

Samuel Johnson proposed that the essential task of a book review is to answer three questions :

- What did the writer try to do?
- How well did she or he do it?
- Was it worth doing in the first place?

People who read a book review want to know if a particular book is worth reading, for their own purposes, before expending their resources buying it or their time reading it. These potential readers want to know the book's subject and its strengths and weaknesses, and they want to obtain this information as easily and quickly as possible. Your goal in writing a book review, therefore, is to help people decide efficiently whether to buy or read a book. Your immediate objectives may be to please your instructor and get a good grade, but these objectives are most likely to be met if you focus on a book review's audience: people who want help in selecting books to read. In the process of writing a book review that reaches this primary goal you will also

- Learn about the book you are reviewing
- Learn about professional standards for book reviews in history
- Learn the essential steps of book reviewing that apply to any academic discipline

Learning to review a book properly has more useful applications than you may imagine at first. First, it teaches you to focus quickly on the essential elements of a book, to draw from a book its informational value not just for other readers but also for yourself. Some of the most successful people in government, business, and the professions speed-read several books a week, more for the knowledge they contain than for enjoyment. These readers then apply this knowledge to substantial advantage in their professions. It is normally not wise to speed-read a book you are reviewing, because you are unlikely to gain enough information from such a fast reading to give it a fair evaluation. Writing book reviews, however, helps you to become proficient in quickly sorting valuable information from material that is not valuable. The ability to make such quick and effective judgments is a fundamental ingredient in professional success.

Writing book reviews also allows you to participate in the discussions of the broader intellectual and professional community of which you are a part. When you write a book review for publication, you are engaging in a dialogue with the book's author, as well as with all the other readers out there who are interested in the subject of the book. You are adding your opinion to their opinions, and in doing so you are helping to shape the general discourse that comprises all the work being done in your field. There are few better ways of forcing yourself to confront a particular issue or idea than committing yourself to review a book on it. It is an instant immersion in a vital flux of thought.

A third benefit of reviewing books is of tremendous potential usefulness to you. No doubt you have often heard that the two best ways to improve your own writing are (1) to read, and (2) to write. If this is true—and it is—then what better way to combine these two crucial activities than to review what you read? Reading a book for review can provide you with practical models of what you should and should not do as a writer. You have a chance to become more conscious of stylistic and organizational strategies than you would if you were reading only for a book's content. Writing a book review gives you practice in assimilating and condensing ideas in order to express them with clarity in as few words as possible. There are not many better ways to improve your thinking and your writing simultaneously than to practice book reviewing.

To get a feel for writing an effective book review, you should spend some time reading a few samples. To do this, you may peruse the pages of any professional history journal. As you know, these publications usually contain a handful of scholarly articles, but they also present a number of reviews of the latest publications in the field. Or, more simply, you may read and study the following examples. One is a positive review; the other is not as complimentary. The first appeared in the October 1998 issue of *Fides et Historia*, the journal of the Conference on Faith and History. The second example was published in the Summer 1990 edition of *The Chronicles of Oklahoma*, the journal of the Oklahoma Historical Society.

9.2 Elements of a Book Review

Book reviews in history contain the same essential elements of reviews in other disciplines. Since history is usually nonfiction, book reviews within the discipline focus less upon a work's writing style and more upon its content and method than do reviews of novels or short story collections. Your book review should generally contain four basic elements, although not always in this order:

- Enticement
- Examination
- Elucidation
- Evaluation

9.2.1 Enticement

A good book review entices the reader to read review, and possibly, the book. Before proceeding with the directions in this chapter, carefully read the following two book reviews.

Pagans and Christians by Robin Lane Fox (New York: Alfred A. Knopf, Inc., 1987. Pp. 681. $35.00.)

Reviewed by Mark Hellstern, Oral Roberts University, Tulsa, Oklahoma

The conflict endured by the embryonic Christian movement before the reign of Constantine is a familiar story. The conflicts that existed within the faith—disputes and tensions both seen and unseen—constitute a significant but lesser-known chapter of that story. The internal and external struggles experienced by Christianity in its rise from persecution to acceptance serve as the basis for Robin Lane Fox's rich portrait, *Pagans and Christians*. This is a vivid, comprehensive, and rewarding crosssectional analysis of religious life in the Roman Empire in the second and third centuries. Fox carefully chronicles the decline of paganism and the concomitant surge of Christianity, but he cogently maintains both that paganism remained alive and well until the very end and that Christians constituted a smaller minority in the Roman world than previous estimates have indicated.

According to Fox, by the second century various forms of paganism were practiced by the overwhelming majority of the inhabitants of the Empire. By this time, however, cult worship had lost most of its genuine zeal and had become ritualized and institutionalized, degenerating into a perfunctory religiosity supported by buttresses of home town pride, love of honor, the preservation of social order, and, of course, tradition. Pagan temples, athletic contests, festivals, and other philanthropic enterprises were created by notables animated less by spiritual devotion and more by intercity competition, intra-class rivalry, and the notables' egotism.

The impression left by Fox of early Christianity is one of confusion and complexity. Early Christians were required to contend not only with the ever-looming threat of persecution, but also with doctrinal disputes, behavior adjustments, spurious claims, and heresies. The melange of ideas which characterized the thought of the early Church represented a broad spectrum. On the one hand were the ascetics—"overachievers," Fox calls them—those who believed Christ's return to be within their lifetime and who advocated strict discipline in personal conduct. On the other extremes were the heretics who either manipulated or restructured the "gospel" to suit their own ends or who freely mixed Christianity with remnants of paganism. Each subtle variety of Christianity was supported either by those who claimed a special, personal revelation or who could authenticate their version with some bogus, apocryphal "gospel," epistle, or "acts."

Fox's work is built upon thorough and impressive research; it is readily apparent that he is in firm command of his evidence. From this wealth of documentation Fox draws conclusions that are remarkably perceptive. His writing style is, for the most part, clean and very often demonstrates a delightfully dry wit.

The flaws in *Pagans and Christians* are few and minor. In the book's introduction, Fox presents six individuals whose lives represent the story of Christianity's triumph over paganism. Only two of these, Cyprian and Constantine, are followed with any detail. The chapter on Constantine near the end of the book seems a bit awkward and over-balanced, as if it were an afterthought. Some of Fox's paragraphs are quite long, others questionably organized, and still others vague in their development.

These small structural defects in no way diminish the worth of this fine study. The demographic and social profiles of the Roman Empire's pagan and Christian communities are of immeasurable value. *Pagans and Christians* is social history at its best. It is certain to achieve the same acceptance and acclaim as that garnered by Fox's biography of Alexander the Great.

The Confederate Cherokees: John Drew's Regiment of Mounted Rifles. By W. Craig Gaines (Baton Rouge: Louisiana State University Press, 1989. Pp. 178. Photographs. Maps. Appendices. Bibliography. Index. $19.95 cloth).

Reviewed by Mark Hellstern, Tulsa Junior College, Tulsa Oklahoma

One of the most familiar chapters which comprises Oklahoma's rich and diverse history is that of the Civil War in Indian Territory. Much has been written on the subject, particularly that phase of the conflict within the Cherokee Nation—a tragic microcosm of the larger war which sundered the tribe, arrayed family members against family members, and left the Cherokee people decimated and destitute by the war's end. In *Confederate Cherokees*, Craig Gaines has unearthed a gem of a story which has been, for the most part, overlooked by previous examinations of the internecine fight. Whereas other studies have focused on the more familiar Cherokee leader Stand Watie, Gaines's work explores and chronicles the formation, military activities, and gradual disintegration of the lesser-known regiment led by mixed-blood entrepreneur and politician John Drew.

Composed mostly of non-slaveholding full-blood Cherokees, the unit known simply as "Drew's Regiment" was armed hastily by Chief John Ross as a safeguard against a possible political coup attempt by a rival mixed-blood regiment organized and led by Ross's old nemesis Stand Watie. Because Drew's full-bloods were never fully committed to the Confederate cause, the story of the regiment is one of repeated en masse desertions and defections to the Union side. By the end of the war, Drew's regiment had ceased to exist. Most of its original members either were serving in Union Kansas regiments or were among the thousands of displaced and confused Cherokee refugees trying to rebuild their lives in a warscarred and neglected land.

Gaines's work is admirable for two reasons. First, he has provided a well-researched and well-synthesized narrative of a heretofore neglected but essential aspect of the Cherokees' civil war. Second, his account is refreshingly even-handed, a welcome departure from the neo-partisanship fostered by recent writers who have been either pro-Ross or pro-Watie.

(The latter is much more common.) Gaines is to be commended for retaining objectivity.

Two things would have made the work more satisfying. First, though the book's jacket indicates otherwise, there is very little material on the man John Drew. There is more said about other Confederate leaders and about those under his command. The sub-title is appropriate; this is about John Drew's regiment. With fewer than 115 pages of actual text, Gaines could have invested more space in a lengthier discussion of Drew's background. Second, the book gives indication of being another Indian history as seen through white eyes. Cherokee full-bloods should not be discredited for acting as full-bloods, yet Gaines has entitled some of his "defection" chapters as "Disgrace" and "Disaster." A fuller examination of the dynamics of "Indianness" must yet be undertaken.

These subjective omissions notwithstanding, Gaines has made a vital contribution to an understanding of the Indian's Civil War. The Confederate Cherokees fills a gap in that understanding without tine' customary judgmentalism. The narrative would be more meaningful, however, had it been set within its broader personal and cultural contexts.

Your first sentence should entice people to read the rest of your review. History does not have to be dull. Try to start your review with a sentence that subtly leads your readers into the rest of the opening paragraph—and make that opening paragraph such an attention-grabber that, before they know it, your readers have finished reading the whole review. In the first example above, the word "conflict" in the first sentence catches readers' eyes, because there is a deep part of our nature that draws us to conflict. (Good literature and good drama are built on the tension and release of conflict and its eventual resolution.) The repetition of the word "conflict(s)" in the second sentence establishes the idea that there is "more to know." After the first two sentences pique the reader's interest, the third sentence then introduces the book being reviewed. This "ready, set, go" (short, short, long) technique involving three sentences to begin a work may seem manipulative. It is. It is also nothing new. Consider the first few measures of Mozart's famous Eine Kleine Nachtmusik or the even more familiar beginning of Beethoven's Symphony # 5:

MOZART

BEETHOVEN

The "ready, set, go" idea, while being perhaps a shameless and mercenary piece of psychological manipulation, has been around for a long time, used by those we consider creative geniuses! Why? Because it works!

In the second example of a book review above, the technique is reversed. This review begins with an extra-long sentence—sixty-eight words—that sinks readers into the topic before they reach the first period! By that time, there is no easy pullout; readers are committed.

Another way to lure readers into continuing to read is to employ words with built-in emotional impact, such as "conflict" in the first example or "rich," "conflict," "tragic," and "decimated" in the second. Instead of the mundane, "Craig Gaines has written a book," you read, "Craig Gaines has unearthed a gem." Which version is more appealing to you?

9.2.2 Examination

Your book review should allow the reader to join you in examining the book. Tell the reader what the book is about. Before you reach the end of your first paragraph, you should have given the reader a capsule summary of the essential content of the book.

When you review a book, write what is actually in the book, not what you think is probably there or what ought to be there. Do not tell how you would have written the book, but instead how the author wrote it. Describe the book in clear, objective terms. Tell enough about the content to identify the author's major points.

On the other hand, you do not want your review to become merely a condensed version of the whole book, a smaller narrative based on the book's narrative. If you find yourself using phrases such as "in the next chapter . . ." or "then the author . . .," you likely have succumbed to the temptation to rehash the book. Remember that you are examining the book, not the same material the book examined.

It is usually not a good idea to borrow the book's organization for the organization of your review. While the book's author, dealing with a much roomier format, has time to build his argument slowly, using detailed arguments and examples, you have very little time to set up and articulate your opinion. Don't let yourself get bogged down explaining a minor point from the book's introduction or recapitulating a supporting line of argument from chapter one at too great a length. Remember, like any other piece of writing, your review must find its own balance, its own form.

9.2.3 Elucidation

Elucidate, or clarify, the book's value and contribution to history by defining (1) what the author is attempting to do and (2) how the author's work fits within current similar efforts in the discipline of history or scholarly inquiry in general. By the end of the first paragraph of the first sample book review above, there should be no doubt in your mind about the author's views on the subject of Pagans and Christians. The review closes with an assessment of the book's overall worth in our search for greater understanding of a vital historical era. The first paragraph of the second sample review, the one dealing with *The Confederate Cherokees*, ends with a straightforward statement of the author's intent, and the review itself again closes with an estimation of the book's worth to the academic community.

The elucidation portion of book reviews often provides additional information about the author. Only one of the two examples above includes such information. It is helpful to know, for example, if a book's author has written other books on the subject. If the book you are reviewing is the first published by that particular author, its place in the literature of the discipline may not be the same as that of the seventh book written by another author on the same subject. On the other hand, an author may have blazed into the professional heavens by offering a truly outstanding first work, one whose research explores areas never covered before or whose thesis is so revolutionary that it should not be ignored by the academic community. You may well not be sure ahead of time what sort of book you have to review, so stay sharp!

9.2.4 Evaluation

Once you explain what the book is attempting to do, you should tell the reader the extent to which the book has succeeded. To evaluate a book effectively, you will need to evaluate the book clearly according to a proper set of criteria. While you may not need to define the criteria specifically in your review, they should be evident to the reader. Your criteria will vary according to the book you are reviewing, and you may discuss them in any order that is helpful to the reader. Consider, however, including the following among the criteria that you establish for your book review:

- How important is the subject to the study of history?
- How complete and thorough is the author's coverage of the subject?
- How carefully is the author's analysis conducted?
- What are the strengths and limitations of the author's methodology?
- What is the quality of the writing? Is it clear, precise, and interesting?
- How does this book compare with others on the subject?

- What contribution does this book make to history?
- Who will enjoy or benefit from the book?

When giving your evaluations according to these criteria, be specific. If you write, "This is a good book; I liked it very much," you have told the reader nothing of interest or value.

9.3 Qualities of Effective History Book Reviews

Remember that no review—including the two examples in this chapter—is perfect. Effective history book reviews

- Serve the reader.
- Are fair.
- Are concise and specific, not vague and general.

Write your review with the potential reader, not yourself or the book's author, in mind. The person who may read the book is, in a manner of speaking, your client.

Your reader wants a fair review of the book. Do not be overly generous to a book of poor quality, but do not be too critical of an honest effort to tackle a complex or difficult problem. If you have a bias that may affect your review, let your reader know it, but do so briefly. Do not shift the focus from the book's ideas to your own. Do not attack a work because of the author's politics or personal agenda. On the other hand, if the author has an obvious bias or agenda that slips through obtrusively, you owe it to your reader to say so.

The reader of your book review is not interested in *your* thoughts about politics or other subjects. A book review is to be an appraisal of the merits of the book, not an occasion for a point/counterpoint debate on the book's subject matter. If the book has stirred your animus to the point that you want to refute it, then do your own research and write your own book! Try to appreciate the author's efforts and goals, and sympathize with the author, even if you do not necessarily agree with every point made. Still, you should try to remain sufficiently detached to identify errors. Try to show the book's strengths and weaknesses as clearly as possible.

Write a review that is interesting, appealing, and even charming, but not at the expense of accuracy or scholarly credibility. Be erudite but not prolix. (To be erudite is to display extensive knowledge. To be prolix is to be wordy and vague.) Your goal is to display substantial knowledge of the book's content, strengths, and weaknesses in as few words as possible.

9.4 Preliminaries: Before Writing a Book Review

Before sitting down to write your review, make sure you do the following:

- Get complete directions from your instructor. Ask if there are special directions beyond those in this manual for the number of pages or content of the review.

- Read the book. Reviewers who skim or merely read a book's jacket do a great disservice to the author. Read the book thoroughly.
- Respond to the book. As you read, make notes on your responses to the book. Organize them into the categories of enticement, examination, elucidation, and evaluation.
- Get to know the subject. Use the library to find a summary of works on the topic. Such a summary may be found in reviews in a journal or in recent textbooks.
- Familiarize yourself with other books by the author. If the author has written other works, learn enough about them to be able to describe them briefly to your readers, if space permits.
- Read reviews of other history books. Most historical journals have book review sections, usually at the end of the issue. Go to the library and browse through some of the reviews in several journals. Not only will you get to know what is expected from a history book review, but you will find many interesting ideas on how books are approached and evaluated.

9.5 Format and Content

The directions for writing papers provided in Chapters 2-5 apply to book reviews as well. Some further instructions specific to book reviews are needed, however. First, list on the title page, along with the standard information required for history papers, data on the book being reviewed: title, author, place and name of publisher, date, and number of pages. In the sample that follows, note that the title of the book should be in italics or underlined, but not both:

```
A Review of

Ties of Common Blood:

A History of Maine's Northeast Boundary Dispute

With Great Britain

by

Geraldine Tidd Scott

Bowie, Maryland: Heritage Books, Inc.

1992. 445 pages.

Reviewed by

Paula Smith

HIST 213

Dr. Michael Arnold

Western University

January 1, 1996
```

9.6 Reflective or Analytical Book Reviews

Two types of book reviews are normally assigned by instructors in the humanities and social sciences: the *reflective* and the *analytical*. Ask your instructor which type of book review you are to write. The purpose of a reflective book review is for the student reviewer to exercise creative analytical judgment without being influenced by the reviews of others. Reflective book reviews contain all the elements covered in this chapter—enticement, examination, elucidation, and evaluation—but they do not include the views of others who have also read the book.

Analytical book reviews contain all the information provided by the reflective reviews but add an analysis of the comments of other reviewers. The purpose is thus to review not only the book itself but also its reception in the professional community.

To write an analytical book review, insert a review analysis section immediately after your summary of the book. To prepare this section, use the *Book Review Digest* and *Book Review Index* in the library to locate other reviews of the same book that have been published in journals and other periodicals. As you read these reviews,

1.   List the criticisms (strengths and weaknesses) of the book that are made in the reviews.
2.   Develop a concise summary of these criticisms; indicate the overall positive or negative tone of the reviews and mention some of the most common comments.
3.   Evaluate the criticisms found in these reviews. Are they basically accurate in their assessment of the book?
4.   Write a review analysis of two pages or less that states and evaluates steps 2 and 3 and place it in your book review immediately after your summary of the book.

9.7 Length of a Book Review

Unless your instructor gives you other directions, a reflective book review should be two to four typed, double-spaced pages in length, and an analytical book review should be three to five pages long. In either case, a brief, specific, concise book review is almost always to be preferred over one of greater length.

10 *Topical History Papers*

10.1 Writing the History of an Event, Trend, or Phenomenon

Of all the various types of history assignments you may be given, the most basic papers are those which require you to focus upon a "topic," in other words, a particular event, social trend, or phenomenon. The topical paper is related to the chronological narrative, with one major difference: Rather than simply tell an unfolding story, as the narrative does, the topical paper permits a deeper examination of human factors, such as gender reactions, worker anger, or voter upheaval. To see the difference between chronological and topical studies, consider the following three ways one might approach the subject of America's Gilded Age of the late nineteenth century:

CHRONOLOGICAL	TOPICAL #1	TOPICAL #2
Election of 1876	The developing Labor Movement:	American Business: Postwar industry
Hayes Administration		Trusts
Election of 1880	The Industrial Revolution	Vertical Integration
Assassination of Garfield	Immigration Factors	Monopolies
Arthur Administration	Rockefeller and Carnegie	The Money Barons
Blaine vs. Cleveland, 1884	The Gospel of Wealth	An Affront to American Enterprise?
Harrison's Interregnum	Effect on Common Americans	Govt. Attempts at Regulation
Cleveland and the Panic of 1893	Early Attempts at Union NLU	
McKinley's "Splendid little War"	The Knights	
	Strikes and Put-Downs	
	The AF of L	

We have said before that history, as a social science, should focus not so much on *what* happened as on *how* and *why* things happened, how and why people acted as they did. This is what the topical approach allows a writer to do: To get to the bottom of historical events, uncovering the motivations behind them and the results that stem from them. Look at the outlines above. Which of these approaches to late nineteenth century America are more conducive to the exploration and explanation of human action, reaction and interaction? There is nothing wrong with chronological narratives; they play an important role in our comprehensive knowledge of the human story. But if you really want to dig deeper into the human aspects of history, we suggest a topical outlook.

10.2 An Example of Topical History: Ante-Bellum Slavery

Few topics within the general field of United States history have generated as much recent scholarship as that of the nature of ante-bellum slavery. Only since the late 1930s have significant primary source materials been available, and the use and interpretation of these have been evolving slowly. The study as a whole, of course, is framed within the larger context of racial tension in American life. The true nature of the Southern slave culture is still a matter of debate among scholars. Because slaveholding affected the minds and morality not only of the African "immigrants" themselves but also of the many whites (and Native Americans) who owned them, the subject of slaveholding has become a fertile area for social and cultural investigation. It is also a subject that is best viewed topically, rather than chronologically, and is therefore a useful example for us to study here.

A Brief History of the Issue

This century's first scholarly account of slave life was written in 1929 by Ulrich B. Phillips, who examined the records kept by ante-bellum slave owners and overseers. Phillips' work is useful to us for three reasons. First, in his study he established certain parameters for assessing the actual conditions experienced by black Americans on Southern plantations. He studied and offered comments on food, housing, working conditions, and so forth. In doing so, he lifted the subject away from the usual chronological narrative common for history writing in his day. Instead of focusing on the larger political aspects of slavery, he provided a look at the human factors associated with the "peculiar institution."

Second, Phillips taught future historians how *not* to research and write history. By looking at the records of white slaveholders, he gave himself only one side of the story to examine. Southern whites saw what they were doing only through their own eyes, their own experiences, and their prejudices. Naturally, their records would supply later researchers with a skewed version of what conditions actually were like. Examining only one side of the story, Phillips concluded that slavery was actually a kind and benevolent institution and that smiling, docile blacks actually were treated well, like members of the owners' families. Phillips argued that by the 1860s slavery had reached its natural, geographical limits and that even in the South it was a dying institution. He reasoned, therefore, that the Civil War was wholly unnecessary, brought about by fanatical Northern abolitionists.

This line of reasoning suggests the third lesson Phillips taught us. He researched and wrote after World War I, a gruesome struggle that Americans in the twenties believed to be wholly unnecessary and wasteful. Phillips himself was a Southerner. His version of history, then, was filtered through the distorted lens of his own times and his own experience. In other words, he allowed a personal agenda to slip into his assessment of the subject.

Shortly after Phillips published his study of the life of slaves, the conditions under which research into the history of American slavery was conducted changed radically. Historians were among those who had been thrown out of work during the Depression of the 1930s, and to provide an income for them the New Deal "primed the pump" with make-work projects, most of them sponsored by a program called the Federal Writers' Project (FWP). Scholars working for the FWP were paid to conduct interviews with older Americans, particularly those of color. Tremendous research tools resulted from this initiative. In the 1930s, there were many black Americans who were old enough to have been slaves early in their lives, and they offered their recollections to federal interviewers. It should be no surprise to you that these people had substantially different stories to tell than those left by white slaveholders!

In 1956, making use of this remarkable body of information, Kenneth Stampp published a book entitled *The Peculiar Institution* which took issue with almost all of Phillips' arguments. According to Stampp, slavery was not dying out in 1860, but was alive and well. He asserted that the institution was cruel and exploitative, not benign and benevolent. Using the same set of parameters established by Phillips, Stampp suggested that Southern blacks were ill-fed, ill-housed, ill-clothed, and subjected to long hours of demanding labor, frequent beatings, and the breakup of marriages and families. Stampp pointed out that fierce slave revolts from time to time proved that blacks were by no means happy with their conditions. We should observe at this point that Stampp's writings, published during the beginning of the Civil Rights movement in the 1950s, reflected the attitudes of his times just as surely as Phillips' ideas had a generation earlier.

Since the 1950s the debate set into motion by Phillips and Stampp has mushroomed. Other historians—Stanley Elkins, John Blassingame, Eugene Genovese, Winthrop Jordan, Leon Litwack, and John Hope Franklin, to name but a few—have offered their studies and ideas to aid our understanding of the life of African-Americans under the yoke of bondage before and after the American Civil War. The current status of thought concerning the life of American slaves is that black families, far from being merely passive participants in a white world, managed to keep alive a remarkable degree of culture and to maintain family and kinship ties in spite of bondage.

What we would like you to see in this discussion of the evolution of academic thought concerning American slavery is the ebb and flow of ideas surrounding a particular historical topic. At no point in the discussion above did we describe an act of Congress or a Supreme Court decision. Nor did we supply dates. This is not to say that a chronological approach is wrong or passé. Such analyses do have their place. After all, if your paper is about an event, you will very probably need to provide a narrative in order to set your findings within a meaningful context. If you are analyzing a trend, you are certainly welcome to use dates. For many college students, however, the tendency when writing a topical history paper is to provide a chronological narrative *only*, without supplying needed analysis.

Prepare by Reading

Suppose that your historical interests lie in areas other than American race relations. You may be interested in nineteenth century British politics, the opening of trade between the United States and Asia, or Julius Caesar's campaigns against the Gauls. Perhaps you are fascinated by the growth of the oil industry in Louisiana or by the plight of women on the Oregon Trail. Maybe archaeological investigations of Bronze Age shipwrecks grab you. No matter where your interests lie, we urge you to begin preparing for your paper by reading a few journal articles. We have suggested this before, and we will do so again. By becoming acquainted with the body of scholarship that already exists in your area, you will accomplish these things:

- You will see what debate parameters scholars have established for your subject. By gaining a comfortable understanding of the work of Phillips, Stampp, and other historians, for example, you will be able either to fit your investigation into the existing framework or venture into new areas of discussion.
- You will come to understand what is expected of a paper in this subject area. Give yourself the opportunity to see what the discipline expects in terms of research, writing, argument, and so forth.
- You should get to know some of the most important resources available in your field. If you are interested in the Civil War in Kansas, read journal articles about the subject, and pay attention to the bibliographies that you find at the ends of the articles.
- You will become more knowledgeable in your field. The more you read about the Hittites, for example, the more sophisticated your questioning and research will become.
- You may see a whole new aspect of the subject that has not been analyzed before. Perhaps most of the existing debate within your topic goes in one direction, while you discover a useful way to explore it from another.
- You may decide that your interests take you elsewhere. It would be better to discover this now rather than when you are six weeks into your research.

Preliminary reading is an essential step that you must not bypass. While it may, at first, seem like a waste of time, in the long run background reading stuff will save you time.

In the next pages, we will offer advice about creating a successful topical paper, the kind of traditional paper you have written before and the kind that may have prompted you to pick up this book. The number of possible topics for such a paper is virtually unlimited, but we will focus here on a few general areas: political and diplomatic, military, business and economic, social and cultural, and archaeological.

10.3 Steps to Writing a Good Topical Paper

The four chapters in Part Two of this book describe in detail the steps necessary for producing a top-quality research paper, from research through preparing the final draft. No more will be said here about the essentials. This chapter is devoted to specifics. It should help you find the best ways to approach some of the most common types of topics. Processes involving library research, note taking, assimilation of information, competent writing, and proper citation will remain the same, no matter what topic you choose. What will change here is the way you perceive your topic. Just as a book review is substantially different from a biography in purpose and method, so a military history paper will differ from an archaeological paper. The differences range from types of sources to mode of preparation and presentation.

Becoming Familiar with Styles, Formats, and Sources

One of the strongest suggestions we can offer you is to read. There is great benefit to be derived from steeping yourself in the type of paper you want to write. If you are thinking of researching a paper on some aspect of United States diplomatic history, you should begin by reading several articles concerning diplomatic history. If you write a paper dealing with military history, your own paper should not be the first of its kind that you have read. The more you read, the more you will become familiar with the standards in that particular field. You will learn what the profession expects of a paper such as the one you are about to write. (This is not something you want to learn when you receive your graded paper and realize that your professor had to buy a new red pen because the old one ran dry on your paper.)

Another essential recommendation we can make is to become familiar with the types of sources most commonly used in the field you are wanting to explore. You should know the names and works of the luminaries who have written on your subject. You should know what kinds of primary sources are available in your area. What significant research could you do on the Civil War, for example, without an acquaintance with the Official Records? The task might be done without using this invaluable resource—but why? You should be on a first-name basis with the essential reference works in your field.

10.4 Finding a Topic

Chapter 1 discussed ways in which you should go about selecting a topic. This task may be eliminated, in part, by the type of assignment your instructor gives you. If you enrolled in a graduate seminar called American Diplomatic History, chances are good that your paper will concern an aspect of American diplomatic history.

If you are in a more general course—The Reformation, for example—your topic choices could run from religion to art, military alliances to music. What then? Again, your instructor may want you to focus on a specific angle, and your choices could limit themselves. If the options are entirely your own, ask yourself the question, "What interests me?" or "What did I hope to learn by enrolling in this course?" If your answer is a practical one—for example, to learn how the reformation affected a particular nation or group of people—there is at least the beginning of your topic selection.

As you arrive at this preliminary destination, begin to read some very basic articles on the subject, perhaps from the first encyclopedia you pick up. We can (almost) guarantee that by the time you finish reading that first article, you will have narrowed your interests and focus. You will have a clearer idea about where you would like your research to go. Remember that topical history generally seeks to examine the more human elements of the past—the effects of events and conditions upon everyday people, as well as the emotional and psychological motivations behind those events and conditions. Let this goal of exploring the humanistic implications of history be stamped on your mind as you proceed through each step of your paper's production.

10.5 Political and Diplomatic Papers

Most of the writing that has been done in the general field of American history has concerned political and diplomatic history. Think of the major events of the twentieth century. They center around two world wars and subsequent military actions in Korea, Vietnam, and other corners of the world. We also tend to define and categorize history according to presidential administrations and even the ascendancy of certain political ideologies—the Progressive Era or McCarthyism, for example.

Americans seem to be obsessed with candidates, campaigns, and elections. Even before one presidential election has ended, the media has the country mulling over possible aspirants for the next contest four years away! Cable television and radio talk shows discuss and/or promote various political viewpoints. Though recent voter turnout seems to indicate otherwise, Americans have a deep interest in politics. If you examine an older American history textbook, the focus will very probably be a political one.

Foreign affairs are also a constant in the American agenda. There have been times when world crises have demanded U.S. involvement and other occasions when the United States itself has initiated the involvement. Even when the

United States has not been plunging into world affairs, or refraining from plunging, we have nevertheless been involved in trade negotiations and treaty ratification, raising or lowering tariff barriers, or trying to decide which regime to recognize as the legitimate government of a third-world nation.

It is a very strong possibility that the paper you have chosen to write will cover some small aspect of political or diplomatic history. Again, the main steps involved in choosing and refining the topic, conducting research, organizing the results, and writing a meaningful paper were covered earlier and will be the same for papers with a focus on the history of diplomacy as for any other type of paper. The significant differences between political and diplomatic papers and those in other fields concern not method but sources.

10.6 Business and Economic Papers

In 1886, an Atlanta pharmacist named John Styth Pemberton mixed a strange brew of cola nuts, coca leaves, and caffeine and called it Coca-Cola. One year later, he sold most of the interest in his new beverage for $283.29. The new owners sold the formula a decade later to another Atlanta pharmacist, Asa G. Candler, for $2,000. By the time Candler sold the product in 1919, its worth was an estimated $25 million (Bryson 1994)!

Before you write off papers dealing with the history of business and economics as beyond your interests, you need to know that there are fascinating historical tales associated with the development of American industry and finance. Exemplary studies such as *The Wealth of a Nation to Be: The American Colonies on the Eve of the Revolution,* by Alice H. Jones, and Bray Hammond's *Banks and Politics in America from the Revolution to the Civil War* tell exciting stories while recording crucial developments in American economic policy. Business papers do not have to be numbing, figure-ridden accounts of historical economic analysis. They can be simple tales of American success stories. They can be about common people who made a local but very important impact. You could explore the boom and bust of a mining town in Colorado or how oil built a thriving community in eastern Oklahoma.

If American economic history is not exactly to your liking, you could examine trade networks in the eastern Mediterranean during the late Bronze Age or economic relationships within the Norse world of the eleventh and twelfth centuries. The possibilities are indeed endless.

10.7 Military Papers

If you are interested in military history, you already know that it is a field with not only a special jargon but also a special way of looking at evidence. Military historians throw around terms such as *phalanx, grapeshot,* and *panzer.* When we hear place names such as Cannae, Agincourt, Shiloh, or the Somme, our minds conjure images of their histories and significance.

One of the things we must keep in mind as we prepare to conduct research in military history is to try to find areas that have not been covered too often. It is possible, for example, that you could uncover a fresh angle on Pickett's Charge at Gettysburg in 1863, but it is unlikely. This moment is one of the most famous—and most discussed—in military history. Unless you find something truly new and exciting to offer, such as an unknown dispatch from Robert E. Lee to James Longstreet hidden in a picture frame in your grandmother's attic, try to find another episode of the Civil War to explore.

The central purpose in writing about military topics is not to give history buffs more trivial details to fantasize about but to gain a better understanding of the use of military force to achieve certain political or geographical objectives. Let the Civil War buffs immerse themselves in the minutiae that interest them. Let the World War Two buffs memorize the armaments aboard a P-51, the top cruising speed of Iowa-class battleships, and other such details that are, in the grand scheme of things, not really important. This is rather stern talk, and perhaps it seems even insensitive, but it is absolutely essential. As historians, we must never lose sight of our raison d'être, which is to shed more light on the ways human beings think and act. This issue is as applicable to military history as to other historical fields.

Consider this example. All of us know that Napoleon revolutionized warfare. The "Little Corsican" was so admired (and worshiped) by generations of military theorists on both sides of the Atlantic that there arose schools of interpretation dedicated to replicating future Napoleons. In the American Civil War, many commanders, North and South, fancied that they would be the "next Napoleon." Note photos taken of General George B. McClellan, commander of the Union forces, trying to look as Napoleonic as he could, complete with hand tucked inside his uniform! Napoleonic tactics were still being employed as late as World War I, but few could figure out why these honored tactics were not working.

It is probable that all the interpreters from Jomini to Halleck to McClellan to Haig missed the point of studying Napoleon's battles. In bathing themselves in the minute details of Napoleonic tactics, they forgot to study Napoleon himself, the man who created the ideas in the first place. What made Napoleon Napoleon were his ability and willingness to be an innovator. He was not concerned with being the "next" this or that. He did not slavishly replicate eighteenth-century military practices. He did what he needed to do to win. In the American Civil War, the closest commander in thinking to Napoleon was not the ineffective, hesitant McClellan, but perhaps William Tecumseh Sherman. Here was a truly Napoleonic innovator, in that he did what he needed to do to win— including departing from the tried-and-not-so-true. So foresighted was Sherman in apprehending modern, total warfare, that the Nazi generals of the 1930s studied Sherman, not McClellan.

The purpose of military science is to improve military effectiveness. This effort may and should involve the study of past tactical procedures. After all, the classic "double envelopment" was just as effective at Cowpens in 1781, as it had been at Cannae in 216 B.C.E. What must not become lost, however, is the study of the effect of basic human nature on warfare. What makes the double envelop-ment work is the human tendency to be lured into a trap. What made George McClellan an ineffective commander was his human tendency to be fooled, frightened, and incapacitated by an opponent's clever tricks. What made Robert E. Lee order a seemingly suicidal charge on the third day at Gettysburg was the human tendency to become overconfident.

It is easy for us as military historians to concentrate so intently on hardware or battlefield maneuver that we forget what we are actually about: the human truths revealed in war rooms and on the battlefield.

10.8 Social and Cultural Papers

It is awe-inspiring to stand in front of the tomb of Napoleon in Paris, to stroll among the notable names in Poets' Corner at Westminster Abbey in London, or to view the monuments in the Valley of the Kings near Luxor in Egypt. These famous places remind us of the lives of famous people. On the other hand, more than a few of us delight in wandering through old, crumbling cemeteries. We do so, not out of morbid curiosity or the lure of the macabre, but because the headstones with old, unusual names and birth and death dates from previous centuries take us into the past and conjure images of long ago. We know what Napoleon did. The life and work of Geoffrey Chaucer is not a great mys-tery. When we see, however, a grave marker that reads "Reuben Schumacher, B. May 6, 1803, D. Feb. 19, 1854," we begin to wonder about Reuben Schumacher. Where was he born? What was his family's business? His occupation? Was he edu-cated? What notable or mundane things did he witness in his life? What political candidates did he support? Was he happy?

Many students consider the field of social and cultural history to be the most entertaining and rewarding in which to work. Here you get to look at the lives of everyday people. It is true that the work of history in the past has cen-tered on kings, battles, generals, treaties, acts of congresses and parliaments, and so forth. How many volumes, for example, were written on the military career of Alexander the Great before someone asked, "What about Hellenistic gender roles?" Authors examined the political causes of the American Civil War long before they began to consider the cultural differences between the North and the South. If history is the study of human experience, interaction, successes, and failures, then social history, perhaps more than any other branch in the dis-cipline, is the high point of our craft.

The areas of interest for social historians seem practically endless. Consider the titles of the four fine articles published in the October 1985 issue of *The Western Historical Quarterly*:

- Susan Armitage, "Women and Men in Western History: A Stereotypical Vision."
- Clark C. Spence, "The Landless Man and the Manless Land."

- William G. Robbins, "The Social Context of Forestry: The Pacific Northwest in the Twentieth Century."
- Robert Oppenheimer, "Acculturation or Assimilation: Mexican Immigrants in Kansas, 1900 to World War II."

Within the parameters of these four articles are interests ranging from gender and ethnic issues to economics and spanning centuries. Social history gives many scholars the opportunity to explore little, dusty corners of history that when studied, prove to be of vital interest, not just to scholars but also to the general reader. In other words, these articles are as fun to research as they are to read, and vice versa.

Years ago, a bright young woman took a course entitled Civil War and Reconstruction. A history major, she had enrolled in the class not because of an enduring love of the American Civil War, but rather to satisfy graduation requirements. During spring break, she spent much of her vacation time researching period documents at the University of Texas at Austin, trying to prepare herself to grind out the usual term paper assignment. At first, she visited the library grudgingly. But one afternoon she discovered a diary left by a soldier who had been hanged as a spy in Tennessee. The pathos of the diary entries intrigued her, and the more she read the more she found she could not leave the story alone.

Most of her classmates that semester were wading through the multivolumed *Official Records of the War of the Rebellion*, the collection of primary sources historians usually consult when researching Civil War topics. This woman had discovered a much more personal, intimate view of the war than the customary battle communiqués written back and forth between the commanders on the scene. The paper she wrote using material from the diary was excellent. She read it at the annual meeting of the Southwestern Social Sciences Association that year in Dallas, and she continued to research her topic into graduate school.

Diaries and letters are gold mines of possibilities for students interested in the personal side of history, because they offer opportunities to examine the way real people have faced and handled life's problems. If in your research you stumble onto such treasures, you will be lucky. On the other hand, you do not have the luxury of simply transcribing or reprinting the documents. You must read and evaluate them, decide what portions of them you need to use, then weave the appropriate parts into a story and a meaningful assessment.

On the following pages, you will see two items. The first is a transcription of one of the pages from the actual diary of E. S. Dodd, the convicted spy. Then you will see an excerpt from the paper written by the student, Karen Martin. Note Ms. Martin's deft analysis of material in the diary, in which she is not content merely to recreate Dodd's story but freely speculates on the possible meanings of the diary's entries. Elias Dodd was not in a glamorous position of command. Until Ms. Martin discovered his diary, he was one of the many nameless, faceless soldiers who participated in America's internecine conflict in the 1860s. Reading his diary, however, is an invaluable tool that can help provide us with a clearer understanding of the deep, inner, personal turmoil that lay beneath the facade of the War of the Rebellion. That is what social history is all about.

Transcription of Excerpt from

Dodd Diary

April

Friday 10th I was very sick last night & hardly able to ride this morning. Command left today, got to Leb…

…anon at daylight. Dr. Hill could not get the medicine for me but gave me a pass to return to the wagons, near McMinnville. I came out to Mr. Bafass and staid all night Saturday 11th. I felt better this morning but very weak. Francis came over this morning or evening. George Tracy was over in the morning, I believe. Sunday 12th rained last night very pleasant this morning. I remained quiet today. 3 or 4 soldiers came by, found that our Brigade had come back [unclear] Spring Crick. Monday 13th My mule taken scratches or something else badly. Cannot ride her, pretty day today. Aunt Nancy came over this evening. Tuesday 14th rained last night again & cleared off this morning. I remained quiet today rained again tonight. Wednesday 15th was misty & damp this morning. I fixed up & went up to Mrs. Larpley's [?] bidding the folks good by at Mr. Bafass's I found the way…

pretty easy. Killed a squirrel & took dinner with them.

Excerpt, Karen Martin

There are three main areas in which he leaves much room for doubt. In situations where Dodd is speaking of towns or people, and these names are quite long, he abbreviates the word by printing only the first letter of the word. This practice is common for him, especially when the elongated form of the word is immediately preceding the abbreviation. But in two special instances, Dodd speaks of someone whose name is abbreviated to one letter, but the elongated form is not mentioned. The first one is a person referred to as "A." There are two names mentioned that both begin with an "A," but both names are short to normal in length and do not need an abbreviation. The person 'tA,' is only mentioned a few times, and no other names beginning with the letter "A" are in close proximity. The second of the two abbreviations is perhaps the most puzzling. The letter "D" is mentioned early in the diary, and not mentioned again until the middle of the diary, with no I'D.' word in the vicinity either time, or anywhere in between. At one point "A" and "D" are mentioned together, but there is no information that would reveal their true identity. The second area Dodd leaves open for speculation is his mention of "papers" and "information." "Papers" can mean cigarette papers or writing papers, even newspapers. But his use of the word information would influence some doubt about the innocence of those *"papers."*

11 Biographies and Oral History

11.1 Biographies

11.1.1 An Overview

A biography, of course, is a narrative and/or analytical account of the life of someone. These may range from a multivolume opus on the life of a former monarch or president to your own grandmother. Whether the subject of the biography is famous or obscure, the person was (or is) a human being, and that alone makes it fascinating and worth doing. Indeed, some of the most hard-to-put-down biographical reading concerns common, everyday, "just-plain-folks."

Biographies are fun to write for at least three reasons. First, they are relatively easy to research. Unless you choose an obscure Medieval Norse raider or Byzantine potentate, your sources are probably near enough to be easily accessible. If your biographical subject is one of your own family members, your sources will be very accessible, and if that family member is still alive, you will have the opportunity to supplement your other research with a first-hand interview.

Second, the life of someone unfolds in a fairly clear, straightforward narrative. This is probably the easiest kind of historical writing to do, because the story almost tells itself. What you must do as the conveyor of the story is to bring it to life with effective organization, clever use of anecdotal material, and a meaningful, succinct assessment to encapsulate the whole.

Third, you will find yourself becoming emotionally involved in the life of the person you are researching. Whether your subject is a grandparent, your favorite aunt, or an obscure native American leader who has been dead for over a century, the deeper you delve into that life, the more meaning it will acquire. You will become, in a way, "friends" with the person.

You are probably astute enough to realize that herein lies a pitfall. The better you come to know your subject as a human being and the more "alive" the person becomes to you, the harder it will be for you to view him or her with objectivity. You may find yourself wanting to protect your person from reputational damage by simply "forgetting" to include less-than-admirable material. We have all read biographies that seem to glorify—almost deify—the subject. This was particularly true of historical and biographical writing during the height of nineteenth-century nationalist fervor.

In the current climate of revisionism and "political correctness," it is almost expected to write from the opposite point of view. Those who write biographies now must take an automatic adversarial point of view toward the subject, find and bring out as much "dirt" as possible, and paint a decidedly unflattering portrait of the subject. Those who do this are called "hard-hitting investigators," while those who do not are dismissed as sycophants.

The truth is, you should refrain from both extremes. While you should not seek to exalt a person by hiding the facts, you should not seek to destroy her or him either. If you find yourself "seeking" to do either, then chances are you have an agenda, and your ability to write objective history is in question! Research the facts, then tell the story—as is!

11.1.2 The Size and Scope of a Biography

This could be a problem. It took Carl Sandburg three volumes to tell the story of Abraham Lincoln, while Douglas Southall Freeman required four volumes to give us Robert E. Lee! If you begin to think that a similar Herculean effort is required of you, it could sour your desire to be a writer of history. How can you as a college or graduate student be expected to render the entire life of someone in a few typewritten pages? The truth is that it cannot be done. You must find ways to limit the size and scope of your biography, and there are a variety of ways to do so.

Limiting by Time

One of the most common ways to limit the scope of a narrative is to confine the inclusive dates to a more manageable proportion. If your subject lived from 1795 until 1866, you do not necessarily have to report on every activity in each of those years. Refine the scope of your study, for example, to the 1830s and explore how the policies of the Jacksonians affected your subject in particular. Instantly, you have released yourself from an overwhelming responsibility by reducing the proportions of your study. Do you feel better yet? (Hint: In this class or writing seminar, focus on the 1830s. Next semester, shift your study to the same subject in the 1840s. Before many semesters have passed, you will have the basis for several chapters of a master's thesis or doctoral dissertation!)

If you want to research and write about a particular American congressman, you could focus on his or her college years, on early pre-Washington campaigns, or on the actual years spent in the House chamber. If the scope needs to be refined further, you could focus on your subject's first campaign or her or his role in the passage of a particular bill.

Limiting by Place

Suppose, for example, that your subject is a World War II veteran, who saw action in several major campaigns in the Pacific theater of the war. If he was present at the invasions of Saipan, Iwo Jima, and Okinawa, you have the option of choosing one of those adventures and focusing on that one alone. By making such a choice, you have already cut the length of your task by two-thirds.

Limiting by Association

You could also limit the scope of your study by connecting your subject with a particular event, trend, or phenomenon. If you are studying, for example, the career of Senator Sam Ervin of North Carolina, you could focus exclusively on his role as chairman of the Select Committee investigating the Watergate matter. You could direct a study of Andrew Jackson toward the formation of his attitudes toward Native Americans.

Family Members

Investigating a family patriarch or matriarch can be a rewarding experience; in fact, we think that you should do so just because it is important, regardless of whether it ever becomes a paper you submit for a grade. Older Americans have fascinating stories to tell, and when they leave us, their precious stories and perspectives will go with them. After a funeral has concluded is a bad time to think about wanting to record a person's recollections. This century has already seen an enormous sweep of history. Just think: It is possible for the same person to have been present at Kitty Hawk to watch the Wright brothers' first successful powered flight and to have been watching television that summer of 1969 when Neil Armstrong stepped into the moon. We urge you to sit down with a tape recorder and that older person sometime and simply chat about the past. You will be surprised how quickly the time passes, and you will not be sorry you did!

11.2 Oral History

In 1918, historian Ulrich Bonnell Phillips published American Negro Slavery, a landmark study of the nature of the South's "peculiar institution." In his book, Phillips asserted, among other things, that slavery was not reprehensible but benign, that slaveholders treated their black "property" with care and kindness, and that blacks themselves did not resent the circumstances of their enslavement. Phillips based his assertions on what he considered to be solid research: He had scoured diaries, journals, and other "primary source" records left by white ante-bellum slaveholders and their overseers. Because his theses were carefully documented, they were rarely challenged, settled comfortably into the historical community, and were taught as fact over the next three decades.

During the Great Depression of the 1930s, the Federal Writers' Project, a subagency of the Works Progress Administration, commissioned historians to interview older black Americans, many of whom had been slaves early in their lives and who had first-hand knowledge of the realities of their past situation. The picture these former slaves painted of the institution was vastly different from the one created by those white records and perpetuated by Ulrich Phillips. The growing awareness of this version set historians' pens and typewriters in motion once again, and works by Kenneth Stampp, Eugene Genovese, and Stanley Elkins, among others, changed forever the way Americans view this regrettable part of their past. Such is the importance and power of first-hand testimony—of the actual eye-witness to history.

Oral history is not new; in fact, it is the oldest form of transmitting the past to the present and future. Details of the legendary Trojan War, for example, were handed from bard to Greek bard through centuries until one (or more) of them, traditionally known as Homer, recorded them in the *Iliad.* Other societies— Gaelic, Mandinka, and Lakota, to name but three—have employed similar historical methods and bestow great honor upon learnéd and talented individuals capable of remembering remote details from remote ages.

There are many Americans alive at this time who have vivid recollections of previous decades of our own history. Many remember what times were really like during the Depression. Others may recall how they felt as they landed on the beaches at Normandy or left home for the first time to go to work in factories geared for full war production. Some may remember the end of World War One, the presidency of Theodore Roosevelt, or even life in a sod house in Indian or Oklahoma Territories. These people and their rich memories are a precious commodity—a true national resource. They are also a dwindling resource, and the passing of each and every older American is the irretrievable loss of knowledge. Every American family has a patriarch or matriarch who is a treasure house of recollections, if someone has the foresight, determination, and time to capture these memories before it is too late. No story is too small or insignificant. One need not have "rubbed shoulders" with presidents, senators, and Supreme Court justices to have a valuable contribution to make. In fact, it is often the seemingly mundane stories that will prove to be the most fascinating. How was ice preserved on the plains of turn-of-the century Nebraska? What did city dwellers do to stay cool during hot summer days in New York or Detroit? What was the job of a radio operator on board a PBM Mariner in World War II?

The Interview

The task of recording oral history obviously centers around an interview with a person whose story or stories should not be lost. This procedure is neither as daunting or as simple as you might suppose. On one hand, this will prove to be one of the most fun, engaging activities you will perform in the field of history. Once the ice is broken, you will find yourself drawn more and more deeply into the life of your subject. Hours may pass without your awareness of time's passing. On the other hand, proper preparation is essential. Failure to acquire a sufficient base knowledge before the interview will produce an awkward, superficial, and mundane reward.

Perhaps you know of an older person whose recollections should be preserved. If so, there are a few steps you should take to insure a successful interview.

1. *Establish a rapport.* Ask some preliminary questions in an informal setting, such as a family get-together, church picnic, or other relaxed situation. You need not be in a hurry to collect every piece of information at this stage of the game. What you need to do now is to become comfortable with the person to whom you wish to speak. Of course, if this is a close friend or family member, this relationship will have been established long ago. You also want to place in your subject's mind the idea that you are sincerely interested.

2. *Become as knowledgeable as possible.* After this initial contact, investigate as much as possible about the stories your person might tell. This will provide you with a reservoir of knowledge from which you can draw additional questions during the interview—questions you may not have planned to ask. For example, say you have a great uncle who was wounded during the 1945 assault on Okinawa in the Pacific. Perhaps you are not a military or World War II "buff." You will need to do some advance reading on subjects such as the nature, strategy, and tactics employed by the armed forces in the Pacific theater of the war, the campaign for Okinawa, the handling of wounded soldiers by medical units, and so forth. Armed with this basic informational resource, you will ask better questions, you will make your subject feel more at ease talking to you, and your interview will prove to be more than a mere chat. It will be a fascinating and useful piece of history.

3. *Be sensitive.* Some people are hesitant to talk about their own past for a variety of reasons—all of them good reasons. Some may not wish to talk at all. Most older Americans love to tell stories about their past, because it gives them a chance to reminisce. We all enjoy that. Others, however, may have painful memories that they may not wish to confront. Veterans who may have experienced the horror of intense combat situations very often do not wish to discuss the matter, period. If this is the case with your prospective interview subject, start over. Your history assignment is not worth antagonizing or hurting someone. Sometimes, an initial "no" answer may evolve into a "maybe," then to a "yes," if you are patient.

4. *Be aware of cultural differences.* The free and open divulgence of the past is not always practiced in some cultures, and many may have certain protocol that must be observed. Native Americans, for example, may feel "used" by granting you an interview, not because of anything you might have done, but because of centuries of having been manipulated by previous generations of white

Americans. (It is a good idea, by the way, to present your prospective native subject with a small gift—a cantaloupe, for instance. The size or price of the gift does not matter; it is their tradition, and the fact that you care enough to try—to "meet them half-way"—will let them know that you consider their dignity to be important.) It is surprising how well we humans respond when our dignity is left intact. No one wants to be—or should be—considered an anthropological specimen to be studied.

5. *Brainstorm ahead of time.* Do not walk into your interview cold. By the time you arrive, you should have fortified yourself with the essential background information necessary to ask meaningful questions. You also should have prepared a list of things you want to know more about. Your interview will probably follow your subject's chronologically. Your uncle's Okinawa story did not begin with his beach landing. You may wish to ask him a little about his own background, his recollections about the early days of the war, his enlistment, training, unit, and preparations for the assault, as well as the battle itself and what happened to him thereafter. After you have organized your questions into basic narrative or topical categories, anticipate some of the directions these answers could go and make sublists of additional, follow-up questions you could ask. Many of these will suggest themselves as you probe deeper into the interview and the process take on more of the feel of a normal conversation. Do not think that you need to use every question you have written; be flexible enough to allow the interview to flow where it will. Do not be afraid to ask questions that will require an opinion from your subject. In other words, along with the "What happened next?" questions, sprinkle in a few of the, "How did you feel about that?" "What was the general mood at that point?" or "What did your buddies have to say?" variety.

6. *Make specific arrangements.* Leave nothing to chance—or misunderstanding. Arrange a definite time and place for the interview, keeping both the comfort and convenience of your volunteer in mind. A schoolroom desk will not be as nice or as conducive to heart-felt revelation as someone's favorite easy chair—unless the person has a preference not to use that chair or that room. Your person is already doing you a great favor. Make the doing of that favor as painless as possible. Be punctual and have everything you need when you arrive. You do not want to be late, making some poor soul wait a half-hour to talk to you. Neither do you want to have to ask for pencil or paper—or to discover that your tape recorder needs batteries or to have to fish around for the right side of the right cassette. Try to have extra batteries and several fresh, blank tapes. Label them with a marker on a piece of masking tape. You do not want to record over an earlier part of the conversation! If you are interviewing several people, you will want to see at a glance what tape is whose story.

7. *Be sensitive during the interview.* Just because you are twenty years old and may be in superb physical shape, your ninety-year-old friend may not be capable of sitting comfortably for a three-hour marathon taping session. As the interview deepens and intensifies, this is often hard to remember. Several sessions may be necessary. It may be necessary even to truncate an interview for the sake of your subject. Simple courtesy must override your needs. You should remember to ask

often during the interview if your volunteer is tired. "Would you like to continue?" "Do you need to take a break?" "Is that enough for today?" We can offer suggestions here, but we cannot think for you during the interview. You must retain your savvy and common sense. "Play it by ear." It may happen that one recollection of the "good old days" could lead to a flood of additional ones, and you might have to find a polite way to end the interview without offending your friend. In other cases, particularly with combat veterans, it may take an hour of preliminary questions to provide the time necessary for "loosening up"—for getting deeper into the story.

8. *Be profuse in your thankfulness.* As we have said, this person has been kind enough to share an important part of life with you—maybe parts never revealed to anyone before. Especially if the interview has become intense or heated, you do not want to click off the recorder, say a curt "Thanks," and walk away. Give the atmosphere time to cool by slowly and subtly directing the conversation to less passionate areas. Follow the usual courtesies. Send a card or a small gift as a token of thanks, and keep your friend up to date on the progress of the assignment.

Now What?

Congratulations! Your interview is finished, and you have three ninety-minute cassette tapes filled with some of the most interesting stuff you have ever heard! Your history professor, unfortunately, would like something in writing—something more useful than three ninety-minute cassette tapes. Your question now has become, "How do I transfer all this great information to paper?" If you are a very fast keyboardist, you could play back the interview and type each and every word onto a diskette. The resulting hard copy will require hours of labor and be dozens of pages long. For all the good it will do, perhaps you should just submit the tapes themselves. There may be, however, an easier, more efficient, and more satisfying way.

It is a good idea to keep your pencil moving during the conversation. If you have made a written sketch of the flow of the interview, it will help you later to find and organize the wealth of material you have collected. It is also a good idea to label each tape as completely you can when you have finished. If your veteran uncle, for example, made a memorable comment about the medical care at evacuation units, locate the tape that contains the "battle" or "postbattle" sequences. Fast-forward past the landing but not past the return stateside. If your recorder or play-back unit has a reliable counter, use it to mark the place on the tape where you may need to return again to find additional details. (Be sure to record the number on your note pad. Also, do not forget to reset the counter when you look for something on a different tape.)

You will obviously need to edit. You will remember from the interview (since you were there) that your subject's comments tended to fall into three categories: background or "setup" material, interesting, "heart-of-the-matter" revelations, and transitional areas. All your friend's valuable statements are there on tape. You need not feel disrespectful if you do not use it all, and you may return to the well to quench additional curiosities in the future. For the time being, however, you must make painful decisions, not so much about what to include, but what you must omit. Some of the preliminaries may not help to establish context or contribute to the story. Include what is necessary to frame the rest of the narrative.

Common sense should help you make decisions about what to omit from the main story. The transitional elements should be included only if they provide essential transitions. This function can be summarized in a paraphrase in your own prose, enabling you to consolidate a huge amount of time and space into a single paragraph. Leave this option open and look for ways to use it.

Putting your interview into a workable form is not your final step. For the sake of your readers, you cannot begin with the first word of the conversation. You must establish context! Plan to begin your presentation with some introductory material of your own composition. This will enable you to suggest a possible thesis and to provide your readers with the same historical framework you may have needed when you began your project. Offer some brief explanations concerning the Pacific war, the Okinawa campaign, the Marine Corps, and so forth.

For many of the same reasons you cannot begin with the interview, you also cannot end with the interview. You cannot simply come to a convenient stopping place and quit. You must theorize, summarize, and cauterize. To make an effective presentation, you must begin and end with both context and perspective.

WRITING ASSIGNMENT   *Oral History*

Think of a friend or relative whose life story needs to be recorded. Following the procedures detailed above, plan, conduct, and present an interview. Remember: Your written presentation should contain these elements:

I.   Prose *introduction* with thesis and historical overview.
II.   Chronological *narrative*
      A.   Events preceding the main issue
      B.   The central, climactic feature of the story
      C.   Personal thoughts and opinions
III. *Summary* and *assessment*

---

12 Having Fun with History: Short Writing Assignments

12.1 The Historical Letter Home

One of the most rewarding and entertaining types of historical documentary evidence you will encounter as a researcher is the "letter home." Before there were telephones, humans were forced to rely on writing to transmit information and ideas across distance and time. Without realizing it, past writers wrote not only to their intended recipient, but also to us. We thank them! Without these primary source gems, we would not know many of the details we know about events both great and mundane. Written speeches, acts of national congresses and parliaments, and the edicts of monarchs and popes are certainly valuable, but the intimate, personal glimpses of the same events add a more human dimension to the human story.

Most of us who care about that sort of thing, know the essentials, for example, of the ebb and flow of the battle of Gettysburg. Terms such as "Little Round Top" and "Pickett's Charge" have become permanent components of our vocabulary. All the current monographs in a library, however, cannot convey to us the essence of the horror like the single, heart-wrenching letter of a Union or Confederate soldier, writing home to his family about the terrifying things he had seen during these three hellish days in July of 1863.

We all have read books and seen movie and television interpretations of the nineteenth-century westward migration of thousands of Americans to Oregon, California, Utah, and other destinations. Our knowledge, however, is often limited to chronologies, the names of famous scouts, or simply a variety of lines across a map. What was it like to be adrift in an ocean of grass on the plains of what would someday be Nebraska? To pass endless hours of tedium and to preserve their sanity, many intrepid pioneer women wrote frequent letters home to loved ones. These dispatches relate the grueling day-by-day realities and hard-ships faced ten or fifteen miles at a time as they made their way toward the set-ting sun. Examine the following excerpt from one woman's experience:

> I never shal see eney of you eny More in this world. We Are Almost three thousand Miles apart. I would like to see My sweet littl Ann And Homer And the other two but I never Shall. . . . And you never Will see Hiram. . . .Hiram drounded in [the] Plat River At the Mouth of Dear Krick. He went Aswiming with some other boys of the Compeny that we Trailed with And he swum Acrost the river and the Water run very fast And he could not reach this side. The young Men tried to save him but he [had the Cramp] And Could swim no more. And they Said o hiram do swim but he said I cannot swim eney More. And one young Man took A pole And started to him And the water ran so fast that he thought he Could not swim eney more so he returned And left him to his fate. And the other boys Called to him and said O hiram O swim. And he said o my god I cannot eney More. They said that he went down in the water seven or eight times before he drounded. And then he said o my god O lord gesus receive My Soul for I am no More. Oyes I think that if ever A young Man went to their lord gesus that he Did for he Always Was a very good boy and that [all who] knew him liked him. So you know All about Hiram's death now. So you need not ask eneything About him eney More for it will not do us eney Good to trouble ourselves About him eney More. It has Almost kild Me but I have to bear it. And if we Are good perhapes then we can meete him in heven. (OCTOBER 10, 1850)

In this assignment, you will become a history-maker yourself, living through a past time or event and creating a primary source. It will require con-siderable knowledge of the moment you intend to record—and a leap of the imagination.

WRITING ASSIGNMENT   *Writing a Letter Home*

1. Choose an event or period in time you would like to relate.
2. Read as much as you can about that historical moment so your description will be his-torically accurate rather than fanciful. (You do not want Jeanne d'Arc, for example, to be a participant in World War I.)
3 Imagine yourself in that particular situation, seeing and living what you would have seen and lived if you had actually been there. Allow yourself to become emotionally involved in the situation. Those who witness ghastly battles or endure a six-month ordeal generally do not remain emotionally detached.
4. Write a letter home to a family member or friend. Describe what you witnessed and experienced. Feel free to let your emotions show through the facts. Don't forget to include lots of concrete detail: sounds, smells, tastes, and textures, as well as sights.

12.2 The Time Machine

The previous assignment, the "Letter Home," required you to transport yourself back through time in order to see and record a moment in history as if you were actually a participant in that moment. This exercise will involve "time travel" as well, but in the opposite direction. Rather than taking yourself backward in time, your research and writing will bring a famous person forward to the present. This will require a thorough acquaintance with the individual you would like to introduce to these times. It will need honesty and objectivity. You will find that the assignment will test your ability to remain neutral as a historian. It will demonstrate the pitfalls inherent in writing about the past through the lens of the present. Consider these examples:

1. *Sacagawea*: What would this Shoshoni woman think of today's development of the northern Plains and Rocky Mountains? Would she be glad that she helped conduct Lewis and Clark across the Continental Divide in 1805?

2. *Thomas Jefferson*: If he had reservations about the role of government under the new Constitution of 1787, what would he think of the size of the federal government today? The members of today's Democratic party consider themselves to be the philosophical heirs of the sage of Monticello. But where would Jefferson place himself in relation to today's political spectrum? Would the versatile Virginian consider himself a Democrat or a Republican? Suppose you could drive Jefferson from Monticello to Washington. What might he say to Congress? What advice would he offer to the current president?

3. *Booker T. Washington*: What would this remarkable American have to say about the progress of the Civil Rights movement since the 1950s? Would he be satisfied with the position of blacks today? Delighted? Disappointed? Would he agree or disagree with the direction pursued by today's black leadership? Would he support continuing affirmative action programs?

Obviously, there are some traps in this exercise that will strain your scholarly objectivity. It will be tempting to superimpose your own ideas, predispositions, and agendas upon your subject. You may be passionate about protecting the environment, and you may "want" Sacagawea to believe as you do—but would she? Likewise, Thomas Jefferson must think like Thomas Jefferson, not like you. If you are a Democrat yourself, there will be a tendency to respond, "Yes, he would be a Democrat today," just because you want it to be that way. But would that be true?

WRITING ASSIGNMENT	*The Time Machine*

1. Choose a person from history whom you would like to introduce to the present.
2. Read as much as you can about that person. Get into the mind of the person so that your transfer will be as historically accurate as possible.

3. You may present the results of your research in several ways:
    a. You could make it an interview. You, as a reporter, could interview the subject to get his or her reaction to certain questions.
    b. You could write a newspaper story about the visit.
    c. You might write your paper from the viewpoint of the historical time traveler, perhaps in the form of diary entries about what he or she was seeing, being careful to include personal viewpoints and reactions.

12.3 The Luminous Detail

You will find this assignment an interesting combination of literary and historical study. In a series of articles published in 1911 and 1912, the poet Ezra Pound, himself a student of history, discussed a process of historical inquiry which he named "the method of the luminous detail." The method involved a search for details in history which, if apprehended imaginatively, would disclose to the student more about the particular time period being studied than do the traditional forms of research. "Certain facts," wrote Pound, "give one a sudden insight into circumjacent conditions, into their causes, their effects, into sequence, and law." Close scrutiny of such crucial moments allows for a vivid apprehension of the contemporary environment. Pound gives an example:

> [W]hen in Burkhardt we come upon a passage: "In this year the Venetians refused to make war upon the Milanese because they held that any war between buyer and seller must prove profitable to neither," we come upon a portent, the old order changes, one conception of war and of the State begins to decline.
> The Middle Ages imperceptibly give ground to the Renaissance. A ruler owning a State and wishing to enlarge his possessions could, under one regime, in a manner opposed to sound economy, make war; but commercial sense is sapping this regime. In the history of the development of civilization . . . we come upon such interesting detail. (1973, 20)

In the excerpt he quoted, Pound focused on a small sentence with big implications. Many, if not most, readers tend to breeze right through such passages, and the matter-of-fact subtlety of the prose renders the larger picture difficult to discern.

This exercise employs Pound's notion of the luminous detail to develop your ability to think for yourself as you sift documents for clues to the life of the past. To complete the task, you must read, to be sure, but with a different purpose. In most of the academic reading you do, your attention to the details in the text is normally employed to provide you with the larger picture. This time, you will look more closely at the details embedded in the text, trying to find the implied picture. The example shows that Pound already possessed a fundamental understanding of the shift in state priorities from the Middle Ages through the Renaissance. What he noticed in the Burkhardt excerpt did not necessarily tell him anything new. Rather, it gave him a sudden, vital apprehension of a historical moment in which the way societies viewed themselves and their neighbors underwent a crucial change. The detail Pound discovered appealed not only to his intellect but to his imagination—and the imagination is a formidable tool to bring to bear on any historical question.

In the same way, this assignment will train you to bring your powers of observation to bear, imaginatively, on a historical document or literary work. You will read between the lines to locate what is sometimes called the "subtext." Can you, for example, spot the political theory known as the "Social Contract" in the Mayflower Compact, the Declaration of Independence, or the Preamble to the United States Constitution? What clues can the Canterbury Tales provide about economic life or gender relations in medieval Britain? What could an excerpt from Andrew Carnegie's Wealth tell about Gilded Age priorities? Was Carnegie a Social Darwinist?

WRITING ASSIGNMENT   *The Luminous Detail*

1. Choose a brief historic document or literary work. (Your instructor could assign one.) You should try to find one that is not readily apparent. For example, the Seneca Falls Declaration is very clear about its intent and its message. A subtext may be difficult to find.
2. Peruse your example carefully, keeping in mind the times and circumstances in which it was written. Why was the document written?
3. Try to locate subtexts—the "luminous details"—which could provide fresh insight into that era. What does the excerpt say about its times? You might read the excerpt several times, looking each time for a different type of information, details, for example, about the ways in which that particular society and time viewed science or business or fashion or the rights of children.
4. Write a brief essay identifying a luminous detail and the fresh view it provides.

12.4 The Art Gallery

When most people visit an art gallery, they stroll leisurely past paintings and sculptures, pausing now and then when something pleases them or catches their eye. Rarely do they linger over any one piece for any length of time. In a huge museum such as the Louvre in Paris or the Uffizi in Florence, there is such an amazing display of art treasures that the casual viewer may feel overwhelmed by it all. Once in a while, you see a dedicated art student who seems to be examining every brush stroke on a canvas, but the vast majority of visitors, pressed for time, can do little more than determine quickly which works they immediately like and which leave them cold.

If history were a museum, it would be far bigger and richer than all the other museums in the world put together because, among other things, it would contain every work of art ever produced. As a visitor to this museum, a historian cannot merely stroll through its galleries; he or she must move slowly, looking closely at evidence. Whether you are researching pre-Columbian lithic material, Vatican codices, the diaries of colonial New England women, or Watergate-era White House tapes, you are bringing all your powers of detection and discernment to bear to try to discover hidden, imbedded clues that could open new understanding about the past. It may be that dozens of other eyes have scanned what you are seeing, but perhaps you will see some tiny detail that has escaped notice before. Sound implausible? It is not. It happens all the time. That is why history books are still being published on subjects you might consider worn-out. Modern historians are still discovering new things, even in old materials, providing new ways of looking at old stories. The point is, they must look closely!

In this assignment you are to focus on a work of art, studying it to see what clues it might have to offer about the person who produced it and the times in which it was produced. Different artifacts tell different stories. An elongated iron statuette may reveal things about Etruscan economics and values. Grave markers from colonial New England can give us insight into the hopes, dreams, and fears of the Puritan founders. We scrutinize literature in similar ways. The words of Andrew Carnegie say something different about America's industrial age than those of Jack London or Stephen Crane.

For these same reasons and with the same results in mind, we can examine closely great (or not so great) works of art. There are messages deeper than the surface of the canvas in a painting, and just as no two historians will agree on the interpretation of a certain historical "fact," most art historians do not share the same interpretation of the meaning of a painting. Botticelli's Birth of Venus has something to say to us about Botticelli—about Renaissance Italy—about the Renaissance itself. Edward Hicks' Peaceable Kingdom has things to say about a wealth of subjects. So do the lithographs of Currier and Ives, the flowers of Georgia O'Keeffe, or the large "concepts" of Cristo. This assignment will help you develop your ability to see beyond the surface, beyond the obvious.

WRITING ASSIGNMENT   *Describing a Work of Art*

1. Find a work of art that you like. It may be a famous treasure from a famous place, a hidden treasure in a local gallery, or one of your aunt's best watercolors.
2. Make a preliminary visual observation of the item. Make written notes about as many of the attributes as you can discern, not simply brush work, perspective, or other techniques, but also things about the painting that could give you clues or insight into the mind and motives of the artist. (For example, why did Jan van Eyck decide to make the woman pregnant in his painting Giovanni Arnolfini and His Wife?)
3. Make preliminary guesses about your painting. When do you think it was painted? Where?

4. Consult a library. Find books on the art of your chosen place and time period. If your painting is not actually present in any book (your aunt's watercolors may not be, though we agree that they should be), try to find similar looking examples so you can cross-reference.

5. Write the results of your examination and investigation. Tell what you believe the painting says about the times in which it was created. Why do you think so? How will this painting and your explanation of its message help us to gain clearer insight into the social, political, economic, or religious climate of its era?

12.5 An Archaeological Paper: Describing an Artifact

12.5.1 Archaeology as a Subdiscipline of History

Because archaeology as an academic discipline is often considered a natural science (like astronomy, botany, and chemistry) as opposed to a social science, there are some who might say that a discussion of it here would be out of place. If you consider that the primary goal of archaeology is to supplement our knowledge of the past, which, in turn, enhances our understanding of ourselves, then its kinship with history becomes clear. Perhaps there is no discipline better suited than archaeology to illustrate that no study exists in a vacuum, independent from other studies; they are all interdependent.

History is the written record of human existence. As we discussed in a previous chapter, there are some areas of that story that are more completely documented than others. There are gaps in the historical record, usually (though not always) found somewhere near the beginning, as human beings were only starting to conceive of the idea of giving permanence to their thoughts, business transactions, and deeds through writing. Where missing bits of the human story exist, we must try to supply them through other means. Historians often make guesses, suppositions, and theories to explain what may have happened. They also rely on archaeology.

Archaeologists evolve and practice techniques to recover those missing puzzle pieces. They also try to make historical sense of the thousands of fragments they find. These clues left by the past are grouped into several categories. For example, immovable structures such as the pyramids of Egypt or the walls of Troy are called *features*. These must be examined where they are (*in situ*), because to move them would be to destroy the context that could later provide additional clues to their decipherment. Smaller objects—things produced by human manufacture that can be transported without altering the objects themselves—are known as *artifacts*. Lithic (stone) projectile points—usually called arrowheads—are artifacts. So are lost arks. Petrified trees, grains, and other, non-manipulated substances are called *ecofacts*. Though they have not been changed in any way by the hand of human beings, they nevertheless provide indirect clues used to unravel the hidden mysteries of the past.

The process of archaeology occurs in two places: the field and the laboratory. Field work is by far the best known—and most romanticized—of the arenas of archaeological investigation. This is the place where ancient (or extra-historical) humans inadvertently left cultural remains for later generations to discover. Field techniques, from traditional spade-and-trowel excavations to remote sensing and other high-tech methods, have been developed to make the most efficient use of artifact deposit sites. Once archaeologists have excavated a site, it has been changed forever. Excavation is like a laboratory experiment that can be performed only once. It is very important, therefore, for archaeologists to dig only when necessary and to keep exact written records of what was found and where.

When artifacts have been collected from a site, they then are transported to a laboratory for analysis, cataloging, and preservation. This may be accomplished by a local university or by a privately run archaeological organization. Archaeologists working in a controlled laboratory environment conduct tests to determine the age and composition of an artifact as well as the manufacturing technique used to produce it. The trained eye of an experienced archaeologist can provide the answers to many questions. Is the projectile point "Folsom" or "Clovis?" Was the sherd found at the same strata as other pieces the same age? Direct visual analysis, coupled with knowledge of the context of the find, can provide an artifact with a relative age, but to date it exactly requires more sophisticated and expensive techniques such as "Carbon 14," "Obsidian Hydration," or "Potassium/Argon."

Once archaeologists have performed all relevant tests, they then categorize and catalogue artifacts by any of their various parameters. But this is not the end. The purpose of archaeology is not to fill the basements of university laboratories with thousands of bits of rock, bone, and broken pottery. Some sense must be made of these clues. The final stage of the investigation is publication of the results of the excavation in a scholarly journal. Historical investigation is a team effort. One group of investigators working in New Mexico, for example, might publish the results of a discovery and analysis that could shed light on the questions of another group working in Florida. Publication is our profession's way of keeping up with itself. A journal article is the final stage of one investigation, but it may also be the first stage in another.

Because writing is one of the final results of an archaeological investigation, it is important to know some of the things this writing entails. That is why we have included the procedure in our list of historical papers.

What You Will Find in Archaeological Papers

To illustrate the kinds of things you can expect to find in a typical archaeological paper, we have chosen to outline briefly for you a fine article published in the Fall 1994 issue of the *Bulletin of the Oklahoma Archaeological Society.*

Robert L. Brooks. 1994. "Variability in Southern Plains Village Cultural Complexes: Archaeological Investigations at the Lonker Site in the Oklahoma Panhandle." *Bulletin of the Oklahoma Archaeological Society* 43: 1-27.

Introduction:

During late prehistoric times, the Southern Plains were occupied by societies who produced numerous recognized cultural complexes. These exhibit a set of common characteristics referred to as the Plains Village tradition (Wedel 1961, 168-169). Thousands of sites belonging to the Plains Village tradition have been recorded on the Southern Plains. Because of the many recorded Plains Village sites and their recent formulation (ca. 1,000 to 500 years ago), they provide excellent research opportunities for studying groups ancestral to historic Plains societies.

I.   Cultural Complexes of the Texas and Oklahoma Panhandles

    A.   Antelope Creek Phase

    B.   The Buried City Complex

II.   Description and History of the Lonker Site

III. Environmental Context

IV.   Methodology

V.   Feature Descriptions

VI.   Radiocarbon Dates and Chronological Placement

VII. Cultural Materials Recovered

    A. Chipped Stone Tools

    B. Chipping Debris

    C. Ground Stone

    D. Ceramic Artifacts

    E. Bone Tools

VIII. Biotic Resources

    A. Faunal Remains

    B. Plant Remains

IX.   Interpretive Results

    A. Cultural Historical Relationships

    B. Settlement/Subsistence Structure

Acknowledgments

References

Note how the article presents all the essentials in a logically unfolding pattern. Brooks begins with a general description of the culture being investigated. He then narrows his field geographically, first to the Panhandle region, then to the Lonker site, and then to an actual description of the "look" of the site. Brooks then presents a record of the methods used to excavate the site as well as specifics about how the site was dated. Next, he provides a detailed report of each of the various types of artifacts and ecofacts found at the site. He concludes with an assessment of the possible meaning of the site and an acknowledgment of the people who helped in each phase of the investigation. No historical paper is complete without a list of sources to lend credence to the writer's conclusion, and this article is no exception.

Study the outline carefully. If you are interested in writing a description of the results of a local archaeological investigation such as this one, you would do well to observe the items that should be included. As you probably can tell, the observations Brooks makes in his article did not originate at the keyboard. Careful methods and procedures must be followed at the site to ensure that the excavation will yield results of value and destroy nothing that could aid later researchers. In fact, you should not attempt such an excavation alone. If you suspect that you have discovered a possible site, contact your local, state, or other academic professionals. They will be able to assist you, perhaps even in arranging a dig at the site. Watch carefully during a dig to learn what procedures the professionals follow. Keep in contact with them. When you have garnered sufficient information about the parameters of the site—geographic, topographic, historic, artifactual and ecofactual—organize your materials for writing your own paper. It is possible that one of the academicians you have consulted will write about the excavation, too, but you are welcome to try your hand as well.

Included in the Brooks article are several charts and photographs used to demonstrate the kinds of evidence found at the Lonker site, their frequency of occurrence, contextual information, and so forth. Look at some of these. They also will help you understand what kinds of information should be present in a satisfactory archaeological paper.

12.5.2 Describing an Artifact

In this assignment, you can play the role of an archaeologist. You need no leather jacket or a fedora tilted at a rakish angle. Nor will your activities require the use of a whip or firearms. You will encounter no repulsive, loathsome arachnids or rodents, and your life probably will not be in constant peril. As we have said, the actual work of the archaeologist may, in fact, take you to exotic locales, but it is very likely that the labor there will be tedious and boring—anything but the swashbuckling romanticism of which movies are made.

As you know, an artifact is any human-made object that can be transported away from the site where it was found. A fire pit, for example, cannot be moved; pottery from that hearth may be. It is the task of professional archaeologists not only to find but also to interpret evidence.

That is the nature of this assignment. To begin, find an artifact. This is not as difficult as it sounds. You may live in a region where pre-Columbian projectile points (laypersons often call them "arrowheads") lie in abundance in fields and creek beds. Perhaps you now have a good excuse to visit local antique shops. Maybe your grandparents have an attic or old barn wherein lie an array of mysterious and intriguing gadgets from past decades. Unless you have been raised in the right environment, you may not know, for example, what hay hooks, cream separators, or spoke shaves are just by looking.

Once you have found some relic you cannot identify, study it carefully, making written observations as you do so. Note the dimensions, colors, shapes, and other attributes you see. Does it have moving parts? What relationship do the parts have with each other? Does the artifact show signs of wear at a particular place? When you have completed this preliminary visual investigation, formulate a hypothesis. For what purpose do you think it may have been used? Could it be an agricultural implement of some kind? Is it part of a larger tool or machine?

Once you have begun to imagine a possible use for your artifact, visit the library to try to locate books with pictures that could provide an example of a similar artifact. Archaeologists' opinions are educated guesses. No one knows with certainty what role an artifact played in the lives of the people who used it; we were not there. If we do know, however, that similar artifacts exist whose purpose is relatively well known, we can surmise that the artifact we hold probably had the same raison d'être. In other words, we cross-reference from what we do know to what we do not know. For this reason, for example, an archaeologist studying the wreck of a Bronze Age ship off the coast of Turkey may consult catalogs of Bronze Age pottery styles to try to match the sherds in the wreck with other known examples. The importance of such match-ups is obvious: A careful examination of the attributes of broken amphorae could help to determine when the ship sailed, where its point of origin was, and what its destination may have been. Answering these questions, in turn, might shed new light a healthy, thriving, nonmilitarist commercial life in the eastern Mediterranean long before Athens was a dominant Greek city-state.

WRITING ASSIGNMENT   *Examining an Artifact*

To perform this assignment will require an observant, discerning eye and the ability to make educated guesses. Your job is to write a brief description of any artifact. Here is a summary of the process:

1. Visit an attic, an antique shop, a junk shop, or a flea market. Find a gadget you cannot identify.
2. Make a preliminary visual observation of the item. Make written notes about as many of the attributes as you can discern.
3. Suggest plausible explanations to define the identity of your artifact.
4. Consult a library to try to find books on antiques, tools, old kitchen items—whatever you can find to cross-reference your hypothesis.

5. Write the results of your examination and investigation. Tell what you believe the object is and why you think so.

12.6 Historical Scripts

The Special Purpose of Scripts

You do not need us to tell you that the methods of presenting history are constantly evolving. No longer do the time-honored books and classroom lectures hold a monopoly on the transmission of stories from the past. Historical drama has been with us for millennia, historical fiction for centuries, and film adaptations of historical events for decades. Few people thought twenty years ago that it would be possible some day to drop a shiny plastic disk into a machine, move a little "mouse" around on a pad, and with a few clicks be able to retrieve a whole encyclopedia, complete with sound and video clips of famous events. In the past, visitors to museums had to be content with static displays such as armor, uniforms, dioramas, and a variety of wall displays. Now they expect video presentations and interactive displays.

Some of the most popular motion pictures ever produced have been based on famous lives or events from history. There are cable television channels that broadcast historical films and documentaries twenty-four hours a day. Someone has to prepare the written lines for the actors or narrator to say. Fascination with the past never ends. As the demand grows for quality historical dramatic or video presentations, so will the need for quality historians who know how to tell a story with accuracy and broad audience appeal.

Historical scripts differ from traditional papers. Though the writing of the script must be preceded by the same high degree of sophisticated research, the way in which raw data are transformed into a visual presentation will require a new approach and new skills. Because your audience will not actually read the script that you write, and because most viewers will not use your work as the basis for further research, you will not need to worry about documenting your material. You will not have the luxury of delving into great detail. Your task is to present the facts in a manner that is clear and straightforward, yet alluring and entertaining.

In a way, you must clear your current understanding of the way to prepare a standard research paper. If, for example, you are writing a video script for a museum presentation, you must reduce the wording you employ, and you must keep the entire work brief—usually ranging from two minutes to ten minutes, depending on the application. You must relate every decision about structure or wording to the camera, because every word you create for the narrator to say will be linked to still or moving visual images.

If your project involves drama, you must keep staging and lighting in mind as you write the dialogue. Always, you must decide who your audience will be and direct your work to reach them.

12.6.1 Types of Scripts

The Documentary

If you watch historical programming on one of the cable history channels, or if your history classes in high school or college included the showing of films, you probably have seen a number of documentaries. These productions are geared toward presenting information using visual images to help convey the facts. In other words, *what* the film says is a higher priority than *how* it is said. This does not necessarily mean that the work has to be boring. A typical documentary may not feature a swashbuckling, long-locked Mel Gibson leading a host of rebel Scots against an English army, but with the right degree of creativity, wit, and visual imagery, a documentary can be fascinating and entertaining. Yes, you have seen classroom films that could barely keep you awake. So have we. There are those that make you wonder why anyone would spend the effort to produce them (and you hope that there is no Part Two to watch later).

There are also films that scratch intellectual itches you did not know you had—those whose dry witticisms provide a few school-day chuckles yet leave you wanting to know even more about the subject. The BBC has always been very good at offering such productions. Perhaps you have had the pleasure of seeing "In Search of the Trojan War," hosted by Michael Wood, a BBC documentary series that has urged more than a few viewers toward a life-long fascination with archaeology. Another successful BBC venture featured Alistaire Cook's America, personal interpretations of American history by a superb interpreter of American History! You may have seen other works such as "Eyes on the Prize," offered by PBS. One of the most popular series ever broadcast by PBS was Ken Burns' "The Civil War" which, night after night during its original telecast in 1990, garnered ratings of which the major networks could be envious. Most of these excellent documentary series are available at your local library. If you have not seen them, please do so!

Dramatic Interpretations

Dramatic historical offerings have been around a long time. Many of Shakespeare's plays were based, as you know, on the lives of England's early monarchs. Historical themes have served as the basis for countless novels as well as scores of motion pictures. Some of these present their historical subject as accurately as possible, while others take extensive artistic license. In other words, *how* the film delivers its message is often a higher priority than *what* the message is.

Have you ever enjoyed an historical movie for its action sequences or acting performances but later found yourself wondering how much of its material was fact and how much was fiction? Old westerns from the 1940s and 1950s often fall into this category, as do 1960s World War II movies and those "cast of thousands" biblical epics. How about TV dramas made from historical romance novels? There should be a law . . .

On the other hand, fine historical motion pictures and television miniseries have been released, particularly in the last two decades. It seems that film screenwriters, producers, and directors have taken a more serious approach to historical subjects, becoming as concerned with accuracy as with cinematic effects. Again, the BBC has provided excellent examples through the years. Perhaps you have seen "The Six Wives of Henry VIII" or its companion, "Elizabeth R." Makers of feature films from *A Man Called Horse* to *Tora! Tora! Tora!* have gone to great lengths to make sure even the smallest historical details were correct. Even fictionalized representations of times and events have had memorable examples in the recent past. Who can forget the impact of the television miniseries made of Alex Haley's *Roots* or the splendor of James Michener's *Centennial?* We can forgive the fact that the real name of Jeremiah Johnson was a more mundane John Johnson. Robert Redford's film portrayal of the mountain man was outstanding.

12.6.2 Script Formats

12.6.3 Basic Considerations

Your script may be used to produce a documentary video, or it may be staged to be viewed by an audience. The purpose of your script will determine how you craft it.

Visuals for Your Documentary

A video will need what are called "visuals." These could include photographs, artists sketches, paintings, or, in some cases, live action sequences. As you write a script for a video production, you should keep in mind the basic fact that everything you write will be accompanied by visuals of some kind.

As you write you should suggest the images you have in mind, hopefully photographic or artistic material you know exists. If the producer who receives your script cannot find photos like the ones you have suggested, he or she may have to turn to an artist to render an interpretation of the missing material. This is normally not a problem, but if the artist's final sketches are not worthy of the rest of the script, you may be sorry that you made it necessary to use that artist.

Live Footage

The problems with live footage involve the usual logistical nightmares associated with filming: costuming, locations and scenery, lighting, permissions, and acting. Often, otherwise fine video productions are ruined because a producer or director decided to insert a dramatic sequence with an actor who thinks he is Lawrence Olivier (but is not) or an actress who believes herself to be the next Meryl Streep (and is not). The more "still" images you can offer, the better your production will be.

Still Images

You want the visual images of your video to change often, usually several photos per paragraph of narrative. Some subjects have very few photographs available and a crew must resort to live footage or sketches to keep the visual interest flowing. When Ken Burns produced his PBS series on the Civil War, he had at his disposal literally thousands of authentic photographs by Matthew Brady and other artists of his day. When a photo needed to be "stretched"—in other words, when it needed to be kept on camera for a relatively lengthy time— Burns would pan in slowly to capture a particular detail of the shot, or he would pan across the whole image from side to side, giving the still photo vitality.

In other words, Burns began with a wealth of visual material and made masterful use of all of it. If your video concerns a subject such as Norse explorations along the coast of Canada, you will have no photographic resources and few, if any, artists' renderings of the events. If your production budget does not permit you to travel to faraway museums or to the Canadian coast itself, perhaps you should select another topic for your effort. Location shooting usually requires elaborate and expensive gear, a knowledgeable crew, and the production facilities to bring everything together into a serious final product.

Drama

You may think you are unfamiliar with dramatic technique, but that is not so. If you took any kind of English or literature class in high school, you probably read though a play or two, perhaps one by Shakespeare. You are basically aware, therefore, of the components needed to write a dramatic script: cast of characters, acts, scenes, entrances and exits, and plot. This is one of the major distinctions between documentaries and dramas. When writing a script for a documentary video, you need not worry about the story, because it will generally tell itself. This is not the case with drama. You must come up with a story that connects in some plausible way with the actual historical narrative. You must also worry about finding the actors who can do justice to your work!

Glossary of History Terms

A.D. - From the Latin *anno domino* (literally "in the year of the Lord"); refers to historical time since the birth of Christ

ancient history - Deals with the period of recorded history from the beginning of civilizations through the rise and fall of near-eastern empires. (C. 3,000 B.C. to c. 300 B.C.

anthropology - A large, comprehensive field of study whose many and various disciplines are devoted to the study of human beings

archaeology - Supplies missing pieces in the study of the past by examining evidences of human activity, either before the historical record began or in the gaps within the record

archive - A repository of historical documents, records, or information

archivist - An historian specially trained in the persecution, organization, storage, and retrieval of historical records

artifact - Any movable item that demonstrates evidence of use or manipulation by humans at any time

B.C. - "Before Christ"; refers to any year or time period before the birth of Christ

B.C.E. - "Before the Common Era"; a more "politically correct" way to denote a time period or year before Christ's birth

B.P. - "Before Present"; useful for geologists, archaeologists, and paleontologists to describe remote periods of pre-history

bibliography - A list of sources used in the research and preparation of an historical work

biography - The narrative and/or interpretive story of a particular individual-famous or obscure-from the past

biohistory - The study of the action of medical or biological forces as they have shaped history

book review - A summary and analysis of a work written by another

Chautauqua - A live, staged, dramatic recreation of a famous individual for educational or entertainment purposes

classical history - Covers the period of Greek and Roman history (c. 500 B.C. to c. A.D. 500)

constitutional history - Studies trends and developments in the interpretation of the United States or any other constitution

cultural history - The study of past human values and thought as expressed through the arts

cyclical interpretation - The view that there are certain attitudes or historical phenomena that follow observable, repeating trends

Dewey Decimal System - A library classification system that divides works into ten basic categories each with one hundred sub-divisions

diplomatic history - A branch of history dealing with the relations between nation-states.

Documentary - A filmed historical narrative or recreation of an historical event.

Drama - A live or filmed re-enactment of an historical event of the life of an individual from the past.

Economic history - A branch of history that traces the interaction between humans and wealth

ethnic history - Historical study devoted exclusively to the experiences of particular racial or ethnic groups

event - Something that happened at a particular place at a particular time

historiography - Essentially the "history of history"; i.e., the study of the way each generation interprets the past through its own lens and with its own agendas

intellectual history - The study of ideas (e.g., Puritanism, Transcendentalism), their expression in literature, and their impact on society

interpretation - Viewing the past with a particular slant, agande, or guiding philosophy

journal - A scholarly periodical devoted to the presentation of current research and interpretation within a discipline or sub-discipline

labor history - A branch of economic history dealing with the efforts of workers to improve their conditions

Library of Congress System - A library classification system that uses letters and numbers to categorize works with less-confusing, more "user-friendly" designations

manuscript - Usually, any hand-written document

medieval history - The period of history from the "Fall" of Rome to the Renaissance (C. A.D. 500 to C. 1450)

microfilm - Any of several methods used by libraries to conserve shelf space by converting paper documents to filmed versions to be read by special machines

military history - A branch of history devoted to the study of warfare, weaponry, strategy, and tactics

oral history - The gathering of historical information from living observers or participants

periodical - Any publication that is printed and distributed on a regular basis

phenomenon - A particularly noteworthy occurance useful to the study of human thought (e.g., the Gold Rush, the Civil Rights movement)

plagiarism - The deliberate or unintentional use of another writer's work as one's own

political history - The study of elections and voting patterns

primary source - A first-hand account or documentary evidence produced by the participants in an historical period or event

psychohistory - A relatively new field of historical inquiry that traces the influence of psychological forces upon the past

regional history - A focus of study on an individual geographical area (e.g., Scandinavian history, the history of the Great Plains)

revisionism - Studying the past with the intention of altering the prevailing understanding of a particular event, trend, phenomenon, or individual

secondary sources - Historical work produced by someone who was not present and who must, therefore, rely on the works of those who were

social history - The study of the way common, ordinary people went about their day-to-day lives

social science - A broad term used to describe the entire realm of inquiry into the way human beings are and were

thesis - An idea, viewpoint, or conclusion reached by a researcher

traditionalism - An interpretation of history that stresses the conventional understanding of a particular event, trend, phenomenon, or person

trend - Tracing the development of an idea or issue through time

References

Boller, Paul F. Jr., and Ronald Story. 1988. *A More Perfect Union: Documents in American History*. Vol. 2, *Since 1865*. 2nd ed. Boston: Houghton Mifflin.

Bryson, Bill. 1995. *Made In America*. London: Reed Consumer Books, Minerva Paperback.

Hellstern, Mark. 1988. Review of *Pagans and Christians*, by Robin Lane Fox. *Fides et Historia* 20 (3):81-83.

———. 1990. Review of *The Confederate Cherokees: John Drew's Regiment of Mounted Rifles*, by Craig Gaines. *The Chronicles of Oklahoma* 68 (Summer): 202, 203.

Lunsford, A., & R. Conners, 1992. *The St. Martin's Handbook*. 2nd ed. New York: St. Martin's.

Oppenheimer, Robert. "Acculturation or Assimilation: Mexican Immigration in Kansas, 1900 to World War II." *The Western Historical Quarterly* 16: 429-448.

Pound, Ezra. 1973. "I Gather the Limbs of Osiris." In *Selected Prose: 1909-1965*. New York: New Directions.

Index